KNOWING THE SCORE

ALSO BY DAVID MORGAN

Monty Python Speaks!

EDITED BY DAVID MORGAN

Sundancing

KNOWING THE SCORE

FILM COMPOSERS TALK ABOUT

THE ART, CRAFT, BLOOD, SWEAT, AND TEARS

OF WRITING FOR CINEMA

DAVID MORGAN

HarperEntertainment
An Imprint of HarperCollins*Publishers*

Photography credits appear on pages 301–302.

KNOWING THE SCORE. Copyright © 2000 by David Morgan. All rights reserved. Printed in the United States of America. No part of this book may be used or reproduced in any manner whatsoever without written permission except in the case of brief quotations embodied in critical articles and reviews. For information address HarperCollins Publishers Inc., 10 East 53rd Street, New York, NY 10022.

HarperCollins books may be purchased for educational, business, or sales promotional use. For information please write: Special Markets Department, HarperCollins Publishers Inc., 10 East 53rd Street, New York, NY 10022.

FIRST EDITION

Designed by Elliott Beard

Printed on acid-free paper

Library of Congress Cataloging-in-Publication Data
    Knowing the score : film composers talk about the art, craft, blood, sweat, and tears of writing for cinema / by David Morgan [interviewer].
        p.   cm.
    Includes index.
    ISBN 0-380-80482-4
    1. Motion picture music—History and criticism.   2. Composers—Interviews.   I. Morgan, David.
    ML2075.K58   2000
    781.5'42'0922—dc21   00-038285

00 01 02 03 04 ❖/RRD 10 9 8 7 6 5 4 3 2 1

CONTENTS

Contents

Contents

ACKNOWLEDGMENTS

My deep thanks to the many composers who generously offered to share their ideas and war stories about their craft and calling, and to their representatives and assistants: Ronnie Chasen and Monique Ward, Brian Loucks at Creative Artists Agency, Helga Wild at the Robert Light Agency, Milina Barry and Malena Watrous of Fine Arts Management, Maggie Rodford and Vicki Quinn at Air-Edel, Annie Ohayon, Linda Dorf at Baker-Winokur-Ryder, April Biggs at Earle-Tones Music, Mi Kyoung Chaing, Deborah Jones, Dean Parker, Jenn Littleton, Rick Kunis, Scott Shukat, Jennifer Bartram, Mary Lou Humphrey of G. Shirmer, Lawrence Taub of the Institute for Regional Education, Randall D. Larson, Katie Barker, Deborah Jones, and Robert Townson of Varèse Sarabande Records.

And *forte* gratitude to Deborah Cabaniss.

Finally, my fondest appreciation to my wife, Tessa Wardlaw. *Bravissima!*

INTRODUCTION

As a youngster, one of my proudest record purchases was of the soundtrack for the animated film *Yellow Submarine*, whose grooves I proceeded to wear down apace. What was unusual, perhaps, was that the tracks on side B (which featured the orchestral background score to the film composed by George Martin, a sprightly pastiche of classical, pop, and humorous vignettes) got as much play—if not more—than the Beatles songs on side A. Such was the attraction of music that captured and evoked the film's visual extravagance, and an early lesson in the power of music to tell a story or a joke.

Like the medium for which it is created, film music is a relatively young art form, although its ancestors—opera, theater music, and, later, radio—have helped set the conventions by which most film music functions: support the atmosphere and drama of a picture without jarring the listener with the seeming incongruity of an unseen orchestra accompanying two lovers or a car chase.

While most cinema is literal—what we see is usually what we get—film music by its very nature allows a filmmaker to expand the scope of a film by introducing nonliteral elements: emotions not evident on the faces of actors, memories of events long gone and undramatized, or contradictory commentary on the actions of characters. When an audience sees an adorable, innocent little boy but hears a hellish, swirling mass chanting praise to Satan, they understand that they are not to believe what they see. Conversely, if we watch a boxer being pummeled and losing a prizefight, but the soundtrack blares a triumphant horn passage, we are being reminded that "victory" and "loss" are not so easily defined. Audiences can be challenged to rethink what they experience, and thus film music can make a film deeper and more resonant than it might otherwise be.

Cinema has offered some of the most vibrant and sophisticated music available to mass audiences, yet film music remains an underappreciated art form. It is easy to denigrate a score for a crass, commercial Hollywood time-waster as having no more merit than the film it inhabits, but it is not unusual for a grade-B picture to sport a classy or inventive piece of music from one of the most talented composers working today. Good film music can rise above its material and even live on outside of the film, long after the drama for which it was written has been forgotten. And it is a testament to the composers featured in this book that Hollywood has given them opportunities to write their music and have it performed in a wide variety of styles and genres that would be almost impossible to match on stage or in the concert hall.

Knowing the Score is a collection of interviews with some of cinema's leading composers, working in both the Hollywood studio system and the independent film community. The interviews have been edited together to form a "symposium," in which their shared or disparate ideas and experiences about working in the film medium are brought together to give readers a rounded and in-depth glimpse into the filmmaking process.

This book is not strictly for the musician, a technical guide to composition or theory; nor is it a primer on synchronizing music to film running at twenty-four frames per second, or on which software programs are best for mixing MIDI recordings with sound effects. Rather, *Knowing the Score* is an appreciation of and inquisitive exploration into the art and craft of film music for film buffs and music fans, as told in the words of some of the form's leading practitioners. They will explore such topics as how film composers decide upon a musical style for a given film, how they collaborate with a director, how they make the choices on what function music should serve in the film, how editing changes in a film can affect their music, and how the process of writing film music changes according to the logistics of the project or the temperaments of their collaborators.

In addition, these composers will examine in depth certain noteworthy scores that helped break new ground or stretched the craft in new directions.

Readers will hopefully come away with a new (or renewed) appreciation of the special talents required to make a film score memorable, even timeless, and perhaps to listen even more carefully the next time the credits roll and the music announces a new adventure, a new world.

■

PANEL

The following were interviewed for this "symposium":

ELMER BERNSTEIN
With a movie career spanning fifty years, Bernstein has written for such diverse films as *The Ten Commandments*, *The Magnificent Seven*, *To Kill a Mockingbird*, *Ghostbusters*, *Heavy Metal*, and *The Age of Innocence*. He won an Academy Award for the musical *Thoroughly Modern Millie*.

CARTER BURWELL
Beginning his film composition career with Joel and Ethan Coen's *Blood Simple* (and continuing on all their subsequent films), Burwell has fashioned an eclectic roster of scores, including *Rob Roy*, *Gods and Monsters,* and *Being John Malkovich.*

ELIA CMIRAL
Cmiral began his music career in Europe before coming to the United States in the mid-1990s. After gaining several indepen-

dent film and TV credits, he was offered the chance to score a high-profile Hollywood studio picture, the John Frankenheimer thriller *Ronin*.

JOHN CORIGLIANO

An acclaimed concert hall composer of concertos and chamber works, Corigliano composed the groundbreaking scores to *Altered States*, *Revolution*, and *The Red Violin*, for which he won the Academy Award. He is perhaps best known for his 1991 opera *The Ghosts of Versailles* and for his Symphony No. 1, also referred to as the "AIDS Symphony," as it was written to the memory of deceased friends.

MYCHAEL DANNA

A Toronto-based composer and musician, Danna has collaborated extensively with director Atom Egoyan (*The Sweet Hereafter*, *Felicia's Journey*), and has recently worked with such Hollywood filmmakers as Joel Schumacher (*8mm*) and Ang Lee (*The Ice Storm*, *Ride with the Devil*).

PATRICK DOYLE

An actor and musical director with Kenneth Branagh's Renaissance Theatre Company, Doyle wrote his first film score for Branagh's *Henry V* and has worked on many of the director's subsequent films. In addition to his Shakespearean scores, Doyle has written lyrical period and contemporary pieces for *Sense and Sensibility*, *A Little Princess*, *Carlito's Way*, and *Great Expectations*.

PHILIP GLASS

One of the most influential of late-twentieth-century composers of concert works, opera, and music-theater productions, Glass has contributed highly iconoclastic music to some iconoclastic films, from Godfrey Reggio's *Koyaanisqatsi* and *Powaqqatsi* to

Paul Schrader's *Mishima* and Martin Scorsese's *Kundun*. He recently composed a new score for the 1931 Tod Browning version of *Dracula*.

ELLIOT GOLDENTHAL

A student of John Corigliano and Aaron Copland, with extensive theater and concert hall credits, Goldenthal has created strikingly original scores using a mélange of styles (orchestral, pop, electronic) for such films as *Drugstore Cowboy, Alien³,* and *The Butcher Boy.* He received Academy Award nominations for *Interview with the Vampire* and *Michael Collins* and recently scored *Titus,* a film adaptation of Shakespeare's *Titus Andronicus* directed by his wife, Julie Taymor.

JERRY GOLDSMITH

Recognized as a leader among Hollywood veterans, a composer of more than 250 film and TV scores, Goldsmith's prolific output is matched only by his own virtuosity in finding unique musical voices for each of his subjects, such as the surreal percussion of *Planet of the Apes,* the echoing trumpets of *Patton,* and the unearthly electronics of *Star Trek: The Motion Picture.* Recipient of eighteen Oscar nominations, he won the Academy Award for his chilling satanic chorales for *The Omen.*

MARK ISHAM

A classically trained performer with a solid jazz streak, Isham was part of such noted San Francisco Bay Area bands as Group 87 and Sons of Champlin before striking out solo, producing several electronic and jazz recordings. Isham has had a similarly varied film résumé, employing electronics, jazz, and orchestral writing, and earning an Oscar nomination for his Celtic-inspired melodies in *A River Runs Through It.*

MICHAEL KAMEN

Kamen graduated from the Juilliard School, and from the New York Rock and Roll Ensemble, into a career writing for the movies. Among his most notable scores are *Die Hard, Brazil, Robin Hood: Prince of Thieves, Don Juan DeMarco,* and *Mr. Holland's Opus.*

ALAN MENKEN

His success with the Off-Broadway musical hit *Little Shop of Horrors* (co-written with Howard Ashman) helped steer Menken to the big screen, where he has become the preeminent composer of musicals, helping to revive two film genres (animation and musical comedy) with *The Little Mermaid* and *Beauty and the Beast.* They and their successors, including *Aladdin, Pocahontas,* and *The Hunchback of Notre Dame,* have earned Menken eight Academy Awards.

BASIL POLEDOURIS

As a film student at USC's School of Cinema in the sixties, Poledouris had the distinction of being the first to direct a script by John Milius (who would later author or co-author *Apocalypse Now* and *The Wind and the Lion*). Poledouris eventually returned to music studies—he had taken piano since he was seven—scoring television and feature films such as *Lonesome Dove, Robocop, The Hunt for Red October, Les Misérables,* and *For Love of the Game.*

JOCELYN POOK

Pook is a violinist/violist who has divided her career between performing and composition. She played on the soundtracks of a few Derek Jarman films (and even appeared on-screen in *Edward II*), and wrote music for dance companies, theater groups, recordings, and several British TV films and documentaries before scoring Stanley Kubrick's final film, *Eyes Wide Shut.*

DAVID RAKSIN

Beginning as an arranger for Charlie Chaplin on *Modern Times*, Raksin is one of the most respected of composers from Hollywood's Golden Age. Celebrated for his rich, sometimes dark scores to such classics as *Laura*, *Forever Amber,* and *The Bad and the Beautiful,* Raksin has also taught a generation or two of film music students, promoting the validity of film music as an intrinsically artful musical form.

DAVID SHIRE

Noted for his works both for the stage (*Closer Than Ever*, *Baby*, *Big*) and for screens big and small (*The Conversation*, *All the President's Men*, *The Hindenburg*, *Last Stand at Saber River*), Shire's chameleonic musical abilities also won him an Oscar for his song from *Norma Rae*, "It Goes Like It Goes."

ROBERT TOWNSON

A record producer who formed the Masters Film Music series of soundtrack recordings, Townson took over Varèse Sarabande, a predominantly classical label, in 1989 and helped turn it into one of the leading producers of original soundtracks and film music recordings, releasing newly recorded classic works by such composers as Bernard Herrmann, Alex North, John Barry, and John Williams.

■

KNOWING THE SCORE

THE ART OF FILM MUSIC

How would you describe the best or most satisfying use of music in a film?

DAVID SHIRE (*All the President's Men, The Conversation*): Film music is so often an art of juxtaposition. When the music is more about subtext—adding an element that isn't on the screen—that's the most satisfying. The most simple-minded scoring is what you get in most B-movies and bad television, where they want happy scenes made as happy as possible, love scenes made as loving as possible, and action scenes made as fast and furious as possible. It's not as creative, and it doesn't leave much room for your imagination, except to try to find some *new* way to write the same old music for the three-hundredth time. And usually they just want the same old music anyway, a generic, same old score that isn't going to tax anybody. I've had scores thrown out because I did a subtext score and they wanted something vanilla, right down the mainstream. You struggle and struggle, and they throw things away, and then I'd hear the score they finally put on the movie and I'd think, "I could have written that with my hands tied behind my back."

The fun is when the score can find an element that weaves into the whole mix—if there's a love scene, instead of making it just more loving, there's an underlying tension. So the melody is saying "love" but there's something underneath that's saying, "Wait a minute, there's something *else* going on here." There's an ambiguity about it.

DAVID RAKSIN (*Laura, The Bad and the Beautiful*): There are times when music is at its best when it's saying what you can see in a *different* way, but actually the whole business of amplifying something that you can't see, [that] you wouldn't otherwise know, is the really defining phrase, and music can do that.

ELMER BERNSTEIN (*The Ten Commandments, The Magnificent Seven*): What you're describing is really a very good use of film music: doing things which are not totally explicit on the screen, to

get behind and inside the character, so to speak. If you have an opportunity to do that, I think that's very effective.

Its real significance is, what does music *do* in the film? That's what it was composed for. If you're writing a piece for film, the film is the spine of the music, because if the music is properly done for the film, the film

Elmer Bernstein

becomes the form. Whereas if you're writing music on its own, it has to have a different kind of spine, a tighter form that stands on *its* own. That's why, generally speaking, if you take symphonic music (like Beethoven symphonies or a Bach fugue), that doesn't work well in a film, because the music has so much a form of its own that the music stands *away* from the film, not *in* the film.

Of course you can change the shape of the film to suit the music; for instance, in *Fantasia*, the Bach "Toccata and Fugue" is fine, but that sequence was designed around the music. I don't want to be accused of citing it as a great artwork; what I'm simply saying is if you have music that has tremendous internal strength then you have to design the film around the music.

I've done a lot of films for Ray and Charles Eames that were little films, one a thirteen-minute film called *Toccata for Toy Trains*. In that instance I wrote a divertissement first and then the film was shot to the music. So the music in that case stands very easily on its own, because it was composed beforehand.

PATRICK DOYLE (*Henry V, Sense and Sensibility*): I suppose film music has to be acceptable *instantly* because it's an instant medium and people have to instantly get ideas. It's not very often films are revisited in the same way that a symphony or a poem or a great piece of literature is; it's very instantaneous, and I try to deliver the instantaneous but to give it a longevity so that it will last through time.

What are your own standards for what makes a successful piece of film music?

DOYLE: Well, first of all it should totally serve the picture. It should always sound like good music, it should always in the end have a structure to it. But basically it should always be musical, and *listenable*. And it should be able to, away from the picture, conjure up the same sort of feelings and images that it was meant to at hand.

Dead Again had so many elements: it had a very strong, romantic feel; it had a lost, melancholy feel; it had the danger of a psychopath; and it had a retrospective quality, because it was harking back to a golden era of Hollywood. All of the elements hopefully still come over when one listens to the music, even after the film's gone.

Maybe the music should be providing something which is not on the screen, or it should be playing *against* what's on the screen—in that case it could be misleading [when heard away from the film], but if one has seen the picture then one knows the intention behind it. That contradicts itself because it may give the listener an idea of what point in the picture it was representing when in fact it would be a red herring.

ELLIOT GOLDENTHAL (*Drugstore Cowboy, Heat*): When Bernard Herrmann in *Psycho* took the sound of a screetchy bird and sort of morphed it into what it might feel like to be stabbed, the music took on a better, more significant role than a sound effect would have in that scene, in the sense that when you abstract something you create a different reality—you've created something more significant because you've entered into a state of dreams. And when you enter into a dream state, things become more and more long-lasting. It's not just hearing a tire screetch, but to hear an orchestration of how that tire screetch makes you *feel,* is one step into the world of art and not just craft.

MYCHAEL DANNA (*The Sweet Hereafter, The Ice Storm*): The role of music is to enlighten the audience about the film from a sonic perspective, and to bring some kind of sonic understanding of the themes of the film. I think the most important thing for me is that what's on the screen visually is a given, and I don't see the need to repeat that very often, or underline it or exaggerate it. If the music can come around and say the same thing that the picture is saying [but] from a different angle, or at least say a theme that the filmmaker wants to say in a completely different way—and in a *provoking* way—then that is when it's just a joy to work at this. That's when the satisfaction begins for me.

I find it really, really boring to just repeat aurally what is already going on visually; I just can't get very interested in doing that. It's much more exciting to be able to spin a parallel story line, or to come up with a concept that will elucidate the themes of the film in an original way.

CARTER BURWELL (*Blood Simple, Fargo*): I prefer doing romantic music, like *Miller's Crossing,* when the music's put up against something *unromantic.* I feel comfortable doing it in those situations because I know it's not exploitative of the emotions of the audience. In other words, in *Miller's Crossing* I'm not pushing anyone's buttons because you're hearing romantic or sentimental music but you're seeing very cold-blooded people acting on screen; whereas in a movie that is openly romantic, doing openly romantic music is a little less interesting for me, and I worry a little that I'm pushing the audience's buttons, or that the result will come out as a cliché; you hope that it doesn't but it concerns me a little more. I'm much happier dealing in, let's face it, darker or more ironic material.

ELIA CMIRAL (*Ronin, Stigmata*): I think the most important decision for us is to find and choose a concept. This concept must come from a complete understanding of the movie, and if the concept is wrong, the composer and director will find out very soon. It's very annoying to see great music written for a movie but with the wrong concept—it doesn't work!

Another annoying thing is we have too much music in films. I feel that maybe we are afraid of silence and that we don't trust our feelings and so we have to *tell* people how they should feel.

BASIL POLEDOURIS (*Conan the Barbarian, For Love of the Game*): I don't think one can start out with a preconceived notion of what the score's going to be like. I think all the techniques mentioned can be applied to a number of situations, and I think the most important thing to do as a composer is to understand the drama, to understand the idea behind the film and the style of the film, and you usually get that by talking to the director, ascertaining what his or her vision is of the finished work. Then within that context that defines the formal limits of what is required, I try to free-associate with it, and the style will usually grow from this process.

Most of the dramatic things I've done are period, for instance *Les Misérables*. I could have done a contemporary score for it but it would have seemed completely out of place given Victor Hugo's writing, given the situation that Valjean finds himself in, given the restraints and the kind of morality of the period that is so strong in the book—I mean, a man gets put in jail for eighteen years for stealing a loaf of bread. That's kind of hard for audiences to accept unless you create a historic environment, and in that sense, both Bille August (the director) and I agreed that the music should really support the period as much as the costumes do. So you try to create a sense that the audience is in the late seventeen hundreds.

What are your responsibilities in contributing a score to a film?

MICHAEL KAMEN (*Robin Hood: Prince of Thieves, The Iron Giant*): There's one overriding principle and that is, as a composer of music for film, I am a storyteller, much like the director, much like the writer, much like in fact everybody who is collaborating in film. And if I respond to the story and the characters in the story I'll be making music that has an emotional truth, and that's what I respond to.

SHIRE: There is one general aesthetic that separates film music from concert hall music: you are writing specific music for specific characters and specific situations. Now, in the theater, the music is sung and it's what I call "foreground music"; in movies, you're using those same aesthetic tools to help tell someone else's story where music *isn't* in the forefront, but it still has a great deal to do with the effectiveness of the story being told. So you still have a sense of music at the service of drama.

JERRY GOLDSMITH (*Patton, Star Trek: The Motion Picture, Basic Instinct*): My opinion is, your first obligation is to the film—*and* you want to write a good piece of music. David Raksin years ago, the guy used to write a good piece of music *and* make it work in the film, too. That's really the perfect example. But sometimes the best pieces of music don't always work for the best effect dramatically. I'm sure if one had enough time, you can come up with the perfect compromise, but sometimes that doesn't happen. You really have to go for what's best for the picture.

RAKSIN: There are times when you have to sacrifice the ability of the thing to stand on its own feet because the dimensions [of the film] do not permit it. In other words, you may not be able to have the correct development or correct proportions in the sequence because you can't be developing something musically when the picture's doing something else. If you're going to write a piece of music which does not acknowledge the narrative, what are you doing? So what you do is you try to write a piece

David Raksin

that has music *in* it. You know, anybody can write film music, the problem is, can you write *music*?

Music from *Laura, The Bad and the Beautiful, Forever Amber,* that gets played in concerts—which does not *validate* it, it's just that some people seem to think it's good enough to play in concerts. When I met Steve Sondheim for the first time, he said to me, "Before we say anything, I want you to know that there are some of us who think that the theme of *The Bad and the Beautiful* is the finest theme ever written in film." So naturally I spent twenty minutes trying to dis-convince him! Actually, what tickles me is, we've become friends since and he's recently said in print it's *one* of the best! Of course I'll settle for that!

If you're a composer who really gives a goddamn, you just watch the film as though you were a yokel and absorb what's going on; if [what you write then] strikes you as right for the film, that's something! If in addition it's *music*, that's even better.

When you listen to film music, do you listen to it analytically as to whether it works both as music in its own right *and* in its service to the drama of the film?

RAKSIN: I never bother with that, it's an automatic response. You know, if the music has an identity of its own and it has a structure of its own, it's music; not only that, if it's just a little tune which is a superb tune, *that's* music.

GOLDSMITH: I'm not terribly analytical about music. If you're talking about concert music, I try to hit on something to learn from constantly, see what directions music is going in. Basically it's not a matter of listening to music analytically; it's listening to music for the joy of listening to music. *That's* what it's about.

JOHN CORIGLIANO (*Altered States, The Red Violin*): My ear is always open. Listening to music you don't like is actually very useful; it's a good way of getting your mind to work on solutions, actively. When I hear something great I just enjoy it, but when it doesn't quite work I ask myself *why*—and this can lead to a useful solution of what I consider a problem.

Minimalism is an example of music I have great reservations about. I like the beautiful sounds, the hypnotic quality—the attention on tiny changes that puts you into a trancelike state. But I'm bothered by the overly repetitious, simplistic material and the lack of architecture and emotional content. So I asked myself: Is it necessary that this sort of music have the bad qualities in order to have the qualities I like? This question led me to try my own sort of minimalist piece in my *Fantasia on an Ostinato*. I based it on a proto-minimalist idea from Beethoven—the ostinato that dominates the *andante* of his Seventh Symphony—and tried to keep the minimalist qualities of beautiful sonorities and trancelike repetition, but avoid the emotional sterility and formlessness. I was trying to solve the problem of listening to something I didn't care for and making it into something I liked.

How do you listen to your own music?

GOLDSMITH: Critically, is how I listen to it. Sometimes I say, "Gee, did *I* write that? It's *good*!" Sometimes I say, "I'm sorry I wrote that; it's *lousy*!" It's funny, I found a cassette of the complete score of *Explorers*. I hadn't heard that in a couple of years, and I put it on and I was sort of amazed; some of the stuff really sounded good, and other stuff . . . It's like all scores—you have an hour of music [to compose]; some of it's really good, and a lot of it may be fine in the picture, but on an album it doesn't hold up.

When you're writing an hour of music in a short period of time, unless it's by some pure luck or something, it's not necessarily going to come out all *that* great.

BERNSTEIN: I never listen to recordings of my music. I'm glad someone else does! But to be perfectly honest I like them best when they're in the film, because that's what it was designed for. That's how I first heard it and that's where it means the most to me.

QUALITY, NOT QUANTITY

Some of David Shire's most celebrated scores are those for small, thoughtful films such as *All the President's Men*, *The Conversation*, and *Straight Time*, providing what he describes as "brain-surgery scores," where a small amount of music, often delicate, would be called upon to paint a succinct character portrait.

SHIRE: People think that if you write less music it's easy; more often than not it's much *more* difficult because you don't have that much room, so the music you do write has to not seem intrusive when it comes in after thirty minutes *without* music.

It's usually lighter. Whereas an action picture would generally have a lot of music and it's fairly steady throughout.

The Conversation was a brain-surgery type of score, of a higher order. Francis Coppola said, "What I need this score to do is to do Harry's inner life." That's a great thing for a director to say.

It was Francis's suggestion to use a piano. He said, "We don't need an electronic score, it's not about that, it's about this man's conscience." He said he heard a piano because it was kind of lonely and cold and alone, and it was the exact right choice. We put it through a synthesizer in places to make it louder or a little weird as a piano, but it was all a piano to begin with.

GOLDSMITH: Some directors like a lot more music, and that's their prerogative—it is a director's medium. I think sometimes you can have too much music. I'm probably more conservative about it than anybody; I don't want to write more than is absolutely necessary. *Patton* had thirty-three minutes of music, and the movie was two and a half hours long.

MELODY

The melodic form of film music is something which *seems* obvious—put in a melody that will captivate an audience and draw it into the drama—but some film music today seems to be more interested in creating sound textures or rhythms rather than melody in order to foster an emotional response, such as tension, fear, or discomfort. In many instances this is perfectly warranted and effective within the film, but when heard outside of the film the music suffers from being repetitive, undeveloped, or boring. Many music cues, particularly those which are very short, have a reason to exist within the narrative (i.e., to bridge one scene with another) but do nothing more musically than recall earlier, full-blown renditions of the main thematic material.

This raises the question of what form film music should ideally take for it to be judged as music of high quality. Is the ability to exist outside of the medium for which it was created, to be able to stand on its own as a "legitimate" piece of music, necessary, or desirable? On the other hand, do dissonance, atonality, or nonmelodic soundscapes that can replicate the montage of a film sequence lessen the legitimacy of the score as a musical statement, because it depends so heavily on a visual association?

One problem that is not the music's fault is the power of the images that are associated with it in the public's mind. Hearing Bernard Herrmann's murder music from *Psycho* will automatically inspire mental images of Janet Leigh, Mother, a knife, and a trail of blood pouring down a bathtub drain. Once you have seen the film, it would be impossible ever to listen to the music without that association. The starkness of the sound and the scene's imagery, rather than any thematic content, gave the music its power.

So in film music, the melodic line may represent the beginning of a composer's inspiration, but not the limit.

▶

RAKSIN: You know, melody has practically disappeared from the world; every so often you get a guy who knows how to write one, but most guys are afraid because, as Oscar Wilde once said, to be understood is to be found out. And the biggest way to risk that is to write a melody.

Also, for a long time it was considered beneath the dignity of a composer to write a melody. It's very interesting to note that that position was espoused mostly by people who couldn't if they *tried*. But you know, for a long time concert music was without melody; it started in the fifties and it got to be a disease. Now it's changing again and guys are running around trying to find some way of writing melodies.

A lot of people are becoming really very interested in what we did [for films] they think film music is very unusual—I've just done my fourth or fifth documentary on this subject—because they recognize it as the last repository of melody.

What do you look for in a film to inspire you?

GOLDSMITH: Basically I am looking for the humanistic values. I want to find a character that I can get inside of, my focal point at least. I don't believe in the leitmotif style of composing something for this, something for that. I want a central character which will motivate the score thematically and I want everything out of the score to develop from there. I'm looking for some meaning or emotional values that are not on the screen. We're not set decorators.

Do you specifically compose melodies for characters in a film?

MARK ISHAM (*Fly Away Home, A River Runs Through It, Cool World*): That is not something I do very often: write "Joe's Theme" or "Mary's Theme." I tend to write more the "Unrequited Love Theme" or the "Family Disintegrating Theme," which are much more about emotion than personality, because that's really what the music is there to do: to heighten the emotion. For *A River Runs Through It*, we could have probably recorded that whole score without click tracks [mechanical or computerized notations that help synchronize music to the film footage on the recording stage]. We could have just gotten the music to sound beautiful and shoved it into the film. Although there was a definite thematic structure to the film—I think there's like five or six themes—they're not specific to *characters*.

I think that in terms of the motival structure, being exact and hitting the action is a stylistic choice, and I just let the films dictate that. For instance in *Timecop*, there were very specific motifs: there was the "plot continues" theme, there was his theme, there was her theme, and it certainly hit the action very squarely on the nose. This is just necessary to the style of more action-oriented films that music be more specific.

THE LEAD INSTRUMENTS

The use of themes in films—deriving a memorable melody or motif that can be associated with a character, a thing, an action—has been prevalent since the days Max Steiner and Erich Wolfgang Korngold accompanied Humphrey Bogart and Errol Flynn on their adventures. And over time, while film music became less Wagnerian and more pop-oriented, that penchant for theme-association continued.

Michael Kamen had collaborated with guitarist Eric Clapton on the score for a 1986 British miniseries, *Edge of Darkness*. It would lead to a successful jazz score that continued the tradition of Korngold while being utterly contemporary.

▶

KAMEN: The editor of *Lethal Weapon I*, Stuart Baird, had visited England at the time *Edge of Darkness* was on television. He heard the score, he got the music, he brought it to L.A., and he temped it into *Lethal Weapon I*. So it was used as temp score,

Michael Kamen

and they liked it and they asked Eric Clapton if he would do the movie. And Eric asked me if I'd do it with him.

I didn't really like action-adventure movies, it wasn't my genre at all, but Stuart said, "Well, what about if you use Eric Clapton's guitar as the Mel Gibson character and use the saxophone as the Danny Glover character?" Now musicians develop a lot of allegiances and as you make friends you hold on to them. One of my greatest friends is David Sanborn, and at that time he was not that well known, but he was known to me as the greatest living sax player. And I was very hesitant because a lot of times people would say, "I have a sax player I want you to use," and if it wasn't David Sanborn I wouldn't be even vaguely interested.

So Stuart Baird said, "Why don't you use the sax for Danny Glover?" And I said, "Yeah, yeah, that's good, I know who to use." And the guy said, "Well, there *is* a sax player I'd like you to use." And I said, "Who's that?" And he said, "Well, there's this fellow, David Sanborn . . ."

And I knew that my life was made!

That film would give me the opportunity to bring my two friends together—one of them the world's leading proponent of the world's leading instrument, the lead guitar, and the other the world's leading proponent in my eyes of the *other* lead instrument in popular music, which is the sax. And the honor and the privilege of being able to put the two of them in the studio and make some music with them was the driving force behind my working on *Lethal Weapon*. The fact that it was an "action-adventure film" was transcended by the fact that I was in the studio with Eric Clapton and David Sanborn. It's not that the film didn't matter; it was that the attention we were going to devote to it was through the prism of our musical sensibilities.

It is not rare for the film editor to have a viewpoint about the music. It was certainly incredibly perceptive of him to recognize that that technique of matching a character with an instrument was right in my line because I'm a big *Peter and the Wolf* fan, and I have always believed that one should do that with a film, as one does that with an opera, a ballet: you identify the characters with their themes. And if they appear again you use a variation.

When I was doing *The Next Man*, to jump back and forth in time, there was a fellow named Carl Prager, who was the music head of United Artists Pictures, which was the distributor. He was an old hand, he had supervised film music for many years, and he taught me a great lesson: He came to my house to listen to the themes that I was writing for *The Next Man*, and I'd say, "Now in this scene I want to use this theme."

He'd say, "That's a great theme, you could use that."

I'd say, "And in the next scene, here's this cue I want to use." I played it, and he said, "Well, where's the *theme*?"

And I said, "I've just played the theme, and *now* I have to do *this*."

He said, "No, no, play the theme again."

"What do you mean?"

"Well, in film you play the theme, and then you play the theme again and then you play the theme and then you play a *variation* of the theme and then you play the theme . . ."

And it was very instructive; I had been writing it like a piece of symphonic music where Theme A comes and then Theme B and then the development section and you might even bring in another theme—not so in film. Monothematic, and with very few exceptions that is the rule of thumb for all films. If you have a melody you drive it home; if you have two or three make sure that they're *related* to each other—*or* completely, starkly opposite.

YOU CAN'T GO HOME AGAIN:
DAVID SHIRE ON *RETURN TO OZ*

It was to *Return to Oz*'s great credit, and ultimately its great distress, that the only thing it shared with its beloved 1939 MGM musical forebear was two letters. The Oz of Walter Murch's fantasy is nevertheless much closer to the spirit of L. Frank Baum's books, both in its design and in the psychological journey which the little girl at its center undergoes. When Dorothy reenters her fantasy world and finds it overrun by a mysterious invader, she collects a group of strange creatures: Jack Pumpkinhead, a jittery walking vegetable; Tik Tok, a spring-activated mechanical man who always seems to wind down at the worst possible moment; the Gump, a living amalgam of sofa, moose head, and wings; and Bellina, her pet chicken, who in her fantasy talks. Together they ultimately destroy the rocklike Nome King, returning the land to its original beauty and herself to a settled life in Kansas.

David Shire used a multithemed approach to portray

Dorothy and the other characters, as well as a theme representing home—the goal of her quest. In addition, Shire looked to turn-of-the-century music as the color of his score (a recording of Charles Ives's music, *Old Songs Deranged/ Music for Theater Orchestra*, was a notable inspiration); Prokofiev and Bartók also figured in the orchestral texture. The resulting score is one of the richest and most resonant in recent memory.

Because of the starkness and darkness of the film (for starters, the dream-prone Dorothy is taken by her auntie Em to a quack for electric shock treatment!), it was rejected by critics and audiences looking for a repeat of the original's Technicolor-coated, vaudevillian spirit. Truly a shame, because in addition to avoiding a fantasy film with some psychological meat to it, a rarity these days, a score wonderfully varied and melodic went unheard.*

▶

Walter Murch was certainly under a lot of pressure from the studio when he was directing *Return to Oz*, both because of his inexperience as a director and because the film was coming out much darker than I'm sure the studio might have liked. Were you under pressure to make a lighter score that would have lightened the film in any respect, make it more jovial, like *The Wizard of Oz*?

DAVID SHIRE: I just scored the film that Walter made. I didn't think of it as dark and light. Actually, if you go back to the

---

*In addition to the author's interview, portions of the following discussion were excerpted from a contemporaneous interview by David Kraft, which appeared in *CinemaScore* magazine in 1987. My thanks to editor Randall D. Larson for his generous permission.

Frank Baum books and the illustrations, Walter's is the more literal adaptation, closer to the spirit of Frank Baum. *The Wizard of Oz* was a bastardization, although I love it as much as anybody. I just saw Walter's movie as Walter's movie, and we worked as closely and long as I've ever worked with a director. It was so satisfying to work on one picture for six months.

How did you get involved?

SHIRE: I knew Walter from *The Conversation** and he called me up and asked me to do it. I love him, working with him is a whole education in itself. It was a multithemed score, it was the kind of score I always wanted to write.

There are nine major themes or thematic groups in *Return to Oz*, and I tried to compose them so they would work as extended pieces of music in addition to their functioning as themes. I wanted the score to hold together like *Pictures at an Exhibition* or *Peter and the Wolf*. I felt this would give the film a musical coherence and make for a soundtrack album that would really tell the story of the picture.

Walter agreed that it should be a score that could stand on its own. It has scope, and when we put the album together we put it together like a long suite—it's solid music.

I tried to find models for each theme from American music that the character of Dorothy could have heard, since the story is, in a sense, Dorothy's dream—she's creating it. I wanted the score to have a truly American flavor and, even though symphonic, to employ various interesting smaller combinations within that texture. I also wanted each of the "little" characters to have a characteristic small ensemble sound and put all of them against the

---

*Murch was the sound designer on that film; his other credits for sound design and editing include *Apocalypse Now* and *The English Patient*.

larger symphonic forces that mostly represent the "large" forces of evil (the Nome King and Mombi) that they are up against.

There are three themes that relate directly to Dorothy. The first is the home theme, which represents Dorothy's feelings about her Kansas home and Aunt Em. It's hymnlike—much like something Dorothy would have heard at Sunday services. The other two are Dorothy's main theme and the theme for Ozma.

The trick with Dorothy was that there were *two* Dorothys: her unconscious one when the story took place in Oz and the conscious Dorothy, and it may sound a little pretentious but composers and directors play these games to get themselves functioning. We had a theme for Dorothy, and I had a theme for Ozma, her doppelgänger, or counterpart in Oz. Ozma is really Dorothy's alter ego—she's the imaginative side of Dorothy that Dorothy is trying to make contact with. The subtext of the movie, according to Walter, is that Dorothy is going back to Oz to rescue (and thus be able to reconcile herself with) Ozma, and somehow find a way to be

David Shire

true to the world of her imagination while living in the real world. And Walter and I felt wouldn't it be neat if the two themes seemed totally independent but went together in counterpoint at the end of the story when Dorothy finally steps into the mirror and becomes one with Ozma. So at that moment of the picture the two themes—one in a violin, one in a cello—come together, and then come together in counterpoint with the home theme, which is where Dorothy was in the beginning. So Dorothy unites as a person, and that character is able to go home again.

There's a lot of stuff like that which I think helped make it so rich, even if I don't expect anybody to notice it in a screening.

I had the Ozma theme early on, and after Walter made his counterpoint suggestion, it took a very long time to get a Dorothy theme that would work with it yet have an equally strong and distinct character of its own. I must have written twenty or twenty-five different Dorothy themes until I came up with one I was really happy with! All the throwaways either didn't work well contrapuntally, or else sounded too much like counterpoints or obligatos rather than distinctive melodies. I didn't want the climax to be telegraphed at all.

Can you describe some of the themes and orchestrations you developed for the other characters?

SHIRE: I wanted to find a fresh musical voice for each of the characters; we thought that each character would have its own instrument, too. Tik Tok was mechanical, but instead of using ratchets and stuff like that (because you see the mechanism and hear it), I figured I had to have a brass band because he's made of brass. So "Tik Tok's Theme" features a brass quintet, which related to his metallic rotundity. Also, in the late nineteenth and early twentieth centuries, there were several cornet players who were big musical stars and loved to play these wonderfully silly

David Shire conducting the London Symphony Orchestra for
Return to Oz.

show-off cadenzas. Walter agreed with me that something like
that would work very well for the end of the fight scene
between Tik Tok and the evil Wheelers—Tik Tok's big triumph.
I gave the Wheelers [their own] distinctive sound by featuring
metallic percussion.

The "Jack Pumpkinhead Theme" is a turn-of-the-century
waltz, again something Dorothy might have heard. I originally
wrote it to feature clarinet, but Walter had me switch the
melody to bass clarinet, an octave lower, because he thought the
clarinet would be in the same audio range as Jack's voice and
would conflict. Oddly enough, Walter thought of this when he
noticed that the bass clarinet (he didn't know what it was) *looked*
like the character of Jack Pumpkinhead! But he was right about
the potential conflict, and its solution.

Dorothy's chicken friend, Bellina, has a motif for nervous high reeds and double reeds, moving quickly in major seconds. As for the evil forces, Mombi's theme employs a mandolin, since she plays her own theme on one in the movie. I used a synthesizer for this to get a slightly unreal mandolin sound that I could better control. The Gump has a clockwork-type vamp, and (when he finally takes off) a big symphonic "movie-music" theme with the six horns triumphantly singing away.

The Nome King's motif uses shifting whole-tone harmonies in the lower end of the orchestra. As he gets meaner and meaner his essentially augmented triad harmonic character shifts to diminished seventh and Bartókian harmony. When he finally disintegrates, the three diminished chords are stacked horrifically, à la the twelve-tone "Wozzeck Chord." I tried to mirror his gradual psychological disintegration with a gradual harmonic one.

I decided to use only string orchestra (with harp and percussion) for the first three reels before Dorothy gets to Oz, so that there would be a musical delineation between the real, somewhat dark world of Kansas and the bright and bizarre world of Oz. The woodwinds and brass are gradually introduced in the storm sequence as Dorothy is swept away to Oz. I especially liked developing all the interrelationships between the themes, such as in the "Rag March," which has a few bars from each of the little characters' themes threaded through it.

My only disappointment with Oz is that it didn't lead to me getting more scores in that genre. Very few people saw it. It was kind of crushing for the picture and the score not to have had the kind of profile I had hoped they would have, except with so many film music buffs, God bless 'em, who have appreciated it.

SUSPICION BREEDS CONFIDENCE:
MICHAEL KAMEN ON *BRAZIL*

Ary Barroso's 1939 song "Brazil" (a.k.a. "Aquarela do Brasil") has been recorded by Eddy Duchin, Xavier Cugat, Geoff Muldaur, and the Ritchie Family. But nowhere in this eclectic discography is suggested an inspiration for an Orwellian, dystopian vision of a bureaucratic society run rampant, or of a petty government functionary given to leaps of fantasy that plunge him squarely in the hunt for real-life terrorists.

Terry Gilliam's visually stunning film called for an equally visual music score, which nevertheless was to be tied to a familiar tune (though, curiously, in Gilliam's first draft the opening song was planned to be "Maria Elena" by Ry Cooder). What went into Michael Kamen's score, however, was very different from what came out, as the basic melody of "Brazil" was shaken and stirred like a martini to suit just about any dramatic or emotional context.

It's no surprise that by the time the project ended, Kamen came away feeling that he had written the original song himself, a song he originally dismissed as a "tacky bar mitzvah tune."

▶

MICHAEL KAMEN: It's such a memorable experience to have participated in, and it's sadly a relatively rare one. I have done sixty-odd films, and I could count on one hand the films that have been totally absorbing in the last fifteen years of my life. And one of them was certainly *Brazil.*

I was in London co-producing Pink Floyd's music for *The Wall* and that led to making a co-production of a Pink Floyd album (their last, called *The Final Cut*). I was in the studio, and we called in Ray Cooper to play percussion. So Ray was listening to our newly recorded orchestra tracks in his headphones, saying, "Who did that orchestra writing, that's really good," and I sheepishly said, "Oh, I did." And he said, "Really? Have you ever done a film?"

And as a matter of fact I had a film that was coming out that day, the ads for it were all over the buses in London, called *Venom* [a thriller about kidnappers crossing paths with a black mamba]. It was not one of my prouder efforts; although it's a nice score, it's just not a very good film. They had Oliver Reed, Sarah Miles, Klaus Kinski, Nicol Williamson, a couple of other actors of great, great merit and not a single fucking memorable line of dialogue in the entire movie, and that to me was inexcusable, to get all this great talent together and give them nothing to do. The snake had more lines!

And I was sheepish about *Venom*, and Ray Cooper looked at me as if I were God and said, "*You* did *Venom*?" It turned out in his other life Ray was the managing director of Handmade Films, and he and George Harrison went to see *Venom* because it was offered to them for distribution. When he said George Harrison had actually sat in a theater and commented favorably on my music, saying it was the only good thing about the film, I felt like going through the roof. My head swelled up, amazing, I was really gratified.

And he said, "Have you ever met Terry Gilliam? He's making a film, it's called *Brazil*, it's with Robert De Niro. I'm going to have him call you, you should do that film." He asked if I had any other music. I had written a ballet score based on Rodin's sculpture, so I gave him a tape of *Rodin Mis en Vie*, and didn't hear from him for a year while Terry made the film. And as they drifted off into the horizon, my vision of *Brazil* was that it was going to be the history of Brazil, with Robert De Niro stripped to the waist samba-dancing through the streets of São Paolo, Rio de Janiero, absolutely besotted with the drunkenness and the revelry and sex and the throbbing pulse of the samba drums. I was really looking forward to it!

They called me back to meet with Terry and talk about the film, whereupon Terry informed me that one of the main features of the film was the *song* "Brazil."

And I said, "Wait a second, that song that they play at bar mitzvahs and weddings?"

And he goes, "Yeah!" He sang the little motif.

I said, "You can find a much *better* song than that. Why use that song? There's really *beautiful* music!" And he laughed: "No, that's the song, it's the *title* of the movie!"

And I was incredulous: "The movie is *about* the song?" I actually tried to talk him out of it. And then I went to see the movie and not only was the song and the melody involved in the movie but so was my ballet score! He had pasted bits of it into the movie. And obviously I was thrilled to pieces. The first version I saw was so confusing I couldn't begin to tell you, but he had created a world, and that world totally engulfed me for about six or eight months, and has never left me. I became totally immersed in it, to the extent that I actually learned the song, and discovered that deep within that Xavier Cugat, tacky bar mitzvah tune was a really reverential, achingly beautiful melody.

Terry's initial image of the film was of somebody sitting at the edge of oil-ladened docks in an industrial wasteland, glued to a shitty transistor radio, and "Brazil," in a tacky, tacky version (played by the Jim Kweskin Jug Band, I think!) was coming over this radio, and it represented in this incredible Death Valley of the twentieth century the last beautiful thing in the world: this tacky version of this melody coming over a transistor radio. A very powerful image that isn't *in* the movie, but doesn't need to be.

And the song became the endless source of theme for that movie: the front end of it backward, low end of it forward, slowed down, sped up, minor key, major key. There are also a couple of melodies of my own in there that are loosely based on the "Brazil" melody, and a bit of insane party music.

What was involved in legally using the Barroso song "Brazil"?

KAMEN: They were going to make a deal for use of the "Brazil" theme, and it was going to be charged by minute of use, so at one point I had to delineate the sections of my score where I felt I had used the unabridged theme. They gave that to a group of musicologists who went through the score and *disagreed* with me; there were some of my variations that they said, "No, that's your original." So when they totaled up the number of minutes of music they decided in my favor rather than Ary Barroso's!

Were there other specific musical inspirations for the characters, such as Sam Lowry, the dreaming functionary at the Ministry of Information?

KAMEN: I told Terry that the film was inspiring thoughts of the hero in Richard Strauss's *Ein Heldenleben*, which I was very fond of and very familiar with, having played it at Juilliard. Sam was a hero and felt like the vanquishing spirit of honesty and purity and strength and all that resolute positive stuff when in fact it was a dream, all a myth that he was aspiring to but didn't know how to handle.

Terry and I took a drive up to George Harrison's house to meet George for the first time, so we rode up the M4 listening to a great recording of *Ein Heldenleben*. And I felt I was riding on a comet. Turner must have done the landscapes and the sky that evening because it was so obliging; the music would hit a huge crescendo and finally climax and there would be a blaze of sunshine through a black cloud that bounced off a mountain and hit another, illuminate a whole other bank of clouds, set them alight with pink flames, and the violins soaring over the French horns, it was incredible.

I thought I would write this valiant heroic violin solo to represent Sam, and the funny thing was we have a fiddle player in London who was my orchestra leader, who is one of the most experienced and talented musicians in the London film music scene, Sid Sax. He's played for Bernard Herrmann, Nelson Riddle, he played violin on "Eleanor Rigby," this guy has credits a mile long, and is a fabulous fellow and fabulous musician, but not any longer a fabulous fiddle player; he can no longer maneuver the instrument as he used to. So I wanted to bring in Pinchas Zuckerman or some other friend of mine to take the solos because otherwise I knew Sid would stand up at a minute's notice and rattle off the whole part, and I wanted to avoid that. One thing led to another, I couldn't get Zuckerman, but I had all these fiddle solos written into the score. Despairing that I was going to have to leave them out and record them later, I didn't know what I was going to do. And then Sid picked up and played them in this wonderfully vulnerable way. They actually made more of a statement about Sam's character—this guy who dreamt that he had hair, that he had muscles, that he could fly—because it was played by this slightly weedy violin who was valiantly playing heroic music, but *only* valiantly. And that was a wonderful marriage of temperament to the story.

I didn't ever try to set it in any particular period. I mean, I used big orchestras, I used solo cello, I used kazoos, I used a thousand people singing and I used one guy singing.

In the temp track there was a little piece of music from *The Dead Zone*, a film that I had recently completed. And Terry liked that bit and I eventually incorporated a bit very much like it in the final work.

Terry and I had funny conversations; he'd say, "What do you think, do you think music can be funny?" I remember saying, "I *guess* music is funny."

A lot of the time my tongue was firmly in my cheek. The first time that I felt I was cracking the nut of the film and coming up with something that was a real contribution in the style of the film was in Kurtzmann's office, that incredible tracking shot as everyone's scuttling to and fro. I remembered a piece of music from my youth, Leroy Anderson's *The Typewriter,* and it used a typewriter with a symphony orchestra. So I had the typewriter beating the "Brazil" rhythm—DING-DING-*DINGGG*, DING-DE-*DING*-DE-*DING*—and I made the whole cue based on that thing, and I said, "Oh, *that's* funny!"

I finished the score, I was really proud of it, was certain that *Okay, now I'm going to be taken as somebody who needs to be reckoned with as a film composer*. And I got a call from my agent saying, "Sit down, welcome to Hollywood. Your score has just been fired." The president of Universal Pictures in his wisdom felt that he could make the film more accessible, more of a "Now Generation" thing and get some rock and roll or God knows what (disco I suppose at that time) and redo the score to make it more accessible to kids.* And I felt like I had been shot.

I wouldn't go outside. I was sure that, like in some weird Luis Buñuel film, people were laughing at me in the street, pointing, "Ah, the guy whose score was fucked!" I was mortified, and with a bit of sweet vengeance and justice, and a big exhalation, the score finally made it onto the film.

You worked after that on Gilliam's *Adventures of Baron Munchausen*, and I understand that in scenes featuring a musical ensemble whose ranks had been decimated by war, parts of the music were purposely left blank that *would* have been played by musicians had they not been killed!

KAMEN: We did part of that. I made a reduced group of disparate instruments—a solo fiddle played by Nigel Kennedy, a trombone, a trumpet, a drum, I think I played oboe, there was a bass but there was no cello, a conglomeration of percussion and very few brass players left—they were the first to go, they were drafted! It was really great fun, we had a wonderful session with this half-a-theater orchestra!

I must say I helped unwittingly to contribute I think in an adverse way to the film. The score to *Munchausen* is beautiful

---

*A very similar reasoning was used by Universal to replace Jerry Goldsmith's wondrous orchestral score for Ridley Scott's *Legend* (also 1985) with an all-electronic score by the group Tangerine Dream for the film's North American release.

and elegant and stylistically correct and all of that, but it's *too* detailed. Terry's whole attention to detail inspires you to paint what in my case could have been too detailed a canvas. Terry made a film that is so crenellated and crusted with gold leaf and florid curlicues of design that the music could have helped the film by being a little more stark, a little less baroque, less Period of Enlightenment. I think I was so motivated to be part of that rich tapestry that I didn't step back enough and just play a single note and allow the film to blossom on its own. It was an intense barrage of images and an intense barrage of *musical* images.

I just needed more theme-dependency. Back to Carl Prager: "Play the theme and then play the theme again and then you play the theme . . ." Perhaps I'm being harsh on myself, but if I could critique my own work, it would be that it was probably too busy. For example, the battle scenes at the end of the movie I did twice; once in Germany in the original recording, and then I rewrote and rerecorded it in England. I made the ideas a little bit more resonant. I felt I needed a little more spine to the idea, because it had been *too* detailed.

Movies at the end of the day are meant to be viewed in a very temporal fashion. They are not a novel that you reread, they are not books, they aren't paintings you can study; they grab you or they *don't* grab you.

■

GETTING A FOOT IN THE DOOR

When surveying how composers got their starts in the industry, it becomes clear that there is no single path to a career writing music for film, and certainly no direct route that leads from a diploma to a Hollywood scoring stage. There is also no key to predicting which composers might succeed or fail in a career that is, at its most basic, writing music to order.

Some noted concert or jazz composers have dipped their toes into film and retreated (David Amram, who wrote a terrific score for the 1962 political thriller *The Manchurian Candidate*, has had music featured in only one theatrical film in the last thirty years, the Beat documentary *The Source*). Others have jumped from rock bands to orchestral writing with a surprising facility. (Danny Elfman, former member of Oingo Boingo, wrote his first major score for the comedy *Pee-wee's Big Adventure*, which is a tuneful circus ride.)

Although universities are offering more courses in the aesthetics and mechanics of film scoring than was the case a couple of decades ago, the education and experience brought to bear in composing music for film comes from the concert hall, the stage, television, radio, commercials, cartoons, and touring bands. Just as important, the chance to pursue a career in the field—as is the case with many film crafts—often comes from serendipity and plain fool luck.

▶

ELMER BERNSTEIN: My initial musical training was as a pianist, and I was started on composition at the same time by a piano teacher. When I was twelve years old she took me to play my pieces for Aaron Copland, who started my composition education. I studied subsequently with Roger Sessions and Stefan Wolpe. Even though I studied composition the whole time and did compose pieces, I perceived myself mostly as a pianist—that was what I was headed for. (I suppose I did my last solo concert on piano at Town Hall in New York in 1950, and then at one other concert appearance after that in New York, a violin/piano sonata recital in 1967.)

I got into writing music for the media totally by accident; it had to do with World War II, curiously enough. One of the guys who was writing the dramatic scores for the propaganda shows they had on the air took an unofficial leave of absence at an awkward time, and the then–music director, Harry Bluestone, knew my background, called me in, and asked if I thought I could do such a thing. Needless to say I'd never done anything like that, but being young and foolish I said, "Sure." And I did it and thought, "Geez, this is fun!"

When I got out of the army in 1946, I tried to find gainful employment doing this, but I couldn't, and I went back to concertizing. And then in 1949, somebody that I knew in the army, a novelist named Millard Lampell, was doing a radio show for the United Nations and asked me to do the music, because I'd worked with him in the army, and I said, "Great!"

A very lucky thing happened: He had written a novel about a football player called *The Hero*, which he had sold to the movies, and he had talked to the producer about me. And by real weirdness, when *Variety* wrote up the radio show they mentioned the music, which was very rare for a radio show. They said something nice about the music, and the producer Sidney Buckman—who was then vice president of Columbia Pictures— heard the music, and to make a long story short Millard convinced them to let me do the music for this film, which was called *Saturday's Hero*. And that's how I got into film scoring.

DAVID SHIRE: I started out primarily wanting to write for the theater, but films were also part of it. I was writing shows in college, and when I came to New York I started supporting myself as a pianist and working in the theater. I had done a few TV scores in New York, but I had some friends who had gone out to Hollywood, and after we wrote a show that closed out of town, I was by myself in L.A. One of my friends took me to Universal Pictures and I got on their list of composers that they were hiring to do television scores, and I started working my way up from there to films.

So I always had this bifurcated career—one foot in the theater and one foot in film. I have had a string of Broadway/Off-Broadway shows that have gotten on, and although none of them have been big hits, they've had tremendous afterlife—hundreds of performances all over the world—so they have become kind of repertoire musicals. And yet I've scored more than a hundred films. I find them both satisfying in different ways.

I lived in L.A. for twenty-five years, but the first ten years of my professional life were spent living in New York, then the next twenty-five paying taxes in L.A., although always having some base of operations back in New York. I was regularly going back and forth between one and the other; I'd get an assignment in L.A., come to New York while I was working on a musical, and then go back to L.A. to record the movie, come back to New York to go to theater rehearsals.

ELIA CMIRAL: I grew up in a very culture-oriented family in Czechoslovakia. My mother was an actress, my father was a director and chief of theater, my grandfather a professor, so in this atmosphere all my childhood, everything I remember, is connected to literature, theater, music, books, so I didn't know anything else. I was painting, I was playing different instruments, I played rock and roll—I was interested in basically anything creative.

I got an offer from my father to write music for one of his theater setups, so that was my first work writing music for the stage. Then I attended a music conservatory in Prague, graduating from composition and double bass. I didn't really do so much afterward; I wrote a couple of small things, small TV cartoons and things like this, nothing really big.

But the political atmosphere was not really friendly at that time, so I actually escaped to Sweden, became a political refugee, and started from the beginning again. I learned Swedish, studied electronic music in Stockholm, and started my musical career there.

The first four years were pretty hard. Then I got my first job writing music for a TV series and from there it just accelerated. I did whatever came: features, commercials, theater music, three ballets, and so on. I was one of maybe three or four film composers in the country. But Sweden is small, eight million people. I'm not saying it's easier, it's definitely not, but the production of film I was interested in writing for was very, very limited. So my idea was to come to the U.S.

So I came here. I studied for one year, at USC in Los Angeles. I learned how to count clicks and all this mechanical stuff. After

Elia Cmiral

I finished USC came a very interesting offer through my Czech friends to score a movie, *Apartment Zero*, because they just fired a composer who was Astor Piazolla, the father of Argentine tango. Of course it's like being asked to replace Stravinsky! *Apartment Zero* was a movie which has the flavors of Argentine tango; it was shot in Buenos Aires, and they asked me to write a score with a flavor of Argentine tango, which I hadn't heard before, so it's like *Ooops!* So they asked me, "Can you write it?" I said, "Of course, no problem"—I learned in one year in the U.S. how to say that! I didn't know how to start writing themes, to hire musicians, I didn't know *anything*. And I had ten days to compose and record the score.

I bought some CDs of Argentine tangos and I incorporated a couple of elements—I didn't copy really because I didn't want to copy, I always write my music. But I think through listening I was able to write something with the flavors, the elements, and I used solo violin for it. So I wrote approximately ten to fifteen minutes of music for fifteen musicians and a solo violin. I recorded it in two days, and the rest of the score I improvised myself directly to the picture in the studio. I rented a bunch of percussion and synthesizers and samplers and so the next five days I just said to the engineer, "Okay, next cue," and they played me a scene and I played directly to the picture.

And the production was very successful, it became a cult movie. My friends told me afterward, "You should stay here and get an agent" and these kind of things. And I was too young and too naive. I was thinking, *I just finished USC, I'm here one year and I scored one movie and I'm already successful. Easy! Hollywood is easy!* I was very naive! I thought you just show that you are talented and willing to work hard and everyone will appreciate it. I didn't know that it was just a happy accident.

So I went back to Sweden—I had gotten a state grant to produce my own record there. I did the CD, I did a couple of other features and TV shows. I was very popular because I came with credits from the U.S., so it was even easier than before.

I came back to the U.S. in 1994, and *Apartment Zero* was forgotten already! So I did a couple of small projects, I did something for Showtime, and then my first break: opening season of *Nash Bridges* with Don Johnson. Then I scored another movie with the same director from *Apartment Zero*, called *Somebody Is Waiting* with Gabriel Byrne and Nastassja Kinski. It's on video but it didn't find a distributor in the U.S., unfortunately. I think it's a very interesting movie. Then it was waiting again, and then came *Ronin*.

MARK ISHAM: Others have had more intention and studied formally, but my generation of film composers has roots not at Juilliard's composition school, but in actually being out there as practical musicians, experiencing all these different types of music. In Hollywood, nobody cares if you have a degree on your résumé. They care if you can deliver.

UNTO THE BREACH: PATRICK DOYLE ON *HENRY V*

Shakespeare—traditionally a reliable source for movie spectaculars and romances—returned as a staple of the multiplex thanks to Kenneth Branagh's 1989 adaptation of *Henry V*. Drawing upon the resources of his Renaissance Theatre Company, Branagh hired his musical director and fellow actor Patrick Doyle to compose the score for his highly charged and cinematic treatment of Henry's efforts to lay claim to the French throne, climaxing at the Battle of Agincourt. The score also captures a playful romanticism as he woos Katherine, the daughter of the French king.

The typical Shakespearean adjectives apply to Doyle's music: noble, stately, touching, inspiring. But Doyle accomplished his task without sounding overly respectful of the period, allowing contemporary audiences to accept Branagh's very modern and cinematic interpretation. The fact that such a lyrical and confident musical score should come from someone completely unknown made its success all the more intriguing.

▶

PATRICK DOYLE: I worked with Kenneth Branagh's Renaissance Theatre Company as a musical director and performer—because of the very nature of the job, it was really part of that kind of repertory [tradition] where people are required to do many, many things. I mean, the name was "Renaissance" in the purest sense of the word. You had to be aware of or be capable of performing in many of the arts.

My very first collaboration with Kenneth was on a stage production of *Twelfth Night*. A mutual friend recommended me to him because he was looking for a musical director/composer, and we met and it seemed a fairly comfortable meeting, it just seemed the most natural thing in the world, and sometimes that happens and sometimes it doesn't. Maybe because both our parents had the same kind of upbringing, I suppose that was part of it, and also we both empathize about many, many different things.

He very much described in detail the visual and editorial approach to this production. The thing with Ken is, he's very succinct and very clear, and his images and descriptions are impossible to misunderstand, to misrepresent. He has very clear ideas and very strong ideas. I was certainly very inspired by his description; in fact the production of *Twelfth Night* ended up being precisely what he had envisioned and was extremely successful.

It was a great opportunity for a composer because Ken likes music, and there are many songs in *Twelfth Night*. In theater, unless there are songs specifically in the production (as there are in many of Shakespeare's plays), then the music tends to link scenes together—very little of it underplays the drama. In fact, in *Twelfth Night* a couple of music passages underlined very quietly the drama onstage, which was unusual. It was, looking back, a very filmic approach.

How does taking a "filmic approach" to a stage play differ from a film score?

Patrick Doyle

DOYLE: There are things you can do theatrically with music cues, but they do have to be very short and snappy because then the play moves on. But obviously in film you've got the luxury of locations and of being able to hone in on individuals, or groups, or on people's facial expressions, and then cut to the wider shots, so the whole language changes completely; the music then obviously has to reflect that. Whereas in theater one has the live aspect coupled with the 3-D image; this adds a different kind of sustenance.

Had you composed any music for a stage production of *Henry V* prior to the film?

DOYLE: I've never been involved in a theater production of *Henry V*. The theater productions I worked with Ken on were *Much Ado About Nothing, Hamlet* (both of which bore no resemblance whatsoever to his films), *Twelfth Night, As You Like It, King Lear*, and *A Midsummer Night's Dream*.

This was not only your first time composing for cinema, it was also Branagh's first time directing. What were you most apprehensive about?

DOYLE: Everything! Everything! Initially there was the whole thing of people all the time pointing out to me that William Walton had written a very successful score for the 1944 version, which Laurence Olivier directed and performed in, so I had to very quickly realize this is a different time; that was a propagandist and glorification-of-war-approach, and Ken's was a very antiwar approach. It would be a fresh, new, modern, of-its-time approach, so I very quickly had to dispel that [anxiety]. But not having spoken to anyone about film music, and not really having studied film scores, I suppose that—not consciously—I pulled on my experience up to that moment in dealing with music on the concert platform, and all my years being a performer and a musical director/composer culminated in this "mini-epic," as it was called.

So really it was all a question of instinct. Ken uses instinct, and the only thing I had was my instinct. And in the end both of us would say, "Well, my instinct tells me this . . ." and that's the only thing I have—and in fact it's still the same now. If somebody else says, "Well, I feel this could work," I have to say, "Well, that's probably very valid, but this is just as valid and as *I* am employed to do the job, then *this* will work." In the end the only thing you have is your instinct because no one *really* knows, otherwise everyone would prepare the perfect score, design, whatever.

As a general rule, judging by continual feedback [I have received], I seem to have a flair for melody. I enjoy writing lyrical music and it is invariably requested. I particularly enjoy writing for the voice as I have a great passion for the instrument. I was brought up in a very musical environment with parents who sang and listened to opera and popular American show music.

I come from a culture that demanded, from a very early age, if you had a voice at all it should be exploited and, as a child, regular gatherings where people performed in my home normally took place; this tradition is carried on today with the emergence of karaoke.

Henry V **is a more modern, contemporary piece than its medieval setting might suggest. What were your particular reasons for not making the score more closely resemble fourteenth- or fifteenth-century music?**

DOYLE: This was mainly to achieve accessibility and modernity for a contemporary audience. There are harmonies and modes which clearly suggest medieval beginnings so as to capture the flavor of the period.

The most popular part of your score was the choral piece "Non Nobis, Domine," the soulful elegy sung over the dead on the battlefield at Agincourt. How was that developed?

DOYLE: Ken requested a hymn for the post–Battle of Agincourt in order to create as much emotion as possible. He knew this would divide the audience in its reaction—some would think it glorified war, and others [would feel] it brought home the tragedy. He was particularly keen that the latter would be the objective and subsequent result.

Ken said, "I want it to start off with a solo voice, and I want it to build and build and build and build." Ken described the shot in detail, [saying] he wanted to use the words of "Non Nobis, Domine,"* and he described the shot—the carnage, dead soldiers, dead horses, mud, gore, spears, overturned carts—and he would be walking through all the mud and gore toward a cart where he would lay a body. He'd be carting one of the boys that were murdered by the French. So the shot ended up just as he described. The music was prerecorded and as the camera tracked following the king, the music was played in order to instill as much emotional assistance and atmosphere as possible for the actors on the set.

You acted in *Henry V* as well as composing the music.

DOYLE: I only had a small part and I had the hymn to sing, the opening of "Non Nobis, Domine." The whole point was to be part of the process in true Renaissance style. Of course by that time Ken and I'd both become friends, and I knew the company—the repertory company is a bit like Orson Welles's, I suppose, a whole crew of people who all knew each other, been together for years, so they're really part of a family, as it were. Plus it was an enormously beneficial position to be in, soaking up the atmosphere, to be there watching literally the whole film while it was being shot. So I knew it had to be useful to do this, but in fact it was only in retrospect, when I started to write and I realized how much I knew this particular adaptation, that I discovered *how* useful it was.

*From Psalm 115: *Non nobis, nobis Domine,*
                  Non nobis Domine,
                  Sed nomine, sed nomine,
                  Tuo da gloria.

Translation: *Not unto us, O Lord, not unto us,*
                  But unto Thy Name give the praise.

It was a terrific picture and a great opportunity for music because it's a very cinematic piece, and I suppose it was a great chance for me and I *knew* that obviously—you'd have to be insane not to realize that. I suppose I ran with it and grabbed it with both hands and embraced it. Ken instilled a lot of confidence, and yes, it was an absolutely huge, huge, life-changing experience in a kind of nonpretentious way. It just changed my life in many, many ways.

Having now worked with many directors and many genres, which of your scores do you have the most affection for?

DOYLE: *Henry V.* Oh, it has to be because it was my very first score. I mean I'm very fond of many of the scores I've written— *Much Ado About Nothing, A Little Princess, Carlito's Way, Indochine,* many of them—and with all due respect to all the other great directors I worked with, I think they would understand because that was my first score, it's got to mean the most because it was an opportunity to have a go at what is a very, very difficult job.

■

SCISSORS CUT PAPER WRAPS STONE: COLLABORATION

One of the first lessons to learn about film music is that it is not created independently of the director. Unless the composer and the director are the same person, such as Mike Figgis (*Leaving Las Vegas*), Tom Tykwer (*Run Lola Run*), or John Carpenter (*Halloween*), the composer will find his musical ideas being filtered through the sensibilities of the director, who may or may not be musically trained, who may or may not have an ear for what works in a given style, and who may or may not understand or appreciate music's dramatic or experimental possibilities. Communication between the collaborators is therefore essential, no matter what roadblock of musical language exists between a maestro and an auteur.

Ironically, the time when communication for a composer is most important comes when the production is almost at a close, when a director is at his most vulnerable:

the budget has been spent, scenes are being recut or even reshot, studio executives are arguing for inserting pop songs to justify an exploitable CD, and a locked release date looms large. If there are things that need to be "fixed" in the film, there are few ways left to do so now that the cinematographer, costume designer, and art director have gone home. Very often, the mantra is that the music will somehow "save" a bad scene or a poor performance, which is not film music's primary purpose.

It is a tender time for a composer to suggest using a sitar or a microtonal scale for his underscore; the last thing the director wants to confront is something he or she may not understand. It is therefore the composer's job to make sure the director doesn't lose faith in the composer's ability to do *his* job.

▶

JOHN CORIGLIANO: With most directors, if they don't trust the composer, he becomes almost an enemy instead of an ally. And I think part of the success of John Williams in the Spielberg films is that Spielberg trusts him; it's that element of trust that allows the composer to realize that if the director (who is not a musician) doesn't know how to describe what he wants, he'll describe something wrong!

I did a Shakespeare play once where this director wanted all these fanfares and he said, "I want baroque, baroque." And I thought, *He doesn't want "baroque"!* You know? So I gave him medieval-sounding things. Despite the fact that he had *said* baroque, he goes, "*Exactly* what I wanted!" And I knew he just didn't know what he was talking about. It was a very famous director, it's just he doesn't know anything about music. And so if I'd given him what he *said* he wanted, he would have hated it!

How would you characterize a successful collaboration between a composer and a director?

CORIGLIANO: "Collaboration" implies equality, and I don't think the situation between composers and directors is one of equality. I think "employee" is more accurate a term. And I don't think that's a bad thing, I think you just have to *know* that.

When you write a concert piece, the performers—be they Georg Solti, James Levine, Marilyn Horne—try to do what the composer wants. When you do an opera, they *half* try to do what the composer wants, but the director, the diva, and other people all have their views on how things should be changed because it's theater and they feel that the composer is not really a theatrical individual (even though I tend to disagree with them). So they intrude upon the compositional process, make cuts and changes and redo things another way, and don't necessarily adhere to the composer. Unless he's *dead—then* they adhere to him! But if he's alive they really don't want to have too much to do with him.

The film world is the extreme example of this, in which the director uses music very often as sound effect, a sound palette, which reinforces the drama of his film. In fact, the sound effects are much louder than the music is—the simple turning of a doorknob is a major event!—because in the dubbing chamber the composer is not present. I was not a part of any of the dubbings of my films. The sound effects people *are* present, and they have a sound effect for every millisecond of the movie. I was in the dubbing room for a very short time and saw that in fact the sound effects people are very active with the director during the dubbing process but the composer is excluded from that, unless you have a relationship like Steven Spielberg probably has with John Williams.

Leonard Bernstein did *On the Waterfront*, and when Marlon Brando was having his love scene with Eva Marie Saint during the beautiful, beautiful music that Bernstein wrote for that scene, Brando let out a little belch, and the director Elia Kazan just turned down the volume of the love music, brought up the belch and then brought back the love music. Can you imagine Leonard Bernstein *not* having control to say "That's ridiculous"?

And then you have people like the Kubricks who basically get in love with the temp tracks that they put behind the films, and end up having film scores commissioned and then thrown out and their temp tracks used. See, you really have no control as a composer. They can take your music out, they can put it in other places, they can cut it up, they can add sounds to it; so I really wouldn't call that a collaboration.

A collaboration is when you really do deal collaboratively. I would say *The Red Violin* [see page 258] has been more collaborative than previous films, because the director knows that this film is about a violin, and is musical, and he's quite willing to listen to reason; I can talk to him, he can talk to me, and we can come to conclusions. On the other hand, he did say that he was going to have the producer of the soundtrack and me up at the dubbing sessions and the next thing we knew we got a phone call saying the film was finished. He said—and I'm sure it's true—that time made that impossible, but it is indicative of the profession that once you've finished composing, you're really asked to go home.

Jerry Goldsmith's collaborations with the late Franklin Schaffner marked some of the finest scores of his career—*Planet of the Apes*, *Patton*, *Papillon*, and *Islands in the Stream* among them. In addition to Schaffner's own musical abilities (the director could read music and, according to

Goldsmith, was articulate in discussing musical ideas), his talent was to help spark Goldsmith to do his best work.

JERRY GOLDSMITH: When you work with somebody like Schaffner for so many years, you know, two words and "Okay, that's it, I know what you're talking about." It's a daily conversation. Every morning at eight he'd call: "Well, what are you going to write today?" I'd tell him what scene, and he'd give me a one-liner on what to do on the scene, what he feels or something like that.

On *Patton*, Frank and I had a lot of discussions and arguments because the picture was also a political, social statement. There were the three different elements in Patton—the religious, the war, and the archaic—and I wanted the religious side to be

Jerry Goldsmith

conveyed by the Doxology, which I would use as a counterpoint to the march (because my feeling is that all wars are religious, anyway). Frank finally called me, though, and said, "Uh-uh, it ain't going to work!" It was a bit of a heavy-handed idea, I must admit. So I wrote my own type of hymn for that. [And] on *Papillon*, Frank was the one who fixed the basic idea from the very beginning: "Montmartre, Montmartre." And I thought, *Where the hell is he getting that from?* But eventually he was right.

It was Franklin's idea in *The Boys from Brazil* to treat Laurence Olivier's character (the aged Nazi hunter) with a light Viennese waltz, and to treat Gregory Peck (the Nazi surgeon living in South America) very Wagnerian. It was a terrific idea. What a marvelous approach! It was not up to the music in this film to say what a monster this man was. For one montage where Peck was performing an operation, it was like "Valhalla in Paraguay." He had such a godlike image of himself, it made a marvelous comment . . .

In Vienna, where they were shooting, Franklin started in saying, "I want nothing but waltzes in the picture." It was very funny, but I thought he was crazy. Then when I started writing months later, it really developed that the chases and a horrifying scene with dogs were all being done in ¾ time, not necessarily strict waltzes, but definitely in that feeling. Here was an example of a suggestion by a director that made sense.

DAVID SHIRE: Coming out of the theater, I welcome and seek collaboration. I feel that's the way good work is done and big mistakes are avoided. And in a way I'd rather directors didn't have specific musical training because what I want is a *dramatic* suggestion. I don't want them to tell me in a given scene, "I hear an oboe here." I want them to say, "I'd like the music to emphasize this aspect of the scene, or the performances here aren't as good as I wanted them to be, could you help out with that, or the performances are terrific here and I don't even know if we should have music but can you write something very subtle in a subliminal way?" That's the kind of input I want from a director. I've been lucky in that most of the directors I've worked with have given me that kind of input.

I insist on playing themes for directors on the piano, or what's asked for more and more now are called "Polaroids," where on synthesizers you make a mock-up of the actual orchestration of the cue. Because I want their input; I want them to say, "Well, I think the rhythm is right but the melody is wrong," or "I love the melody but it doesn't have enough energy." Or "Gee, I love this piece but the oboe seems a funny choice, what would it sound like on another instrument?" That's what I want.

BASIL POLEDOURIS: I have a tremendous respect for directors, I don't know how any of them go out there and do it; they're bombarded by millions of questions on the set, they're bombarded by hundreds of issues of finance and marketing, and yet somehow they maintain all that and put ideas and characters on film. Now they work with a lot of people and it seems to me the best of them put together a cadre, a team of people that they work with, but nonetheless everything comes down to the director. And so I have this amazing amount of respect for somebody who can multitask like that—particularly when they've got a really good movie! There's some people who talk a great game and when you see what they've done you go, "Well, maybe we should do this with subtitles instead of music if you really want to get *all* those concepts in the music against this particular picture—it's not going to happen."

But with the good ones I think it's just the willingness to help them realize what it is they're going after. And that can be frightening [for them]. It takes a very special director to want to turn the film over to a composer—some directors are really terrified to let someone else have that much control over how the film's going to sound, and for that reason I think they find a lot of security in the so-called temporary track, because it's a *given*. They kind of have an idea of what it is, and it may have been successful with preview audiences so therefore that music has become a part of the film. Those are the ones I find I can offer the least to, because I'm not interested in being an arranger. If somebody falls in love with a particular piece of music or particular bunches of pieces of music from other composers, they should hire those composers, or hire a really good arranger to copy it all without getting sued.

Toward the end of production, directors are at their most vulnerable. And it's at that time when they may not risk going with something untried musically because they'll have heard some piece of music on their temp track and go, "Oh, *that* works."

POLEDOURIS: And oftentimes it will, for a moment or two. There are always pieces of music that will work against any particular scene. But they won't *sustain*, there'll be no continuity to it, but it gives them an idea.

At its best would be a director like Paul Verhoeven, who will have all these ideas—he spends hours and hours listening to CDs against his film, but he gets an idea about what he wants out of the music: a tempo, a density of orchestration, an attitude, whether it's seriously edgy or romantic or whatever. And he's extraordinarily intelligent and he'll redefine those things in terms of his movie and in terms of the chosen composer's style. So he doesn't just play this piece of music for you and go, "Here, make it sound like this." I've had directors say, "Look, I really love this, just change the notes!"

Paul analyzes it and figures out what it is about the music he likes. What he wants out of almost everyone involved in the productions is themselves; he wants them to bring something to his film. He'll define the parameters but then within that he expects to be surprised, delightfully. And I love that, I love that! He lays the gauntlet down and he'll make no bones; he says, "Look, I know a lot about this, and this is what I really like and this is *why* I like it, but if you've got a better idea, *show* me!"

So I want to be challenged, and that aspect of my personality I think is a plus. I've run across directors that are clueless, they don't want to have to think about it; they've hired me because I'm an expert on the subject and they want me to do it. I've got no problem with that. I rather like that as long as I have their trust.

I assume they're hiring me because they find something of musical value, something of an approach over a body of work— "I like what this particular composer does with a scene."

I do think the fact that directors may like a particular film I've done enters into it. Verhoeven hired me for *Robocop* because of my work in *Conan the Barbarian*, and the way in which the music matched the visuals. But the visuals were very powerful and they needed something strong to match them. Paul always likes to go for the throat, and I like that. And Bille August is the exact opposite; he likes everything to be somewhat restrained and have a kind of tension which is produced by that sense of restraint— completely different approaches. Between the way music matches visuals and how it can enhance the drama, I think they both saw something, and that's why they've hired me.

GOLDSMITH: Joe Dante in a way is sort of an anachronism among young directors. His pictures are in today's style, yet he thinks and he works much like a Capra would. Whereas so many of these guys, they idolize Capra but, you know, they don't really incorporate it. Joe still makes pictures like, I think, pictures *should* be made. And he communicates well with the people making the film. He's not an auteur, which is to me . . . [*grimacing*] the director who feels he's quite capable of scoring the film himself, among all the other functions of the film. But that to me is such a load of rubbish. Film is a collaborative medium, and it always will be.

I think if one looks back at the history of great films, they're going to find that the great films were not done by the auteurs as far as I'm concerned, and I think as far as history is concerned. It's by contributions of a number of extremely gifted and creative people, all under the guidance of a good director whose main job is just to assemble all these massive egos, keep them in line, and try and coax the best out of them all. And I think the key to all the individuals involved in the film is to keep them aware of how important their contribution is to the final product, which is the totality of it all. *That's* a great director as far as I'm concerned.

BACKWARD PRISON GANGS, SCANDINAVIAN HYMNS, "DANNY BOY," AND YODELING: CARTER BURWELL ON THE COEN BROTHERS

Carter Burwell was a performer in New York City in the early 1980s when he hooked up with the filmmaking team of Joel and Ethan Coen—a relationship that has lasted and prospered to this day. Among all contemporary composer-director teams, Burwell and the Coens have probably produced more stylish and yet stylistically *dissimilar* works than any other team, from the gleeful anarchy of *Raising Arizona* to the claustrophobia of *Barton Fink* and the dirge-like *Fargo*.

▶

CARTER BURWELL: When the Coens were working on *Blood Simple,* their first movie, they were trying to find a composer who would do the job for essentially nothing, it being a low-budget independent film. They were talking to a lot of different composers and musicians, mostly in the New York area, and their sound editor, Skip Lievsay, who knew my work from bands in New York, asked me if I would be interested. As a general rule, when people ask me to do things I haven't done before I always say yes—it would be interesting.

Of course I didn't have a demo reel or anything like that to play for the Coens. So I just went in, saw a reel from the movie, went home, thought up some thematic material on the piano and

Carter Burwell

synthesizers, made a tape, took it to them a couple of days later, and they seemed to like a couple of the things there. But they went on for months talking to lots of different composers— partly because the people who put money into the film, having backed these two guys who had no demonstrable experience at directing or producing, didn't really want the Coens to just keep hiring *other* people who had no experience either! If not a name, at least someone who knew how it worked technically; I didn't know *anything* about it at all. In the end they decided to hire me because they had just liked the themes that I'd written from my first reaction to the film, and those were the themes we ended up using.

At that time I was largely a performing musician, and one of the things that *Blood Simple* gave me the opportunity to do was to work in a studio. I can't do tape manipulations or these hyp- notic musical forms live, so this was an opportunity to do a lot more experimental things.

But technically, *none* of us knew how to approach a film score. I paid no attention to what other film composers were doing, and paid no attention to what the technological solutions were to the problems we were addressing—I knew that there must *be* solutions out there but we just didn't have time to learn them. I'd written those themes very early on, but at the point at which they hired me I had three weeks to finish it up.

I didn't know how really to synchronize music to a film, and they didn't know how to do it except after the fact, so we stum- bled around with it. We'd say, "Well, I guess this scene's about a minute and a half long, so I'll just write a minute and a half of music." Joel was an "experienced" editor at that point, so we all kind of assumed that whatever I did he'd be able to edit it into shape. So it was a bunch of people who knew *nothing* about the medium of film music working on it. It's still one of my favorite scores, I think partly *because* we didn't know what we were doing—because unlike everything I've written since then, the music of *Blood Simple* was not really attending that carefully to what was on the screen. The pieces were written as pieces of music, because we thought that we could later *make* them fit the movie.

What is an example of the uncommon approach you took to the music of *Blood Simple*?

BURWELL: I thought if we had voices, vocal music buried so deep under the other stuff I was doing that you could barely hear it—so that even if you heard it you couldn't identify it—that might give it an interesting and disquieting air. You would *just* be aware of it. Because there's something about the human voice that tickles the brain in a way. Through hundreds of thousands of years of evolution we really have learned to focus in whenever we hear a human voice. But if you manipulate it—for instance, just playing it backward—it would just be a little bit discomfiting.

I had these recordings that are publicly available that Alan Lomax did of some prisoners working on a chain gang singing songs,* so I played them backward underneath that piece of music. And it was nice; the piece of music already has this kind of humid, heavy feeling to it, and I guess that's what made me think about this particular piece of vocal music to put against the film, the humidity and the lumbering weight of it.

The interaction between the music and what's happening on the screen is one of my favorite things in this field. These days I'm *always* watching what's happening on-screen while I'm writing the music to it—I'm interweaving the music around the dialogue and the action. None of that happened in *Blood Simple*.

*Negro Prison Songs, reissued on CD as *Prison Songs: Historical Recordings from Parchman Farm 1947–48*, by Rounder Records.

But it works in a different way somehow; the music's really basically mood, partly because it *ignores* action. It's like the ceiling fans that they have going in all those scenes, just to give it a sort of *noir*ish mood—the music works that way, too. Sometimes I wonder whether I should try going back to that approach, but the fact is I really love scoring music to what's happening in the picture and the way music can change the context of a piece of dialogue or action.

I have very fond memories of *Blood Simple*, partly just because we had no idea what we were doing. We're actually right now doing a reworking of *Blood Simple* because someone wants to rerelease it, and do a stereo release—the original mix we did was mono—and Joel, because he's an editor, can't keep his hands off it, so he's reediting the movie, too. It's really more a reconstruction of *Blood Simple*.

How did the Coens communicate to you what musical ideas they had in mind, about what worked and what didn't work?

BURWELL: I think that, like a lot of directors, they're best at reacting to something that they hear, rather than putting into words right up front what music they might think is appropriate. If they're presented with a piece of music, they can say whether they like it or not, why it might work, why it might not. On *Blood Simple* I think they really didn't know what they wanted; that's why they talked to all those composers over many months, and I'm sure they heard lots of different things. I think someone may have even started writing an electronic music score for the movie before I was hired and that was when they realized they *didn't* want electronic music. But I don't think they knew what they wanted beforehand; I don't think there's any question about that.

What developed as we worked on it during those three weeks was the piano became a more important element than we thought it was going to be. The movie was in a way kind of glossy and the characters have intimate relationships, but the way Joel and Ethan tend to shoot a movie doesn't create a sense of intimacy, it creates a sense of coldness. So in the end, as we'd work on a piece, the piano might be a part of it, and more and more Joel or Ethan might say, "Well, why don't we just use the piano there?" and what it would do was create a sense of intimacy and warmth. Obviously that's not what I used the backward chain gang for—intimacy and warmth!—but there are points in the movie when that was a nice element that I'm sure they hadn't planned on. In fact, they hardly ever plan on intimacy and warmth in their movies! And I sometimes twist their arm to push the music in that direction, if only for ironical reasons, to *go against* what's going on on-screen. *Miller's Crossing* is an example.

Often I will write a piece of music from the point of view of a character. In *Miller's Crossing* it's from Gabriel Byrne's character; in *Barton Fink* it's from Fink's character, and it plays his childlike nature in a way.

For *Raising Arizona*, whose point of view did the yodeler take?

BURWELL: I believe while Joel was shooting the movie he was thinking about yodeling. Joel and Ethan are both into country music, and Ethan actually does yodel, but I think yodeling was Joel's idea. I give him credit for that because it's a brilliant idea.

The music treats the movie kind of like a cartoon; *no one's really ever going to get hurt in this movie* is what the music tells you. People can be firing shotguns at each other and no one's going to get any more hurt than Bugs Bunny would in a similar situation. And the yodeling and banjo helped to tell you that. It's a crazy ride we're going on in this film, and the music really is kind of playing Nicolas Cage. It's used right over the intro to the movie before the credits and introduces him, and it's all scored with that banjo and yodeling stuff. What it does is it plays him as a latter-day cowboy who wants to live free on the prairie, so to speak, in his own fashion, and no matter what situation he's in, it reminds you that he's got this cartoon cowboy aspect to him.

Of all your scores, your work for the Coens seems to be the most noteworthy, or the most popular; it's certainly the least conventional.

BURWELL: The scores I've done for their movies are my main reason for being in this business. If I weren't working on their movies, if they stopped making movies for some reason, I don't know if I'd really keep doing this. They are by far the most interesting, and Joel and Ethan rarely prevent me from doing anything that I want. I mean, there are very few external considerations. In Hollywood it's not unusual to have people say, "Well, we want to save this place for a song, or the end credits for a song, because the studio is owned by a conglomerate which has a record label associated with it which has a new band that's coming out"—things like that enter into it. But I've rarely heard Joel and Ethan discuss *anything* that wasn't just about how to make the movie better. We rarely discuss the audience. Once in a while I'll say, "Do you think this point is clear, that point is clear?" But we never think about the audience when we work. I know I for one am just trying to entertain *myself*.

And the other thing I have to say on that subject is, *Miller's Crossing* was the first orchestral score I did. There is nobody else who would've hired me to do an orchestral score knowing that I

Burwell during the recording of Mathieu Kassovitz's French thriller *Assassin(s)* (1997).

knew nothing about orchestral music; they're much too conservative. I've met a few people who *have* hired me to do something I hadn't done before, but nothing that risky, where they put hundreds of thousands of dollars of the music budget in the hands of someone who, again, knows nothing about orchestral music.

From the time we read the script together, before they even shot it, we all agreed it probably would be nice to use kind of a big orchestra. We didn't know what a really big orchestra *was*, but something that *sounds* like one—bigger than a banjo and a yodeler! So while they were shooting I was learning about orchestration and how the whole thing works, and it was really fun. And I also had an *excess* of time, three months, to write the score, which is a lot more than I usually get. And, also uniquely, they had money left over after the shoot—they'd actually come in under budget on the movie—so we could afford a big orchestra and do everything that we wanted to do. So it was a great experience. I love whenever this business gives you an opportunity to do something new.

I was writing it to sound symphonic, in other words more counterpoint in parts; that's definitely what I was attempting to do. Our interest was to have a large orchestra but have it play simply, which I do sometimes. I mean, *Fargo* was pretty simple writing and it's only something like forty players, but in *Miller's Crossing* the point of having a large orchestra was to get a big, lush, traditional sound because of the period the movie takes place in, and the mind-set of the characters. When you see the film on a big screen you see how much attention was spent on costumes and stuff like this. The music had to fit into that environment where it would be rich and maybe even a little ostentatious from time to time—that may not be the right word, but it would be an Irish gangster's *idea* of ostentation in a way, that the music should be big and sentimental and lush.

And "Danny Boy" playing on the record player under the attempted assassination of Albert Finney's mob boss was obviously an Irish gangster's idea of relaxing mood music!

BURWELL: Well, it's actually a little *too* obvious, yes! The Coens knew that something had to be playing on Albert Finney's record player when the assassins arrive. The first thought was, "Well, we'll stick in 'Danny Boy,'" but the assumption was always *we'll find something else to put in,* because it was just too obvious. And wouldn't it be nice if we found another Irish piece that people weren't as familiar with that would work as well? But they cut the scene to "Danny Boy" and after trying lots of different traditional Irish pieces there, nothing was really quite as good. So in the end we settled on "Danny Boy." Well, it certainly works!

The version of "Danny Boy" they cut to mostly worked but there were some things we wanted to change, moments when it would really improve dramatically if we could rerecord it—as the car is careening off into the distance once its driver has been shot, before the car hits the tree, could he hold this note longer? Little things like that. And that raised lots of interesting questions: For example, if we rerecorded it we'd have to find someone who could do the Irish tenor, and also find someone who could do one of these really traditional orchestra arrangements, which *I* didn't have the knowledge to do. I was just learning about orchestral music in the first place—to try and learn about 1920s pop orchestra arrangements was beyond me.

Ethan looked up the person who just happened to be singing the version of "Danny Boy" they had, Frank Patterson. He is sort of *the* Irish tenor of our time and it just so happened that he was in New York, so we got in touch with his agent (who is also his wife) and asked if he'd like to come over, take a look at this movie, and see if we could interest him at all in singing a version of "Danny Boy" for this. Frank was very interested; he sort of thought, "This film will introduce 'Danny Boy' to a whole new audience!" He didn't seem at all off-put by the actual content of the scene, some guy getting his head blown off! He was very excited by it.

And we found this ancient guy, Larry Wilcox, to do the arrangement. He was in his eighties, so his period of experience as an arranger almost goes back that far, in fact it probably did. He died a few years after we did *Miller's Crossing,* I think. But he did the arrangement and we recorded it in this extremely old-fashioned approach which I'm thrilled that I had a chance to see.

Frank would watch the film with us, and Joel and Ethan would say, "Now that word, if you could hit that word while this action happens, that would be perfect, because then we could set up and hold the syllable during *this* shot, and hit this word *here . . ."* He basically memorized the visual cues that he was trying to hit with his performance of the song. Then we went into the recording studio, Frank watched the film while he was singing, the conductor (who was also the arranger) listened to Frank and watched *him* and conducted the orchestra to follow along, which is the way that piece would have been recorded in the twenties—the singer would sing, and the orchestra would follow along via the conductor. That's just not done that much anymore. And I think Frank got it in two takes. It was kind of amazing.

THE LOST SHEEP

In *Fargo*, I did two things that are somewhat at odds with each other: I took the fact that the film is presented as a true crime story, and I thought, well, *I* never looked at the story that way, but what if I *do* play it that way so that occasionally the music gives that over-the-top banging timpani kind of thing that you would expect from true crime stories? And at the same time contrast that with this very lonely and pathetic hymn, which would hopefully play and make *amusing* some of the most tragic parts of the film. Because it plays the hopeless efforts of these characters and their ambitions.

It comes off as very sad that the husband, who is trying to get rid of his wife to save himself in some way, bumbles it at every move, and the same with the guys that he hires; basically they're all lost in some way, but the music would in a sense play their hopes that are always confounded, and perhaps that would really actually help people laugh at some of these things that are going on—you'd laugh, and yet it wouldn't distance you from the characters.

Honestly, *Fargo* was one of the more risky scores I've done with the Coens. For instance, doing Big Crime Music, that would only work if the audience actually *believes* that; if they think they're watching a comedy or a "Coen Brothers movie," the music may seem like it's overwhelming the film, because often there's not much happening—the opening credits is just a guy driving a car through the snow, and the music gets *very* big. If you don't want the music to swamp the film, hopefully what happens is the music gets big and your feeling is, "Wow, something *important* is going on." You don't want to feel the music is just here for its own sake. So it was a little risky from my point of view.

I started listening to a lot of Scandinavian music after I read the script. I thought that might be an interesting source—not necessarily that I was going to take any melodies from that, but just learning about the fiddle styles that they used, and the Hardanger fiddle,* which we did end up using. Because these people all have Scandinavian names and the frame is often this white frame of snow, I thought learning about the *sound* of Scandinavian music might be a nice source.

I'd been working on some themes of my own, different melodies, when I found a Norwegian folk song–turned–hymn called "The Lost Sheep." My reaction was, "Well, that's really perfect; I guess I *could* go on for a few more weeks *trying* to write something that's better than that . . ." It certainly plays the pathetic quality of Bill Macy's character, and the fact that it's *called* "The Lost Sheep" seemed perfect, also.

The version of "Lost Sheep" I heard was played on solo violin. The first thing I did was take that and try a bombastic orchestral approach to the melody—and it worked, it was *funny*! I played it for the Coens and they saw it right away.

Usually they see what I'm trying to do right away. The only

*Developed in Norway in the seventeenth century, this folk instrument's sympathetic strings running beneath the fingerboard add an echoing overtone, creating a dronelike polyphonic quality.

movie where we've ever had any difficulty with that was *Hud-sucker Proxy*, which was very hard to finally get a musical approach that we were all satisfied with, but on all the other movies we're usually in sync without having to talk about it much.

The first public screening I went to of *Barton Fink*—I love that movie, it's probably my favorite of their films—I was the only person in the audience laughing. They seemed to think it was a serious critique of the creative process or something; I just think it's hilarious! I find John Goodman hysterical from beginning to end. But at this point I think people maybe know Joel and Ethan's work enough that a large part of the audience comes prepared to laugh at material that doesn't say on its face, "It's time to laugh." People come understanding that there's a tongue-in-cheek quality, and they'll laugh. It has so much to do with expectations.

The first audience I went to see *Blood Simple* with was stone quiet the whole time. And after it'd been playing at midnight shows for about three months I went and saw it again, and people were laughing and screaming, people had memorized the dialogue and were shouting it out, it was completely different, and the only difference is their expectations. They've come to see the movie in a certain way; when it was first released people thought it was an art movie and as it survived people began to realize it was this . . . I guess it's sort of a genre unto itself, film noir comedy.

ENTERING DUDEVILLE

The Big Lebowski is the only film which the Coens have done which has songs in it. I think they knew you would have to have a lot of recognizable songs to capture that feeling of the Dude (Jeff Bridges), this guy who's kind of trapped in the seventies—"trapped" is not the right word, but in any case is living in his own time and space, and that time and space is certainly *not* the early nineties, which is when the action takes place. So I think using source music [songs which are played "inside" the film, heard by the characters] to do that is a good idea. I think also Joel and Ethan always try to do something that they haven't done before, and in a way working with songs, putting together a song album, is an aspect of the film biz that they hadn't under-taken, so I think just doing that interested them. But it had a lot to do with that character; songs are going to be the way to paint the Dude—he's wearing his Walkman a lot of the time, and lis-tening to his car radio. So a lot of those songs, for instance, Creedence Clearwater Revival and Bob Dylan, they were all written into the script, they were all there before I got involved. And then once the idea had been established that there would be a lot of songs in the movie, we pretty quickly decided that there shouldn't be *anything* that's recognizable as score that would pull you *out* of "Dudeville."

T-Bone Burnett was listed as music archivist on the movie credits, and he was really in charge of one, getting them access to the songs they wanted; and two, when they couldn't get a song they wanted or when there was a place that needed a song, he would try to find things that were appropriate. And T-Bone *knows* the Dude! He's good at that.

I did about six original pieces for the movie, but I intention-ally made them all *sound* like songs, so that they're virtually imperceptible as anything but source. I'd have to draw you a map to show you where my music is in the movie. For instance, at the end when the bowlers finally battle the Nihilists—sup-posedly ex-members of a German techno-pop band—the Nihilists have a boom box with them that's playing one of their "songs" from the seventies, and so I wrote that song. And there's one when Jon Polito, who plays a private dick, appears; there's kind of a jazz piece happening that starts almost like score (when

Jeff Bridges comes out of his apartment), but then it *turns into* car radio source (when Polito steps out of his Volkswagen). It's all things like that, all couched as pieces of source, which was interesting. But Joel promises me we'll have a *real* score in the next movie, which is more fun!

■

IMMERSION: BEGINNING THE PROCESS

This chapter explores the process by which a composer chooses his projects, selects a musical approach, and decides (usually with the director) where and how often music is to be played in a film.

When a rough cut is screened, it can sometimes contain a "temp track"—bits of music pulled from other sources—which may have helped an editor pace the cutting of his scenes, but most often serves as an annoyance or hindrance to the composer seeking an original take on a film.

DRAWING STRAWS

How do you typically choose films to score—and do you actively solicit work from directors or projects you're interested in, or do they come to you?

CARTER BURWELL: It's a good question, and I don't think there's any simple answer. Almost always they come to me—*that* part of the question's easy to answer.

Do they come saying "You wrote a score for such-and-such, we want a score just like that"?

BURWELL: That's common, it was much more common at the beginning of my career. After I did *Raising Arizona*, Ethan Coen said, "You know, you're going to get a lot of calls for farm comedies now." And it was a genre I was unfamiliar with, I didn't know existed, but it turns out there *are* such things as farm comedies, and people *did* call me. "So, you want banjos? Call Carter Burwell!" Of course I don't want to work in situations like that where someone calls me because they want me to do something like what I've done before. Hopefully, I don't repeat myself; I'd feel bad if I thought that I was.

I'm much more intrigued by a project which asks me to do something I haven't done before. And there are personalities that intrigue me, directors whose work I have admired. When they call and say, "Why don't we work on something," in some such situations I'll say yes just because I really want to work with them. I worked with Todd Haines on *Velvet Goldmine*, and I'm really glad I did. I thought he was someone who is smart, capable, and also a nice person. You know, there are not *that* many of those people in this business, so I love meeting another!

But the thing that's most likely to get me into a film is just that it seems to offer me the chance to do something that I haven't done before, the exception being (as you might have guessed from what I was just saying before about romance) the romantic comedy genre, which is the hardest for me to conceive. I really feel at a loss for what to play when someone is walking down the street and they're in love. I can do love music when someone is getting their brains bashed out, but you know, the idea of just doing music which *sincerely* plays what people are feeling just doesn't interest me. It doesn't interest me in real life, when everything all comes together and we've got everyone feeling the same thing and we can all agree and we can express it well—it's just not *interesting* in real life, and it doesn't interest me in films either.

I think what's interesting in films, especially for a composer, are things that can't be expressed in any other way. You know, when the characters aren't able to put something into words or maybe when the director or writer hasn't put it on the screen and you get to express it in music, that's what I enjoy. Romantic comedies don't usually have enough depth or complexity of emotional honesty. A lot of people won't know what I'm talking about, because a lot of people *like* those films and feel that they *have* that depth of emotion, but to me it's not depth—all the emotion's on the surface. I've done a couple of those, I find them really hard, and I do try as a general rule, when someone asks me to do one, to say, "You know, you're really hiring the wrong person, I'm really not good at this."

But the best thing is for someone to ask me to do something I haven't done before.

Are you more interested in characters or the film's atmosphere?

BURWELL: Rarely the characters. I'm not generally that involved in characters or plot in films—I'm not speaking just as a composer, but when I go to films, that doesn't interest me that much. I'm very taken by things like, is it well written? Even a romantic comedy, if it's well written I *guess* I can enjoy it! In fact, I enjoy working with people who are trying to do something new in film that hasn't been done before. I was talking today with Andy Bergman about this film he's making that's based on the life of Jacqueline Susann, and in a way it doesn't sound really like my cup of tea (at least as far as my "romantic comedy problem" is concerned), but it's really *not* romantic. It's written *almost* as though it were a romantic comedy and a farce, quite funny, but what's going on is often quite tragic. Her life was really just horrible: she had cancer, a mastectomy, an autistic child, life just screwed her at every turn. And all she ever wanted to be was famous and she had failed at it continuously until she realized that she was dying of cancer; she for some reason had this idea, *I'm just going to write a book about all the crap I know about everyone in show business*, and amazingly it became a best-seller and she finally got her dream. But the movie is really a tragedy. And so I'm eager to work on that, it's just a strange approach to the material.

So things like that really attract me. If anyone's going to do something new and different, I take my hat off to them. Because feature filmmaking is a very conservative medium, and whenever anybody tries to do anything different, I always say I'll help. A friend of mine made a movie with singing and dancing cockroaches called *Joe's Apartment*. He called—when it was still just a script—and asked if I would be interested. I said if you can get someone to put money into this, you can count me in. Anyone who will make a movie about singing and dancing cockroaches, I'll help!

I honestly can't remember a film which I've done because I liked the character, but I'll often do a film because I like the writing, and often because I like the directing.

JERRY GOLDSMITH: Working with a director for the first time, for me, is very awkward, as I'm sure it is for the director. It's like going out with a girl for the first time, that first date. Everything's very proper. You're very polite with each other and don't want to make waves. [You don't have] the same kind of freedom of expression to feel the other guy out. And *he* doesn't want to hurt anybody's feelings either.

ELMER BERNSTEIN: These days I'm probably more influenced by what I think the working relationship is going to be as much as the subject matter. I'm really at a stage in life where I really don't want to work with anybody that's difficult, and I certainly don't want to work with any music abusers! I like the idea of people who like what they're doing, they're involved in what they're doing.

I think really good filmmakers enjoy that kind of association with composers. Certainly it's rare. I've had it on Alan Pakula's films, I had a good working relationship with John Sturges, certainly it happened on *Ten Commandments* with Cecil B. DeMille. It's not as common these days because things are a little more slapdash and fast. There's a tendency for much less thought to go into scores today. That's not consistently true, but there is a tendency.

What dictates your being offered a particular assignment?

BERNSTEIN: I suppose it's the luck of the draw. I did those comedies for ten years: *Animal House*, *Meatballs*, *Airplane!*, *Trading Places*, and on and on. And after ten years of that I began to get nervous because that was the only kind of picture I was offered. So finally, I think it was in 1989, I said, "No more." Of course, I didn't work for a year as a result!

In my case I just got lucky because of a promise I had once made a very long time ago to a dear friend, Noel Pearson, that if he ever produced a film I would do the music for it, and that film turned out to be *My Left Foot*. That was a very good way to break out of the comedy routine. I was lucky then. I don't know what would have happened if Noel hadn't come along with *My Left Foot*. It's very hard to break out of that kind of a mold easily, especially when the comedies that I was doing were so successful. In a way, it would have been easier if they didn't make any money!

I have relatively little to do with whether a picture makes money or not, but nevertheless if you're associated with money-making, successful projects, then everybody wants you for that kind of project; I've had that several times in my career. When I did *The Man with the Golden Arm*, all that anybody wanted off me were jazz scores, and that went on for quite a while; and then when I did *The Magnificent Seven*, I had ten years of westerns, then ten years of comedies. But I've always quite actively, quite consciously pursued a varied career; I never wanted to be typed.

DAVID SHIRE: Because of my background in the theater and everything, I guess I prefer melodic-oriented pictures to action pictures where you're just writing a lot of music and sound effects, except *The Taking of Pelham One Two Three* was very satisfying. I like going from one genre to another; the worst thing is to do a western after a western, or a psychological thriller right after a psychological thriller.

MARK ISHAM: I've been booked almost a year in advance sometimes, and other times I've actually been out of work, because of schedules just colliding and, well, *that* film is moving six months away, and all of a sudden there's nothing for four months. That's a very tough part of it from a business point of view, just keeping the schedules going, because it's very volatile; I don't know if there's any real pattern to it.

I knew about Alan Rudolph's *Afterglow* the day that the studio said, "Make the film." He called me and said we're going to do it: "See you in about twelve months!" But a film like that has a very tight budget so the schedule's very exact; they're not going to change much—they don't have the money to change! So I can put it on the calendar and be pretty sure that that's when they'll need me. It's usually the big blockbuster films which are the worst, because they've spent so much money they don't mind spending *more* to keep the film open, or all of a sudden if some other blockbuster film moves opposite them they'll pounce on a new release date, and my deadline changes.

GOLDSMITH: A problem I've been having is that for every one picture I do I get nine other pictures [offered]. And they wait so long till the picture's shot, 99 percent chance I can't do it, there's a conflict. Every once in a while one comes up where it's completed; *Hoosiers* was one. They didn't think they had the money for me when they started the picture, and so down the line when they finished, they realized they had something special and they came to me and I happened to be free at the time to do it.

I'd be happy if I were doing *Hoosiers* all the time. Or *A Patch of Blue* or *Chinatown* or *Patton*. I'd love to have done *On Golden Pond* or *Irreconcilable Differences*. That's what I try to find, a picture with relationships. The problem is, I don't think that people really think of me generally in those terms. If you look at the pictures I've done, most of them are action, epic kind of pictures; the small, intimate pictures I never seem to get. Occasionally, every two years, [one] comes along for me. But they don't *make* too many of those pictures; they're all hardware pictures. But the challenge of those pictures is trying to get the emotion *into* them.

BASIL POLEDOURIS: Carroll Ballard probably thought I was a stalker when he was doing *Wind*. I'd been sailing all my life, and when I heard about *Wind* [a 1992 fictionalized account of the America's Cup yacht races], it's like I camped out on his doorstep in San Francisco. I must tell you, for me there's always been this fine line between selling yourself and begging, and it just depends, like anything else, I guess, on the attitude with which one pursues it. That was a film I was born to write, and I knew it, and I just wanted to make sure that *he* knew it, too. I think that was probably the most aggressive pursuit of a film ever.

Economics entered into it in the early part of my career. There was a time where I didn't turn down films because the thought that somebody's paying me money to make music was extraordinary; I mean, to get paid to do something I really loved to do? I've turned down a lot of violent films, which sounds silly for a person that did *Conan* and *Robocop*, but I've never done a slasher film, or a horror movie. They scare me!

But with *Robocop*, it's almost a satire of violent films.

POLEDOURIS: Yes, but it certainly opened up people's consciousness to what violence could be. It borders on being irresponsible, because it innures us. I think any kind of film like that, that takes people to new levels of violence and cruelty, can be dangerous. I'm certainly not a proponent for censorship, but we do have a responsibility to our audience.

The music gave it its comic element, its attitude, but to understate the music or to play it counter to [the violence] or to give it a sense of tragedy or sadness, whatever, that would have been wrong. That's not Paul Verhoeven, that's not his vision—particularly that film, where *exaggeration* was its style.

Is your first impression of a project based on a reading of the screenplay, or on viewing the rough cut?

POLEDOURIS: The ideal way would be to see the film for the first time, but in order to secure work, or to see if you're even interested in doing it, the script is really the item of currency.

Did you ever read a script and have your own image of the style of the film, and then see a rough cut where the director went in a different direction, so that you had to drastically reorient your approach to the music to match his vision?

POLEDOURIS: It depends on the character of the script. Certainly a script that's basically montage and stylized can take a different interpretation. A script which is basically character-rooted and dialogue-driven is pretty much the same; there's very little you can do differently if the characters are strong and well delineated.

When I read a script I *see* it, because I studied directing; I think of it as a film as opposed to a piece of literature. Generally the finished product is better than what I imagined—that's why I'm a composer and not a director!

I'll give you an example: *Breakdown* was an incredible script, I think it was the quickest read I've ever had, a real page-turner. It was kind of a gestalt the way it read, very clean, very clear, it wasn't burdened with all kinds of camera directions and scene descriptions and blocking and things like that. Jonathan Mostow took it and gave it a real style quite different from the way I thought it would be. What I look for is a consistency in the style of the film because I think a score should have a consistency too, and if the film's all over the board—unless it's intended to be—I think it creates problems for scoring.

When you saw the film *Breakdown* how did it change your take on it?

POLEDOURIS: It was much sparser than I'd imagined. It would be the difference between *The Wild Bunch* and . . . well, *Breakdown*! *Wild Bunch* was very epic, full of grandeur, and *Breakdown* is much more internal. I thought originally *Breakdown* would have a fuller sound with a larger orchestra representing the heroic kinds of things, whereas in fact it's about a guy who is not a fighter; he's not a cop, he's just a guy, an Everyman who finds the strength to overcome that terror to save his life. But he doesn't do it with trumpets and French horns! The music is sparse, not paranoid but definitely edgy.

ELLIOT GOLDENTHAL: For a composer, it's not just the story, it's not just the mood. It's the swooping of the camera or the stillness of the camera, it's the art direction, it's the attitude of the costumes, of the acting, the split-second decision behind the eyes of an actor. All of these things come into play that allow you to know when it's the proper time to release an emotional musical response, and all of these things cannot just be conjured out of a script or seen as an afterthought after watching the movie once.

In the case of *Michael Collins* I was very concerned after reading the script that there wasn't a strong female presence. During a war, female presence is very, very unnoticed but *there*, especially in the case of Ireland and the history of participation among females (like Bernadette Devlin), so I wanted a female chorus singing in Gaelic throughout the movie to sort of counterbalance the lack of femaleness. And that was way before the movie was made. And then as the movie went on, Neil Jordan and I were concerned about how much Irishness there should be in the movie in terms of the score—the more it went on, the less that became an important factor. The score became less stereotypically Irish because we wanted it to be more about the drama and not necessarily about the territory or the geography.

There are a great deal of variables when it comes to composing for film, and one of those variables (which is a changing variable) is cuts. Editors quite often will change things to shorten a scene, which creates a domino effect; the film might not have all of the emotional and dramatic responses that it had before. So with each shortening of the movie, you have a *different* movie. One has to keep up the whole time with all the changeable arts that go into making a movie.

APPROPRIATE/INAPPROPRIATE

Often there might be a really great score in a really bad movie—even if the movie is bad, the composer somehow found some inspiration and produced a wonderful score.

BERNSTEIN: Well, that happens a lot. But if you're a composer and you're interested in your career, you're better off with a bad score in a good movie. Because you can write a great score in a bad movie and nobody cares, except film music buffs. But in terms of one's career it's the success of the movies that counts.

But if you're working on a low-budget or independent film that will have a smaller audience—in other words, the studio isn't taking much of a financial risk—maybe you have the latitude to try more experimental work, whereas a formula, big-budget picture's producers will want a formula score.

BERNSTEIN: Well, if it's a formula picture, a formula score is probably appropriate. I think that when they hire people, they expect to get certain things out of specific people.

I can't tell you how many times people called me during the days I was doing westerns, they wanted another score like *The Magnificent Seven*, and I'd say, "Well, I already wrote that."

ISHAM: Yeah, definitely some of that goes on, that's part of the process of how they come to pick you. They listen to your previous work, they take some of it and put it into a temporary score that they're compiling for their film. But I've had people who have hired me for films tell me, "I don't think you've ever done a film like this, I just like your sensibility." So I've probably had all kinds of points of view.

GOLDSMITH: You can't let people pin you down and say you're this kind of composer; if that happens, you not only lose a lot of work but you go a little dead inside. For a creative person, that's the beginning of the end.

ISHAM: What's intrigued me about film music is that I'll start off writing a score and say, "You know, this [genre] is totally unlike me and I don't know what I'm doing," but by the end I feel it *is* totally me—I will have just expanded my view of music. Certainly the first action films I did I sort of felt that way—*Point Break*, *Timecop*—but by the time I got to *Kiss the Girls*, for instance, I felt totally at home, that I totally have my own point of view in that genre. In fact, in *Kiss the Girls* I came up with a fairly unique point of view for that film, and felt totally that it was mine without any reservations about it.

I don't think there's any film score that sticks out as in "Where did *that* one come from?" I think that's really what the process is about: discovering what your own point of view is in each of these films.

If a director or producer comes to you hoping that music will save a flawed film, does that create more anxiety?

MICHAEL KAMEN: When that happens you have to remind yourself you're dealing with a problem that no one can solve, if it hasn't been solved in the storytelling, the acting, and the shooting. Music is not ever going to save a bad film. I don't know if bad music can destroy a *good* film—maybe for a musician it could—and in general I don't think good music is ever inappropriate, but I don't think it can save a bad film. You can add taste, you can add a variety of emotions, from abject terror to sublime majesty and serenity. If it ain't on the screen, you're not going to convince anybody, really, that it *is* on the screen.

And you're a collaborator, so it's no good for you to be acting brilliantly and the guy up on-screen acting like a fool.

But do you come across people who *think* music can save it?

KAMEN: If it's really terrible they'll believe *anything* because they're deeply in trouble. You know, if you've just spent fifty or sixty or seventy million dollars and you've had a cast and crew and equipment and sets and story and script and everything else and it *still* isn't there, you can't really turn to a composer and expect him to bail you out. People will walk out going, "Yeah, the music's good—*terrible* film!"

Music is a collaborator in film, and we are as good as the film. We fall and prosper as the film does, is a more accurate way of saying it. In fact, some of my favorite cues were made for films that very few people have seen.

Is it troubling when a score you're proud of is attached to a film that ultimately does not find an audience?

KAMEN: It's always disappointing when something doesn't rise to the head of the class, but after a while you get used to the fact that life is not a series of goals for number-one records. They happen from time to time, and that's enough. The work itself is what has to guide you. And it would be very easy to get your sensibilities blunted by repeated failure.

TEMP TRACKS

Is working off a temporary soundtrack made up of cues from your own scores easier than working off a temp featuring other composers' work?

ISHAM: I'll find that if they put my own music in there and they feel it's working very well, that'll be the most difficult, because it's like, "Well, I've already done that—now I have to rip *myself* off?" I mean, if I feel it works very well and it's my own stuff, it's hard because I have to come up with a whole other way of doing the exact same thing.

I've found a lot of times, though, they'll put some of my stuff in there and they'll think it works great, but I have so much attachment to that music coming from a specific area, communicating a specific thing, that I won't agree that it works there. In fact, I'm up against this right now. I'm starting a Val Kilmer film in about a month (*At First Sight*) and they sent me their first assembly the other day and it's full of my music and I just think it's completely wrong, but they obviously see something there that they like, so it'll be an interesting discussion once we get started, what their point of view is.

I mean in this case it's a romantic drama and the whole first part of the movie is when this couple is meeting and falling in love, and they temped it with a lot of my music from *Of Mice and Men*. Now to me, that music was very specifically tragic music—*Of Mice and Men* is a tragedy, and so written into the music was a very specific idea that these guys are trapped, they're stuck, it's not going to be *good*! The music is very sweet and painfully beautiful, but it has the essence of a real tragedy, and I really was very happy that (I felt) the music communicated that without just being "gloom and doom" all the time. So, to me, when I hear this music over a series of scenes where this young couple is falling in love, it puts this whole tone on it that I think is completely wrong, and yet *they* don't have that direct association that that is what the music was communicating in the other film; they obviously don't hear it.

I'll just have a discussion with them. I'll just tell them, "Look, I really feel that the music here needs to be very romantic and basically say *All is going to be fantastic with these guys*;

that's what the film needs." Now, things *do* go awry for their relationship, but it's not like Lenny and George in *Of Mice and Men*, which is just pure tragedy. That's not what this other story is about.

Ultimately it will mean saying to them, "No, how about something like this," and playing it for them and they'll go, "Yeah"—or I'll find that they really do *want* a sense of foreboding gloom in the beginning, and then we'll have to discuss how much and how to do it. I usually express it verbally, but ultimately the only thing that really works is to hear the music.

Have you written music *before* seeing a rough cut?

ISHAM: Alan Rudolph had written a lot of the script for *Afterglow* when he was listening to my last record, and he told me that. He said, "I really feel that intimate modern jazz thing is going to be exactly what we'll want for this." I actually prewrote a couple of things for him, because Alan loves that; he loves to be wandering around the set with headphones on! So I wrote a couple of pieces for him for that and then he could throw them in during assemblies.

ELLIOT GOLDENTHAL: Temp tracks are a quagmire for a composer. My nightmare is when a director puts on a temp track of the Brandenburg Concerto: "Now, *you* do one."

Now in a case like that you can't argue that the music is *bad*, but can you argue that it's inappropriate?

GOLDENTHAL: You can't argue that it's inappropriate; you might as well just acquire that piece.

There are certain things in music that are arguably unreattainable. I don't think the Beethoven Fifth Symphony is re-attainable—by Beethoven or by anybody else. Something that is that perfect, I don't see how you can do *another* one.

Have you been asked to repeat your own music?

GOLDENTHAL: From time to time people have temped with my own music, and then they say, "Well, give me one of those." And in everyone's life they have their own little moments, something that is perfectly them and *right*, and if that happens to be something you have to *repeat*, it's deadly!

Let's say they find something of yours that works perfectly [on the temp track]. Well, what good does *that* do you? You have to reinvent your own wheel. You've lost the joy of screwing up six or seven times before you actually get to that perfect, perfect thing for that scene. In essence it's like you've taken the river away from the salmon.

SHIRE: I have very mixed feelings about temp tracks. They send you the movie and it's the first time you've seen it and it's got somebody else's music on it. And often unrealistically so. I just turned down a picture which I would have loved to do but they scored it with *To Kill a Mockingbird*, and I knew they wanted that kind of score, and they had a budget which only allowed a synth score. And I said, "I wouldn't do a synth score for this movie. You were *right*; *To Kill a Mockingbird*, that's the kind of score you need, not some synthesizers."

Now what's good about temp tracks—especially working on the time schedules for TV where you've got to almost go home and pick up your pencil and start writing *immediately* or you won't make the date—is it gives you the general ballpark as to the kind of score they want. But you have to be very careful. I often ask them, "Do you *like* this particular cue?" And sometimes they'll say, "Well, no, but we needed *something* to show the network."

"So I should just ignore it, right?"

"Yeah, kind of."

If I hadn't asked them I would have thought this is what they *want*, they thought it was good. You have to be very careful.

On many projects I tell them that I want to see the picture first without a temp score—strip the temp score off of the tape—then I'll listen to the temp score later. I want to know what my first impulses are. I want to see what pops into my head which wouldn't pop into my head if I was listening to somebody else's score [attached to it].

Have you been offered films where they show you a cut with temp tracks?

PHILIP GLASS (*Koyaanisqatsi, Mishima, Kundun*): Once the temp track was my own music. It's impossible, simply impossible. Once I find out the editor is working with a temp track, the deal is over, I won't do it. It's not worth it.

Basically you're not being invited to do your best work, you're being invited to help someone who can't write music write the music that he *thinks* he wants to hear. It's like someone who can't dance dances for you, and then saying, "Now make a dance like *I* just danced." And it's just as completely stupid.

SPOTTING

The process of spotting—selecting those scenes or transitions in a film where music is needed (or not needed), the length of a cue, its style—is the most important occasion when a director and composer will confer. By communicating what he feels his film needs, the director helps set the broad parameters for the music's style and content and what dramatic function music is to serve. The composer meanwhile must speak up for what he feels music can or cannot be asked to contribute.

MARK ISHAM: The very first meeting I had with Sidney Lumet on *Night Falls on Manhattan*, he was very straightforward, very up front with me: He said, "Look, I've made, I don't know, fifty films, and fifteen of them have had no music"—I don't know if those figures are right, the idea being he's not attached to *having* to have music in a film—"so if I thought that this film didn't need any music I would be the first one to say let's just not have any music. But I really feel this film needs *some* sort of music, and there're a couple of places where I feel that it needs to be scored, but the previous composer had written a *lot* of music and nobody felt good about that magnitude of music, especially me.

"The truth of the matter is I am now *confused*, so I'd like to just have you spot this, and take your own pass at it so then I can react to someone else on it." Which I did. I wrote a few bits and pieces in the way that I would approach it and then flew out to New York and spotted it with him, and we came up with a very minimal spotting, and we recorded it. In fact I took the opposite approach [to most action films], because every time everything got quiet was when I entered!

And then the studio saw the picture and quite honestly I think they were a little upset that they had paid me for so *little* music; they felt they needed more notes per dollar or something, you know? And they had me go back. Sidney was very funny. He said, "You probably should pay attention to the studio, but don't work *too* hard because *I* have final cut!"

So I went back and wrote about another fifteen minutes of music, and sent it over, and sure enough, Sidney didn't put it in the film. And personally I thought it was very right. Since then

I've gone back and looked at a lot more of Sidney's films and I see his whole style, and I think it's very correct for the way he makes films.

How hard is it communicating musical ideas with someone who is not musically educated?

ISHAM: I think most directors have a pretty good handle on that. The only time it gets a little funny is when they're nervous about a particular scene. They feel that they have never gotten the right performance from a particular actor or couldn't get that special angle that they wanted to superimpose that made the scene feel a certain way, and they want *something* out of the scene that they can't get from their picture and their dialogue and the performance. So then they come to the music, and say, "Well, you need to give me this because I didn't get it anywhere else." That could work out fine sometimes, but if it's something that is in fact totally alien to the scene it can put the music in a rather awkward position of trying to communicate something that really isn't *in* the scene at all—it makes the music feel like it's pushing too hard. But those things usually get hammered out in the process.

SHIRE: Generally the producer or director knows what he wants, but sometimes they're not sure about a particular place. They might say, "We want a cue here," and I'll say, "Well, what's the music *about* here?" They'll say, "Well, we just want music!" But that's like saying to a comedian, *Say something funny*. They can't do it. If you ask him, *Say something funny about a guy walking through Central Park at night*, then they can do it.

And then when describing what they want they sometimes use the phrase "neutral music." No music is neutral! You can make one pluck on a harp or one note on an oboe, it's going to color a scene. It's not neutral; it's a value. It's like saying "Put a neutral color on a set." *Any* color on a set is going to affect that scene.

Sometimes they'll want music on a scene and it'll be a terrifically acted scene with somebody like Glenn Close. And I'll say "Why? I wouldn't *touch* it, I wouldn't go near it, the scene is wonderful, it doesn't need anything." And they say, "Really?" Often you can give them objectivity about their pictures, because composers are usually the first one in after it's completed. They want that input.

So often I'll make them realize they didn't really want music, or I'll force them to define their terms. And if I still don't agree I'll write a cue—I might think of *something*—and they can always throw it away. The worst is to not write a cue and then have them really need it and not have it.

Sometimes they'll say "We don't want music here," and I'll have an idea and say, "Let me try something, you can always throw it away." Other times they seem to want too much music and I'll point out that by having a ten-minute cue here it's not going to be as effective as being in for three minutes, going out and then coming back in later. Because if it starts being wall-to-wall, the music steps on its own foot.

Sometimes—it doesn't happen that often—I'll say, "I've got ten days to write this, I cannot write ninety minutes of music, and if I did you're not going to like it, so let's pick our shots." Besides, there have been very few pictures that need that much music. *All the President's Men* is a two-hour-and-ten-minute movie and I think there's twenty-five minutes of music in it, although we wrote more than we used. It's very lightly scored.

GOLDSMITH: When we were spotting *Freud*, John Huston pointed out one scene and said he thought it should have music in it, and I really didn't feel it. I hadn't done too many pictures at that time, and I was in complete awe of Huston anyway, but nevertheless I still had great reservations about the scene. I worked on it, but he sensed my doubts. So we discussed it, and he said, "Listen, what's the point of you spending your time on something you don't believe in and not using your energies on something you do believe? So forget it."

WORK HABITS

Do you write at the piano or on computer?

ALAN MENKEN (*The Little Mermaid, Beauty and the Beast*): I compose basically on computer. It's called a controller, and I have a program called Digital Performer, which is a MIDI-sequencing program and also a digital audio program. They basically can go from scratch, from conceiving a song all the way through producing it (complete with vocal and arrangements) right in your studio without another person involved. And it's great to a point; [but] you still get the best results with people working together collaborating with you.

Are there drawbacks to composing on the computer, limitations in any way?

MENKEN: If you use short cuts it can actually affect your writing, and that is something you have to watch for. One can do the first part of the song and then just go "repeat," and then you hear the second half of the song; and yet if you're playing it on the piano, very likely when you come to the second part of the song you would have added something, so there's that difference. Another big drawback is when you store everything on computer, you could play it very slowly and then speed it up, get everything perfectly in there, and you end up having a finished song without ever having really married it into your fingers. So if someone asked me to sit down at the piano and play a song from a show I've done on computer, sometimes I have to start from scratch and learn that song on the piano, because I haven't repeated it and played it over and over and over the way I used to.

But the advantage is that you're holding five projects in a state of development as opposed to one or two.

I do piano score. Sometimes within the piano score there can be things that couldn't possibly be played on a piano. I generally won't write a percussion line, but I will indicate to my orchestrator, "I think we should have percussion carrying what the left hand is doing here." Or "I need this to be a grand fanfare and then I need it softer here in the strings"; "I want that passage there to be evocative of *Appalachian Spring.*"

Do you work out your music on a keyboard as you're writing?

BERNSTEIN: No, no, no! I work mostly with my head! If I need an instrument to play on, it'll be a piano, but after all these years, the sound is pretty well in my head. I don't really need to try to approximate them to know whether they *sound* right.

SAMPLING

Synthesizers and computer programs that can mimic an acoustic group or symphony orchestra are both a boon and a curse to the composer. While the tools can be useful in experimenting with or auditioning a music cue before the recording stage (where most of a film's music budget may be spent), it can also attract producers looking to save money on music by replacing human players. What's

worse, the ease with which these programs can make musical sounds can mask their inability to create real music without the intervention of human talent.

ISHAM: I think the downside of the technology is that if you're writing an orchestral piece from orchestral samples, you start to write to the limits of those samples. If all you've got are mezzo forte bowings, then you just end up writing only that. There's a tremendous vocabulary that an orchestra can create, little nuances on each individual acoustic instrument, and it's very difficult to have all of that available in the electronic medium. So one thing I always try to do is to always be aware that I am writing for an orchestra even though I'm writing through the electronic medium, and not be afraid to have a piece of paper here and say, "Well, in bar forty-seven I want the col legno strings"—when they hit it with the back of the bow—or things like that, where you're writing *intelligence* for the orchestra.

You can tell sometimes with certain composers that they write from electronic samples because there's a certain one-dimensionality to their orchestral writing, and I think it comes purely from not having forced themselves into experiencing the more traditional writing approach, where you *imagine* something that you might not have a sample for and actually put it in there.

Does sampling allow you to experiment with unusual groups of instruments, and perhaps convince a director (or even yourself) that it would work?

MARK ISHAM: That's true. If I felt I'm going to write for an accordion for instance, I will, if it takes me a week, go out and find a good accordion sample.

Do you ever bring in a player to record parts of a score, as a test?

MARK ISHAM: I have done that. I have done demo recordings of tracks because I just knew I'm never going to get a mock-up of this to convince a director that this is going to work. I will actually book a little session, do it quickly and efficiently, and get the guys to play it. With certain types of jazz scores or rock scores, where it really depends upon a performance, you just write into the budget that you're going to have to do a few demo sessions to convince the producers that it's going to work.

SHIRE: You hear often a piece of music that sounds terrific as a piece of music but it's the wrong piece of music when put against the film. Smart directors can say, "Well, I think your theme is right but can you give me a cassette of it, I want to run it against the picture." Now with synthesizers more and more directors are insisting on it. And I have a whole electronic setup in my studio, I'm able to do it. I'm able to write something and sync it up and watch it on the video and come back after a day or two and go, "Yeah, that needs some more there." So we have a lot more tools to really do that. At the same time, those tools have made it more possible to write chintzy, cheap, fast, what are called "garage scores," as in kids in their garages with synthesizers who write "repetition music." So when a producer has a nephew who does that, he tries to put it on. I've scored a couple of pictures (as I think all of us have) where they threw away one of those scores and at the last minute came to a *composer*! There's something always a little satisfying about that—once in a while they *have* to use a composer!

BAIT-AND-SWITCH:
ELMER BERNSTEIN ON *THE GRIFTERS*

The playful yet rueful crime melodrama *The Grifters*, based on a novel by Jim Thompson, captures a segment of Los Angeles's dark underbelly populated by con artists, gamblers, and numbers runners. Elmer Bernstein has not composed works for many dark or disturbing subjects since *The Man with the Golden Arm*, but for this 1990 drama he crafted a typically memorable but unsentimental tune, played on one of his favorite instruments, the Ondes-Martenot.

Like the shell games that comprise the labyrinthine plot, the path the score took to the film's final release version was itself a matter of mixed signals and sleight of hand.

▶

ELMER BERNSTEIN: My association with Stephen Frears on *The Grifters* was a very interesting and puzzling one. We worked very closely together, we had a wonderful time in the work process, we had a fine time with the recording. But the peculiarity of what happened in that film is something which is very difficult to understand, because Frears must have had a very different concept of what to *do* with the music than I did. Although he seemed to like the score very, very much and used it extensively—I must say more extensively than *I* intended for the film—he *reordered* the score. It's all the same music, but the pieces are in places for which they weren't originally intended, which is very, very odd.

I think it's a brilliant film of the genre, but I perceived it almost as a fable, not as a piece of reality, and the way my score was originally organized the music started very softly, very easily, sort of bittersweet, sprightly, with the idea of drawing the audience into this fable bit by bit. It intensifies and intensifies and intensifies as the film gets darker and more violent.

I think Stephen would be the first person to admit that he knew nothing about music, and is not at all sophisticated about the use of music in films. If you're going to talk about working relationships with directors, my working relationship is different with every single director; what I do and what they do depends a lot on many, many different factors. On *The Grifters*, Stephen was the kind of person that really enjoyed having all the members of his crew really involved in the picture-making process. So he really enjoyed finding out what I was doing.

Now *The Grifters* I wrote, it's a very unusual score, and certainly an unusual score for me. This is not like anything I've ever done before; one of the strengths of the film is that it's not much like anything *anybody's* ever done before. Now in a picture which is driven by atmosphere as opposed to action, films like *To Kill a Mockingbird* or *Birdman of Alcatraz*, the challenge is really to find something which conveys the atmosphere. So *Bird-*

man of *Alcatraz* was a jailhouse atmosphere, and *To Kill a Mock-ingbird* was a children-in-the-impoverished-South atmosphere. But *The Grifters* was rather different because it's not really a normal atmosphere in any sense. It has a totally *abnormal* atmosphere, an odd atmosphere. Which made it fun to do, to try to find the thing which made the atmosphere work, or enhanced it.

So I was looking for what I hoped would be specific to the film. I had a feeling for this little tune that you hear, a sort of monotonous, mordant tune which is not quite jazz and it's not quite *not* jazz. It can be best described like early-thirties Germany. Thematically it reminds me most of Kurt Weill's *Threepenny Opera*. And Stephen was very involved with that all the way along.

A lot of the score was electronic. I was working with my synthesist, Cynthia Millar, because she had the equipment to do a mock-up of the music electronically, so I played the stuff for Stephen so he'd have a chance to hear what it sounded like. He was so enthusiastic, very supportive and very interested in the process, and we had a great time while we were working on the film and all through the recording. I think the score was composed in about six weeks. After the recording was over, Stephen—although he loved the score, he almost loved it death actually!—started to push the pieces around within the context of the film.

I think what happened was, Stephen began to have a slightly different perception of the film itself, which made him start moving the music about. So curiously enough you wind up with a score in which I think only three pieces are in their original positions. But the reason it was possible to do that with this score without totally destroying it is that what I was going for was just overall atmosphere. It wasn't a very "cuey" score in that sense [tied to specific actions]. The atmosphere would be the same no matter where you put the pieces.

He put a lot more music in the film than I originally wrote for it simply by repeating things. And it was very odd, very strange. Often I've had experiences where a piece comes out in the dub, but this is the first time I've ever experienced having practically the entire score moved about. Oddly enough, Stephen couldn't really verbalize why he did that, because he's not very verbal about music; he just goes with feeling.

A lot of other directors are not musically trained, if they've come up from the ranks of writers, actors, or cameramen, and so can't verbalize music either.

BERNSTEIN: No, but they rarely change their minds, as Stephen did about what the particular dramatic *intent* of a cue is in a particular place. I don't think he was ever able to explain to me what it was he wanted to do ultimately; but from what he did to the score I would say he wanted to start in a harder, driving way right from the beginning. He took some of the harder pieces which were intended to be near the end of the film and brought them up earlier. As an example, the piece which is now the main title of the film was originally in reel nine.

Were you involved with the mixing at all?

BERNSTEIN: I rarely go to dubs. I had Cynthia Millar supervise the dub. At which time all the pieces were put in precisely as they had been planned. We then took the picture to New York and showed it to Martin Scorsese (one of the film's producers), and everything seemed fine. I don't think that anybody was unhappy with anything. I think it was Stephen, who is a very hard worker, and he keeps *thinking* all the time.

But it's kind of an amazing phenomenon that—as far as the public was concerned—apparently whatever Stephen did didn't destroy the impact of the score. In terms of its impact it's an important score for me; it was a score that was very much noted.

For the CD, I restored all the pieces in the order in which they originally were in the film. If one compares them one might see what the effect would have been if the original order were kept.

■

COLLABORATION WITH OTHER COMPOSERS

Would a producer or director come to you with a song and say, "I want to put this song into my picture, so write around it"? Or is it more often your decision as the composer to decide whether a film should have a song—either by you or by someone else?

DAVID SHIRE: Generally they know if they want a song. They either hire you to do it or they have an existing one, and then you have to decide if you want to score a picture with somebody else's songs. Sometimes they just want the song to be there and the score to have nothing to do with it; other times they want a score written on a song, and most times I'll say, "Well, that's an arranger's job; I'm really in the business of writing original music and I'd have to score the whole picture." Except I scored *Saturday Night Fever*, which was a very good decision, because it financed a lot of other experimental works. It was also a director who was an old friend of mine whom I had done some pictures for and I wanted to work with him. Again, you have to weigh each job.

If they want the score to help sell the songs, is there pressure on you to make your music reflect the songs?

SHIRE: If they want them to. I did a picture called *Double Platinum*, with Diana Ross and Brandy as a mother and daughter who are pop singers. And there are six spots in the show with original songs where they're in concert. And when the producer sent it to me the first thing I asked was, "Do you want the score to use the themes of the songs?" And he said, "No, absolutely not. We want the score to be totally about the two of them and not have anything to do with the songs." So I took the job. Otherwise I don't think I would have taken it because there are people, arrangers, who could do it better.

In *Explorers*, there is a scene of an atrocious, pseudo–*Star Wars* science fiction film being shown at a drive-in. Its music is heavily bombastic and wonderfully bad, quite the antithesis of the dreamy score you wrote for the film proper.

JERRY GOLDSMITH: I can't relate to that style, and I had a ton of music to write without doing that other "movie," so I got Alexander Courage (whose credits include TV's *Star Trek*) to do it. I asked for two minutes of music, and Sandy wrote all these notes, chromatic scales up and down—and he didn't even see the picture. Yet when we recorded it we ran the picture along with it and everything hit, all by accident, on one take. And we were all on the floor—it was so corny it was hysterical!

JOCELYN POOK (*Eyes Wide Shut*): I did a TV film called *Butterfly Catchers* which was a strange situation: it was *two* composers, there were two of us working on it. We started off being given very separate sections: I was given lots of flashbacks and scenes with a sinister atmosphere, and he was supposed to do more naturalistic scenes. I got the bits that were more dreamlike and for where the music takes on a stronger voice; my music tends to be used in that way more, rather than my doing different kind of pastiche, using certain film writing techniques that I don't particularly have.

Did you work with the other composer, making your music fit with his in some way?

POOK: No, but in the end he kind of used themes of mine. I wrote this main song called "Butterfly Song," and then he ended up using that theme in his music, but I didn't do that with his themes. It was new ground for me. It's like having two designers for a set—one had to kind of dominate slightly more, and we didn't know who that would be particularly.

Was his use of your themes a result of his discussions with the director?

POOK: No, not really, he just started doing it. It was a very odd situation, and in the end it did seem to be that one voice *had* to emerge. So I was grateful that he did that rather than my having to try to write around *his* things because I wouldn't have known how to do that!

A FRIEND LIKE ME: ALAN MENKEN ON HOWARD ASHMAN AND THE REBIRTH OF THE FILM MUSICAL

Alan Menken rose to popular recognition on the laurels of a man-eating plant. His Off-Broadway musical adaptation with Howard Ashman of a cheesy 1960 Roger Corman monster movie, *Little Shop of Horrors*, was both a winking valentine to sci-fi flicks and a vibrant, melodic showcase for Menken and Ashman's gifts for soulful ballads and satiric lyrics.

Following the success of *Little Shop* (which would eventually make it to the screen as a big-budget live-action extravaganza), the duo wrote the songs and score for *The Little Mermaid*, whose tongue-in-cheek romance and calypso beat revitalized—and steered in a new direction—the style of Disney animated features. It was a testament to the filmmakers' craft and savviness that subsequent animated films eagerly copied that film's blueprint; by the mid- to late nineties, few animated films would be produced which did not contain a bevy of songs. More tellingly, very few *live-action* musicals would be produced, and even fewer would meet with financial success, as animation seemed to own the territory.

Several months before the premiere of Menken and Ashman's second animated feature, *Beauty and the Beast*, and during preproduction of *Aladdin*, Ashman succumbed to AIDS. Not only did Broadway and Hollywood lose a singular musical talent whose humor and determination had helped bring musical theater (and film musicals especially) back from the dead, but Menken lost a valuable sounding board, a partner whose success had been inextricably interwined with his own.

In 1992, at a time when he was being courted to work on countless projects, from live-action films (*Newsies*) to documentaries (ABC's *Lincoln*) and Off-Broadway musicals, Menken spoke of the nature of collaboration and of pursuing his career post–Howard Ashman. While the eventual success of *Aladdin*, *Pocahontas*, *The Hunchback of Notre Dame*, and *Hercules* would prove his ability to collaborate with others just as effectively, Menken's feelings about the give-and-take of writing partnerships clearly show how important a part collaborators play in the compositional process. (This conversation is followed by a 1999 interview in which Menken reconsidered the status of film musicals.)

▶

ALAN MENKEN: We had our first preview of *Aladdin* last night—I wasn't there, but I got the notes from Jeffrey Katzenberg, the whole aspect of how he wants things scored, and changes he wants. The songs are done, and I'm writing the underscore. They used temp tracks for a lot of the movie.

Alan Menken

Did you have input with the music editor in terms of what temp tracks are put in?

MENKEN: No, not really. If I'd wanted to have input on that I could have, but I didn't have time. So I basically let them do what feels good to them, and they come back with that, and I try to accommodate it. Obviously the disadvantages are that they can fall in love with a style that I may feel is inappropriate, in which case I have to try to yank it back *this* way, and that's what generally happens if you choose live-action score music to go under these scenes.

When I put in a little musical—"musical" meaning musical

theater—underscore in, or an animated style of scoring in, it's sometimes jarring for them to take in.

Because they've become accustomed to what they have been working with?

MENKEN: Right, so I then cheat back to music being basically a little more of a support, less of a prime element. But so far that tension has worked between the live-action score and the purely musical score, cartoon score.

When Jerry Goldsmith scored the animated feature *The Secret of NIMH*, he didn't use a stereotypical cartoon approach, "Mickey-Mousing" the music by constantly hitting on the action, but instead treated it like a live-action film albeit with shorter, faster-paced scenes.

MENKEN: Well, I have more elements to consider than he did in that case, because besides being an animated project *Aladdin*'s also a musical. So no matter what, I'm going to be supporting song themes which tend to be broader. It's more noticeable, and so in making the song material *less* noticeable you sometimes have to weave it in a different way.

My approach has been to study the classic animation style of scoring and then to pull back from there, as opposed to going for a live-action style and accommodating the animation. But remember, I come with a pretty blank slate; this is my first film scoring work. Also, my work has been [primarily] for animated pictures, so in a way we're sort of defining our own little universe here, which may not be relevant to a lot of other universes. And the results have been obviously phenomenal. People have really appreciated our efforts.

In a lot of cases it's not calculated. I don't know what we're doing except we're walking a line between musical and animation *and* film. And it's my job certainly to support the dramatic truth of a scene, to make sure that if something needs to be funny or moving or exciting, that I'm enhancing that; and to make sure that the songs basically tell the story, and that the song themes are threaded throughout in a way which allows the film to convey the musical experience without the music being obtrusive.

In live-action films perhaps half of the movie is underscored, whereas in animation there may be 80 percent, 90 percent, or more that is underscored. Of course that's a lot more work, but it's also putting more pressure on the music to *not* be obtrusive.

MENKEN: It's a real balancing act. We did eleven minutes of scoring last week which was pretty great and yet at the preview Jeffrey felt it was obtrusive in places. Of course the directors (with whom I worked on *Little Mermaid*) may ask for one thing, Jeffrey may want something else, so there are a lot of masters to serve. I very much trust Jeffrey's instincts, it's very important to have people whose instincts you trust give you notes on your score. Because I think given a free hand, I might make the score too densely packed musically. It's very important to thin it out, and to know *where* to do that.

What was the genesis of your work on *Aladdin* with Howard Ashman?

MENKEN: Howard Ashman and I did our first work on *Aladdin* prior to *Beauty and the Beast*, and I think prior to the release of *Little Mermaid*. So I guess it was holiday season 1987, into 1988. We wrote an entire score for *Aladdin* and he wrote an entire treatment. Of that treatment not much remains. Of that score, basically a song and a half remain: one full song and a song that's been very cut down. And then he and I wrote the remainder of the score before Howard passed away. After he passed away a number of songs were removed and Tim Rice came in, and he and I wrote basically another whole half of the score again.

Considering the original music that remains, did you consciously try to keep the new music within that same style, or did you find yourself pulling away from that direction?

MENKEN: The original songs basically charted the course. That's usually what happens when you start a project: You write a couple of songs and if they land correctly, that becomes the DNA for the rest of the work. The songs that remain are "Friend Like Me," which is written in a sort of Fats Waller/Cab Calloway style, and "Arabian Nights," which is written in your orthodox Arabic/Middle Eastern style, and that basically sums it up. Howard and I had a ballad called "Proud of Your Boy," which was our style of ballad, and those ballads tend to be the elements that are not linked too closely to a specific time or place. Those tend to be the inner emotional life of the central character, so they don't tend to change much from project to project.

Howard and I also wrote a song called "Prince Ali," which is in a Fred Astaire/Ginger Rogers, "Doing the Continental" style, so there's an element of the score that is forties hip jazz, there's an element that is Arabic, and there is an element that is the "Menken pop theater" style—that's in the ballads more than anywhere else. Tim and I wrote a fast Charleston; although it's in a minor key it starts in a sort of frenetic Arabic vamp, written to a scene that's a chase in which we first meet Aladdin. And the ballad "A Whole New World" that I wrote with Tim is in my style but it is closer to the kind of things that Tim wrote with Andrew Lloyd Webber, a little broader musically, a little more exotic than what Howard and I did. It's something that really felt right for when I worked with Tim.

They're not head decisions; you feel them in your body, you kind of get the idea when you play it and hum it. It fits.

Having started on *Aladdin* before you did *Beauty and the Beast*, did the process of working on *Beauty* change how you approached the drama of *Aladdin*'s story? Because *Beauty* turned out to be less tongue in cheek than *Little Mermaid*.

MENKEN: That really didn't enter into the decision in terms of having "One Jump" be a Charleston. "One Jump" really grew out of what I felt the ideal chase music would be for this particular scene, and then when it came to writing the song, overlaying what was going on with Aladdin and the crowds as he went through this marketplace being chased to that music and giving it what I felt would be ideally the most comfortable form. I don't think that song is particularly tongue in cheek, it's pretty dead-on in terms of *I'm being chased and I'm one jump ahead of them, and I gotta run, gotta go, goodbye!* If there's any place where it's tongue in cheek it's simply in the use of the choruses: people who either like or dislike Aladdin comment on him, doing it to a real Charleston beat and feel.

At the recording sessions for *Beauty and the Beast* (from left): Alan Menken, Howard Ashman, orchestrator Danny Troob, and conductor David Friedman.

But the tongue in cheek of *The Little Mermaid* was the entire concept of being under the sea, and that in itself *isn't* tongue in cheek, it's I suppose the intelligence of the adult writers coming through the characters so that there's something for the adults to have fun with [while] the kids gets the basic story and the music.

I'm sort of (no pun intended) floundering around with this question you've given me, because so many of the dramatic decisions on *Mermaid* and *Beauty* were made by Howard; so how the tongue-in-cheek quality of the "under the sea" world affected the score of *Mermaid* as opposed to how we made decisions on *Aladdin* is a very complex question. It also goes to the heart of life with Howard Ashman and life after Howard Ashman and the collaborators I'm choosing and the way I'm choosing to work. On *Aladdin*, Tim Rice stepped in to help complete the score and it was really my job to make decisions as to where songs might go, what the stylistic choices we made in terms of what the songs are going to be, who's going to sing them, so the new songs in *Aladdin* basically represent that for me. Whereas on *Pocahontas*, for a lot of reasons (schedule and all sorts of things), Stephen Schwartz has been taking a very active role in choosing stylistically where the songs might go and who might sing. I've been involved but not nearly with the same burden of responsibility I have on *Aladdin*.

Howard Ashman was really a master of tongue in cheek, of having a take on a song that would really maximize the humor. That's why I think "Gaston" (from *Beauty and the Beast*) is as tongue in cheek a song as was ever written; it's a song in praise of this half-witted bully, sung by his cronies. The whole concept of the song is funny and Howard's execution of the song is very funny; very clearly the choice of what you write *already* puts you over the top.

"Prince Ali" of *Aladdin* is the most like that. It's this parade where Aladdin has turned into this prince and the Genie leads the parade bringing him into town in praise of Prince Ali, and of course all exaggeration and fun.

In continuing *Aladdin*'s score with another collaborator, have you felt more responsibility to keeping true to Ashman's original ideas and intents, of being more protective of them?

MENKEN: Any protective instincts I may have toward Howard have kind of been shoved aside by the process. A number of times I sort of dug my heels in only to find that the forces that were pulling me were much stronger than my poor little heels. So I tried to keep a musical consistency, and I certainly wanted Tim's lyrics to be compatible with Howard's lyrics. But at the same time I think it would be not appropriate to have Tim blatantly try to mimic Howard's style—and believe me, if one can mimic Howard's style, I'd collaborate with that person in a second! It's not easily doable. Because he was probably the greatest musical theater genius of our generation. I feel protective, but there's a limit to how much influence I have to protect.

How much do your working methods change from one collaborator to another?

MENKEN: They change a lot. A lot from the inside, not a lot from the outside. I could work music first; I could work lyrics first; I could work title first and then I write the music; I can write idea first, write the music, let someone come back with a lyric that's an entirely different scan but has drawn from the sound of the music.

I always like to work in the room with my collaborator. But as far as who is the arbiter of what's working and what's not working, that changes to various degrees. Howard was a very strong collaborator in the room and yet very reliant on me at the same time. Tim Rice is very laid back and hands-off, and at the same time, as you go into production he becomes very firm in what he wants; that's something I've learned about him.

Did you feel initially Rice was hands-off because he was anxious about filling Ashman's shoes in your partnership, so he held back or deferred more?

MENKEN: I think Tim's basically a Type B. He's not a compulsive person. But as something comes closer to being real, he begins to hone his choices, making them more and more firm. Howard Ashman would walk in, *Boom!* There would be this steel form in front of you that's unbreakable. And sometimes it was hard for him to change things. It's just different personalities.

In the case of *Newsies* [a 1992 live-action musical inspired by a turn-of-the-century strike by young newspaper carriers], the material entirely dictated the style—pretty much the music came first, and Jack Feldman (the lyricist) would be basically dealing with the people [the director and writers of *Newsies*) to make sure we were keeping the logic consistent with what was going to be happening on the screen as we updated the songs. But it was really impossible to keep that process as effective as it is on the animated projects because there's simply much more time and more support on the animated projects.

How did your partnership with Ashman begin?

MENKEN: In 1970, out of college, I'd joined something called the BMI Musical Workshop with Lehman Engel; I essentially was a pianist/musician/composer/lyricist. I brought to my songwriting a love of old musicals that I'd grown up listening to, but it was when I joined the workshop that I really began to learn the craft of writing for the theater. I wrote a number of musicals and showcased them—we would have annual showcases of our work, usually at the Edison Theater. And it was through that workshop that I met Howard. He was looking for a collaborator for *God Bless You, Mr. Rosewater*, based on a Kurt Vonnegut novel that he had gotten the rights to, and he was meeting with various songwriters around town. Lehman suggested we meet and we hit it off. We began our writing careers together; from that point on, I was aware that I was in a collaboration with an extraordinarily talented writer.

While he was alive, that was the strongest collaboration I

had. I've worked with many other people; I had a show produced by Michael Bennett that I'd written with Steve Brown, called *Atina: Evil Queen of the Galaxy*, a show produced at Manhattan Theatre Club called *Real Life Funnies*, and songs performed in cabarets all over New York. But I felt that there was always something special with Howard Ashman that went beyond.

Would he offer criticism or advice on your collaborations with others?

MENKEN: He was always constructive. A good friend, a brilliant guy. I hate the fact that he's gone. And yet, he and I both pulled at that collaboration, wanting to have success with other people; we didn't want to just be a team. He so wanted *Smile* [a 1986 musical stage adaptation of the Michael Ritchie film] to be the moment when he came through and really saved this show—he'd stepped in as director after Carolyn Leigh died—and it didn't work out well. And I was coming on *Kicks* at the same time, working with Tom Eyen. So we were competitive, but we had a lot of respect for each other. You hate when your talents are wasted; my talents were never wasted with Howard. I think he felt the same way about working with me, that I was always able to give him support musically for what he was able to provide dramatically.

Was *Little Shop of Horrors* your first film work?

MENKEN: Except for one little film I wrote one song for, a little B picture, *Little Shop of Horrors* was my very first film work. *Little Mermaid* was my second.

What was involved in adapting *Little Shop* for film? Did you compose new material?

MENKEN: Howard and I wrote about six songs for that, of which two are in the film ("Some Fun Now" and "Mean Green Mother from Outer Space"). Howard adapted the screenplay and it really wasn't much problem. Fitting new songs in was harder because *Little Shop* was a pretty completely conceived piece onstage, and yet as you know when you work in Hollywood, you're not eligible for any kind of recognition for anything written for another medium; traditionally, when you adapt a musical you always add one or two new songs. And that was, I suppose, the toughest aspect of it. Neither of us were directly involved in the making of the movie of *Little Shop*. He visited the set, I visited the set, he sent me over at one point for a troubleshooting trip because the tempos seemed to be slow. Essentially he was on to other things and I was on to other things. He had spent years going around the world directing *Little Shop,* so the last thing he wanted to do was take more of his time with it.

I understand they then decided to rework the ending at the last minute?

MENKEN: That happened very quickly. There was a preview shortly before the film was released that was true to our ending but expanded it greatly.

Where the monster takes over New York City?

MENKEN: Uh-hmm. And audiences sat there with their jaws dropping! They loved the picture but from the point when Audrey gets eaten and Seymour gets eaten and the plant goes

Audrey II, the man-eating plant, conquers New York, in the original ending of *Little Shop of Horrors.*

after the whole world, the picture went off this way and they wanted it to go that way. It was very clear, what worked on stage with a nine-foot Muppet was not happening on film. I think Frank Oz did a terrific job, but I don't know if anybody could have accommodated the ending (basically the plant eating the world) in a way that made you *laugh*! So very quickly Howard rewrote the ending. It was amazing how economically they were able to do some reshooting and make it work. I think essentially it did work. I don't think it ever worked the way it worked on stage, but it was pretty respectable.

When you compose the background score to a film with your songs, do you purposely interpolate the songs' themes into the score, or do you think that limits your creative choices by doing so?

MENKEN: Well, I don't know if I experience adapting song themes as a limitation; I experience it as a unifying element that helps me define a score. It makes the choices easier. Generally, the bulk of what I'm doing is songs and score. And I admit I feel now a lack if I just do songs and not do a score, and I certainly would feel a great lack if I did score and not songs. On *Newsies* I didn't do the score because of schedule, and I wish I had.

So the way the schedule works is, I will work exclusively on getting, as I say, the DNA, those first few songs that establish a style for a project and then having a strong collaborator who can take meetings when I can't, and then as responsibly as I can divide my time between the various projects that we're doing. I was more apt to do one project exclusively when I was working with Howard, because between the two of us we were like a full-service industry; we would do everything including all the voices on our demos. I just don't have right now that collaboration that feels that complete or has that much invested in it, so at this point it would be very difficult for me to just do one project. So I usually have one or two others going at the same time.

Do you have problems with discipline, working that way?

MENKEN: No, not anymore. My problems now are trying not to be a workaholic, because if you do this amount of work, all your satisfaction tends to derive from work-related things. And I have children, I have a family, and I have a life that I'm increasingly pulled from because of my work. So the hard thing for me is to make the adjustment from work to not-work, trying to have a well-rounded life, and as far as my career goes just not getting burned out, not losing the excitement that I feel with a new project. That can happen.

Or if a project goes on too long, as some animated features do.

MENKEN: Well, that isn't as difficult as bouncing between different projects so that you get tired of opening up and then closing up and getting on to something else and opening up and closing up.

As a composer you do have to open up to the rhythms, the emotions, the sensibilities of the project. And your best work is not calculated, it comes from this gift you have to filter the dramatic experiences through your talent and have it come out feeling like something unique to that property, and also reflective of what people associate with a time or a place or a style. Making those choices comes from being *open*, like an actor would be.

Do you have approval over the way your music is used—for example, the orchestrations, or if changes are made in the music to accommodate some other media?

MENKEN: Not on paper, but effectively if I was embarrassed by something I could. A contract is only as good as the paper it's written on. I want them to be happy, they want me to be happy. I think it's to everybody's advantage that work be high quality. So far that problem hasn't occurred with the people at Disney.

Basically I'm very pleased and proud when material is used. I don't really want to have hands-on control over *how* it's used because I'd be nothing but a caretaker of this catalog of material, and I'd rather write new material. Besides, "Be Our Guest" or "Under the Sea" could stand twenty-five awful performances and still not be hurt by it; the material stands up on its own.

How does the film process compare to the stage process, or to the animated-film process? Is one medium more conducive to collaboration, when honing and revising a show, than another?

MENKEN: If you confine it to purely production aspects there are a couple of more steps in film. As you go through the writing and conception to the result there's an incredible number of steps in terms of getting a stage production in place that you don't have in film—you're continually having to run the gauntlet of producers and investors and directors and choreographers and opinions and rewrites and readings and workshops and showcases.

Has that process been made easier for you onstage because of the success of the animated features?

MENKEN: Yeah, it improved to the point where I got a show Off-Broadway without that process, and [now] the show's not going to run!

I think the process exists for a reason, and you can't short-circuit that process. I think the stage process in general is more conducive to the musical than the film process, as it stands now. Animation is an exception. Animation has become *more* than an exception, animation has become now, I suppose, the true champion of new musicals, and the kind of musicals that probably could never work onstage—or if it did it would be a whole other trick to pull it off.

Was *Newsies* a project brought to you?

MENKEN: Yes. And the script was changed, in some cases rather radically. I clearly lost a good deal of control in the process. Ken Ortega was a wonderful collaborator in terms of staying in touch and being open and amenable to our opinions, I can't fault him in terms of that. It's just there wasn't any really strong overseer.

In a musical you could have a brilliant song, but if you don't set up right what that song promises and it isn't carried through, then the song's power is dissipated, diffused. And much of that happened on *Newsies*. It probably means that I and my collaborators have to take a more active role in film musicals in the future if it's going to be more fully realized. Besides all that, I really did feel that the studio could have waited beyond one week before pulling all their ads. I felt bad that something that we'd put so much effort into essentially was left hanging with no support. But I can't fault the studio in terms of their support on my other things. So they made a decision, that the box office their first weekend said this is a film that people don't want to see—and basically, by pulling the ads, they *assured* that nobody was going to see it.

Many is the time on the stage when something gets up in front of an audience and you can't change it much, either because of the actors or because of the rehearsal schedule or because the money's not there. So it's hard for me to paint it with a very broad brush and say that one medium allows you more input than the other. People at Disney would give me as much input as I want and I really have to take the responsibility for the fact that I live on the East Coast, not there. There are liabilities to living on the East Coast and working on the West Coast, and one of them is you simply can't stay on top of everything.

You're just finishing *Aladdin* now?

MENKEN: I've just done streamlining of the scoring. It's a pain in the neck, but I have to do it by tomorrow morning. Probably the most depressing thing though is going back and redoing old work. Even if you're not particularly pleased with it, even if you're just in-an-average-way pleased, going back and tearing things down again and building it back up is obviously a pain. There's a lot of work to get done, sixty minutes of score. And by the way, we've already done twelve minutes on top of that and that doesn't include any of the songs, so seventy-two, I believe eighteen minutes of songs, brings it up to ninety minutes, and I'm thinking, *An eighty-minute film and I'm writing ninety minutes of music?* So we miscalculated!

But these scores, they become a world unto themselves and you can get lost in them, after all the themes and all these characters and all the work that has to be done. And inevitably there are those points where someone doesn't like what you've done, you go back and redo them, and I'm tempted to stand up and say, "Now wait a second, I did this and don't you tell me . . ." but that's damaging. You shut up, listen to the comments, and if there's any validity there, go with it, because the most valuable thing you can get is perspective.

I'm used to change. I've worked with so many people during Howard and after Howard, that's not an unusual thing for me; the hard thing is not having that particular sureness. And it's strange—Howard dies, Steve Brown dies, Michael Bennett dies, goes on and on and on, all these great close collaborators. It seems like we all go on as if it should feel normal—people go on to write musicals in the face of tragedies, and getting statuettes and doing phenomenally well, and going, *Boy, I should be pretty darn happy.* And I *am*, but it's a strange feeling you get: Isn't Howard supposed to be here? Shouldn't Michael Bennett be around *doing* things? Steve Brown? They were all in their forties or younger. You're supposed to step into their shoes and somehow pretend that you can replace them. So it becomes—I was about to say thankless, but it's *not* thankless because the fact that you're thrust into that is a great honor, and a great thrill, and responsibility. And for a studio to be placing the kind of faith and reliance on one composer that they're placing on me makes me shake my head, when they come to me doing *Pocahontas* and we're talking about the next animated feature. *Don't they want to get someone else?* I know I do feel proud of the work I do and I do feel that not a lot of people do what I do at all, so I don't want to be disingenuous about it—I know what I do is good—but it's an extraordinary situation to be placing that kind of reliance on *a* composer. That's what makes me work my tail off, because I don't want to lose it. It's not the kind of circumstance that I necessarily ever expected but maybe in my dreams dreamt of—being in it now makes you want to say, "I'll work as hard as I can not to lose it because it's so wonderful," but you know at some point you've got to move on.

And be clear about when to say no.

MENKEN: That's becoming this year's challenge! The biggest stars in the world have asked to do musicals with me or have me write something for them. It's flattering, yes, but the only drawback is I have a life and I can't actually do *all* these things. Not all of them are swell ideas, but the prospect of working with this guy, that woman—I can't mention names—this is to laugh, how can you say no? "No" is definitely a challenge.

GOD HELP THE OUTCASTS

By 1999, Menken had moved beyond *Aladdin, Pocahontas, The Hunchback of Notre Dame,* and *Hercules*—all highly successful. He had adapted *Beauty and the Beast* to a live theatrical production, which was beginning its sixth year on Broadway, and has been involved with several other legitimate shows. Busy on his latest Disney animated project, he spoke of the latest developments in the genre of film musicals.

▶▶

Have you learned how to say no?

MENKEN: I still think I am bad at saying no! It doesn't mean I *don't* say no, it's just when I do, I sometimes handle it badly because I wait so long. I have a knee-jerk response, which is "no," immediately. Then when I get past that I actually get into, "Well, wait a second, don't jump to it immediately, let me find out more." Once I find out more, inevitably I end up getting interested in what somebody's saying and find it hard then to cut off the communication without at least looking at the material. And that's where I *really* get myself into big trouble because I don't have *time* to look at the material, so it sits and it sits and they call and then I feel guilty; they've already got you not wanting to say no because you feel you've already kept them hanging on for so long you better have an intelligent *reason* for saying no. Especially because it's not a matter of looking at a film and deciding if you want to score it. For me it's a matter of looking at material and asking myself, *Do I want to adapt it?* And there are so many factors involved, once I start looking into it, then I trap myself in a process. So "no" is never easy for me because of that. Lately I've had less of a problem saying no because frankly there's not quite the rush for song-driven projects that there was five years ago. Seven years ago it was all cresting upward. It has subsequently in films slid downward.

Yet Disney, Warners, DreamWorks, and Fox are all doing animation, and it seems nearly every animated film now *has* to have a musical song score.

MENKEN: Yes, but you'll find now that it has stopped, like if you put the brakes on a train it takes a while for it to screech to a halt. I think the era of the animated musical is kind of waning. It doesn't mean there won't be animated musicals; I'm working on one now, it's a western for Disney. Animated film musicals still regularly make a hundred million dollars a picture. But most of the projects coming up from Disney have songs under the material (like *Tarzan*), or don't have songs at all. And that, I presume, is a phase.

Why now?

MENKEN: Oh, I saw it happening after *Pocahontas*. I got a sense that the public for the most part was saying, "Oh yes, an animated musical; I know what *those* are," and not getting into the *differences* between *Hunchback of Notre Dame* and *Hercules*, or any of the other projects that have come along with distinctions. When I saw that those distinctions were not being seen, I realized that people were not looking at them with a fresh eye anymore—they'd just became a genre that you either want to see or you don't.

There has been a resurgence in live-action musicals on TV, such as *Gypsy* and *Annie*.

MENKEN: Yes, but those don't count, not at all, because they're not original.

But do you think the fact they're being produced at all bodes well for the production of an original musical? Because for a long time no one was doing anything in that genre.

MENKEN: I don't know that it bodes well for original musicals. I think the signs were a lot better at the time I did *Newsies;* there was a receptivity at that point. I think the door has somewhat shut. And now musicals are relegated to television. There's basically nothing *wrong* with television, but television is not film.

I'm a holdout, I'm waiting for the big live-action film musical, and I was working on one at Disney that has now gone back into a development phase. So there's nothing actively in production as far as live-action film musicals. That's something I want to see happen. I think the studios are very wary because live-action film musicals are not cheap at all, and that's a huge burden; and also in order to put them across people feel they need to be accompanied by a lot of fantastic special effects, whether it's visuals like in old Hollywood film musicals or the tricks you would do in a *Roger Rabbit*, and it ups the ante considerably. The same kind of fantastic things that fuel an animated musical would need to fuel a live-action musical.

People expect more from a live-action musical because they've grown accustomed to the fantastic elements of animated musicals?

MENKEN: I think so. It's the way of thinking at the studio that in order to hold people's attention in a film musical, it has to have a real twist to it. However, those things require a large commitment as far as money. Now, at Disney, this is not the time they are most apt to be jumping into gigantic big-budget pictures.

▶▶

During the past few years, what has been most satisfying creatively for you?

MENKEN: A continuation of my work on the stage. I've loved my work in film, but I live on the East Coast and I am closer to the theater community. And the process of writing a stage musical is much more in the author's hands, and it remains in the author's hands all the way through production. In film it's much more collaborative with other people just to coordinate what's to be done.

I have had a perennial Christmas musical that is going into its sixth year, *A Christmas Carol*. That's been a wonderful thing for me. We did an adaptation of *Hunchback of Notre Dame* in Berlin and there are plans to bring it to Broadway; that was an extension of what we started with *Beauty and the Beast*, and what Disney did with *The Lion King*. It's the next installment of bringing an animated musical to the stage.

I opened the New Amsterdam Theatre with *King David*, which you could definitely call a mixed experience; it was fantastically received by the audiences, pretty much disliked by the critics. And I'm now working on doing it in a concert in Jerusalem. I'm doing a new musical that Howard and I had begun before he died and we never got a chance to complete, it's called *Big Street*, a Damon Runyon story. I'm revisiting a musical I was working on at that time I came over to Disney to do *Little Mermaid*, *The Apprenticeship of Duddy Kravitz*. I had done it in Philadelphia, but way back when Howard and I had begun our work on *Mermaid*.

I'm also doing a new musical with Larry Gelbart and David Zippel; I have a new collaborator I'm working with at Disney who I'm looking at doing some musicals with; revising my show *Kicks;* and doing an album with Alice Cooper. So there's a lot of stuff! But I'm getting to stay closer to home, which is important to me, and it probably will stay that way for the foreseeable future.

But as far as new challenges, new horizons, I guess you could say *King David* represents that. It's purely music from beginning to end, an oratorio, and it's more serious. But I welcome the opportunity to do the animated features. The one I'm doing at Disney now is completely light and comedic and a lot of fun to do.

I would love to do a film musical. What's interesting is my kids are at an age now where they've rediscovered *Newsies*, and I've found out that there's a wellspring of people all over the world who love *Newsies*—this film that grossed about a dollar fifty at the box office for some reason has a cult following. It's something that I observe and am very interested in, and I occasionally mention it to people at Disney: "Do you notice that there's this going on out there? How about rereleasing it or theatricalizing it, or how about a *new* film musical?" But there seems to be cold feet right now.

It would take a live-action musical succeeding for them to warm up to that?

MENKEN: Yes, it's that catch-22. It would take that, or it would take a resurgence of the huge box office of animated pictures again. Or it would take an executive with the power who cared passionately about doing a film musical. I know of some people who are working on them, and maybe will get them on. But the ones I've worked on have either not succeeded or had the plug pulled on them. That's a frustration.

That is something I would love to change, but we're in a different era; this isn't the thirties. Songs play a different kind of role, and theater songs play a different kind of role in our culture. The animated musical was the one thing that altered that for a brief moment, but whether that moment has passed or waned to a degree is the question.

■

BENDING THE RULES

Although much has been discussed about specific procedures or goals for film music, this is not to suggest that there are hard-and-fast rules about what can or cannot work when marrying music to image. Because the style and subject matter of films vary greatly, so too do the styles and purposes of film music. But as the following examples show, even if there are no rules, they are sometimes bent anyway—or rather, our *expectations* are bent.

Sometimes composers whose primary work is outside of cinema—in the concert hall, on Broadway, in rock bands—will be hired. If an unconventional film requires an unconventional choice for composer, the results can revivify the craft by expanding its boundaries.

SOUNDS OF APOCALYPSE:
JOHN CORIGLIANO ON *ALTERED STATES*

Ken Russell's films, noted for their visual and aural excesses, are often downright giddy in their self-awareness of how far cinema can take an idea to its most notorious, scandalous, or funky extreme. The creator of several television documentaries and features on the lives of composers and artists, Russell has always brought a keen ear to his films, with iconoclastic scores commissioned for *The Devils* (Peter Maxwell Davies) and *Gothic* (Thomas Dolby)—not to mention a star-filled adaptation of the Who's rock opera *Tommy*.

He took on—with a vengeance—the science fiction/horror genre with his 1980 film *Altered States*. It tells of a scientist experimenting with altered states of consciousness (brought about by hallucinogenic drugs and sensory deprivation chambers) who experiences wildly cataclysmic visions of apocalypse, religious iconography, and morphing flesh. All innocent fun—that is, until the visions take on physical shape when he devolves into a specimen of prehistoric man.

To compose music for such a phantasmagorical joyride, Russell turned to respected concert composer John Corigliano. Corigliano typically eschews the minimalism of many of his contemporaries, relying on a more melodic style of writing, though the brazenness, even cheekiness of his orchestrations sometimes becomes a highly theatrical feature of his works (which no doubt caught the attention of Russell). Its flair for matching the visual fireworks makes *Altered States* a highly cinematic score, although some sections have been performed in the concert hall and as the basis of a ballet (*Three Hallucinations for Orchestra*).

▶

Did you have any experience writing for film before *Altered States*?

JOHN CORIGLIANO: I only did one thing, a short called *A Williamsburg Sampler*, for tourists to see before taking a tour of the colonial Virginia town. It won a Cine Golden Eagle award, but I wouldn't call it a *film* in the major sense of the word.

I got the job for *Altered States* because Ken Russell, the director, happened to hear my clarinet concerto* with Zubin Mehta and the Los Angeles Philharmonic while he was shooting the film. He actually went to hear Strauss's giant tone-poem *Also Sprach Zarathustra* and it was good luck that my music was on the same program.

I was first attracted to the offer because I knew Ken's love of clas-

---

*A 1977 composition, recorded for New World Records by Zubin Mehta and the New York Philharmonic with Stanley Drucker as soloist.

sical music (many of his films deal with the lives of the great composers) and I felt that he would deal with the music well when mixing it in the dubbing room. Secondly, unlike the stereotype, Ken and Daniel Melnick (the producer) wanted me to use all of my advanced techniques in the writing. It was quite the reverse of "We want the Beach Boys"; they said, "We want you to go even *further* and *wilder*, and do the wildest score you've ever done. Go for it, and we'll give you any resource you need to do it." Of course, that's very intriguing

John Corigliano

for a composer! And the third thing was that there were eight- or nine-minute sections where there were *no words*, where the apeman is running around, and where only music (and sound effects) are available, and therefore I didn't feel that it was just music under dialogue all the time. So it was a combination of the fact that the director was the right director, the project asked me not to limit myself but in fact to *expand*, and there were a lot of places for the music to be the force that drove the movie. And it was exciting. I had never done it, and I love to do things I haven't done.

Altered States gave me a chance to try a lot of things which I then incorporated into my concert music. And there are things in my concert music that are in *Altered States*, like reshapened parts of my clarinet concerto which I saw could fit in.

The film had been temp-tracked with music by Bartók and Stravinsky, among others, music styles which are not

unknown to horror film fans. Was that what the director was looking for?

CORIGLIANO: Whenever you see a "Creature Features" horror movie you hear strong influences from the primeval scores of Bartók and Stravinsky—film composers have used these techniques so often that they have taken on the quality of a cliché, and they type the film as a genre piece. To take [the film] seriously, the music had to take it to a whole different kind of primitivism, which was much closer to our time. That is the primitivism of making an orchestra *almost* electronic, not real, which is produced through different techniques—having sounds and sonorities coming out of instruments in which the instruments themselves are sometimes unrecognizable, [because] the kinds of clusters and ways of playing the instruments so distort them that they become primitive, not in the primitivism of the 1940s, but a *new* kind of primitivism.

What is an example of having instruments played in an unconventional manner, as you have had done in some of your concert works?

CORIGLIANO: Well, in the film's first hallucination sequence (where the flutes sound like ancient horns), that's a buzz technique, used by playing like a trumpet *into* the flute rather than blowing across it, producing a major seventh below the finger pitch. That was taught to me by the well-known flutist Ransom Wilson and I'd never used it before writing *Altered States*.

Ken Russell wanted something wild—he didn't even know how to express it—but when I gave it to him he loved it because he knew it was the right thing.

What I knew about the film was that it had a high level of motion activity, and that I needed to write a lot of notes, but because film composing has to be done in such a short amount of time, I wanted to be able to develop a few simple symbols that would result in furious activity in the orchestra, and so I developed a whole bunch of what I called "motion sonorities." One of them that I use all the time now is the idea of putting a box around two notes (say a fourth apart or a fifth apart) and telling the player to play *in between and including* those notes—random figures—as fast as possible. It's very useful because you can play them legato or mercato, and you can play them in a rhythm or as fast as possible.

If you have a box enclosing two notes a fifth apart, that would indicate a half-tone cluster between the two (say C, C-sharp, D, E-flat, E, F, F-sharp, and G). You could then write the two notes with a time value (say a half note) and you could then indicate (by lines through the stem of the half note) how the players would play the notes between and including given pitches—one slash, eighth notes; two slashes, sixteenth notes; three, unmeasured (as fast as possible). If you indicate eighth notes, it would mean that the player would play eighth notes wandering *between and including* those pitches—if you give it to a whole string section that means sixteen people doing it. And it could be even legato, or say breathed like a horn would be, or it could be marcato staccato, with the bow changing all the time producing a kind of boiling sound. It's a single symbol, yet it produces many different kinds of motion sounds.

Another would be the starting of a run indicating the first half-dozen notes, and then *x*'s to a particular high note, and a slash meaning "play as fast as possible," and then bracket it and put the value of the run (like a half note or a dotted quarter), so that you can play as many notes as possible to get to the top note rather than indicating *which* notes they are and how many to play. And this means you can play it more virtuosically.

I had to stop composing the *Pied Piper Fantasy* [a 1982 con-

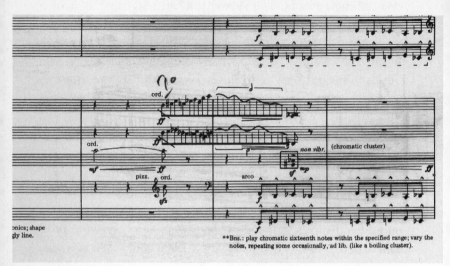

ɔnics; shape
gly line.

**Bns.: play chromatic sixteenth notes within the specified range; vary the notes, repeating some occasionally, ad lib. (like a boiling cluster).

(Above) A recipe for boiling music: Some of Corigliano's "motion sonorities." (Below) Effects to inspire a most visual score, from *Altered States*.

certo for flute and orchestra, based on the folk tale] to write *Altered States*, and afterward I incorporated all those techniques in *Pied Piper*, the battle scenes with the rats, so these techniques intermingled, they cross-pollinated, and that's all very good. And the "War Lament," an adagio played over a frantic battle between the Americans and the British in *Revolution* [Hugh Hudson's 1985 film about the American War of Independence] became the basis for the first movement of my symphony, so again there's a cross-pollination.

Film deadlines are shorter [than for concert works], but it's easier to write film music because you have so many "givens." You're given exact durations, emotional shapes, places where you have to be quiet for dialogue, you're even given recorded examples of things it should *sound* like. I mean, it makes it a lot easier to do that than just a blank page and thirty minutes of music to construct. And with standard film work now, everyone gets a lot of help—the composer composes, the orchestrator orchestrates, the producer produces.

Altered States in fact has an orchestration credit on the film even though I always orchestrate my own music, and the reason for that is that the man who laid out my score—I gave him a short score where everything was labeled and he laid it out on a full score while I was composing the next cue—had to get paid by being listed as "orchestrator," otherwise he couldn't have gotten the money. So we allowed him that credit on the film, but if you notice the CD, it credits him with "Score Preparation."

There was a lyrical waltz, quite different from the majority of the score, which is on the soundtrack album but didn't make it into the film.

CORIGLIANO: That was part of the hallucination intercut with the Hinchi mushroom dance, the section with Blair Brown feeding William Hurt ice cream under a parasol and a slithering python that ended up enveloping Hurt. That was an individual, separate section, and what happened was when the people at Warners saw it they said the hallucinations weren't schizophrenic enough! So Russell took that whole section and he intercut it with the Hinchi dance, to discombobulate the dance by intercutting it with things that were completely different. So we lost that section.

The other thing is, Ken is not a fan of chamber music, and he never really liked the idea that there were only three instruments playing. That's the thing about Ken: he always likes a *lot* of instruments playing! And I was underplaying with a trio because of that huge python. I wanted it to be, suddenly he's holding the python but this trio is playing as if it were the Palm Court of the Plaza Hotel, and the shock would [come from] playing *against* it. Ken didn't want that, he wanted a reaction musically to the python. I said, "No, play against it, just ignore it, it'll be much more frightening, crazier." But we ended up not doing it because the scene was chopped up. So we stuck it on the record.

On the other hand, there's one cue he played in the wrong place and I really hate it because it does sound very "Creature Features"-y. It's a cue that I wrote for when the little ape-man got caught in the zoo, and it's based on my clarinet concerto, a kind of primeval sound; he sort of hobbles around the elephants and rhinoceros and all that. And because Ken needed more music after he saw the whole film, he used it again when the ape-man was in the laboratory. Now when he used it *there*, the music almost was satirical to me, because it has been used in so many movies that way. But the actual primitivism of being in the jungle, [and] the irony of him leaping into a world of elephants and creatures that heralded back in time out of the city, *that* kind of primeval music made sense to me. So he used it where I did like it, it's just that he used it again in another place where I didn't like it, and I didn't know until the movie came out that he had put it in there. I said, "This is not what I meant!" But there's nothing you can do.

What was your experience with the recording, which was done by pickup musicians in Los Angeles conducted by Christopher Keene?

CORIGLIANO: They were the best session players in Los Angeles and they played better than any orchestra, any major symphony can play. I've never heard a horn player who doesn't know how ever to make a mistake, and never cracks and only plays everything perfectly no matter how many takes you take of it. And they literally read through the score, read a cue, record it, read a cue, record it, like that. We're dealing with very high quality people. You get what you pay for in Los Angeles!

Why does there not seem to be much crossover of composers between the concert hall and Hollywood?

CORIGLIANO: I know a lot of concert composers who would love to write film music. Some of them are not suited for it because to write film music you have to write in a variety of techniques and languages dictated by the director and that is what you are expected to do. In my case I only accept films in which I feel I *can* adapt my technique and language.

Basically some concert composers cannot write excepting for the way they write, and therefore that would eliminate them from anything but the right film. Philip Glass, for example—his score for the Scorsese film *Kundun* was successful because of the subject matter of that film, but Philip Glass wrote "Philip Glass music" and they played it while the film was going on, basically. It was not the same thing as him writing to order. I don't think that a lot of composers would be willing to do it, or capable of doing that.

The onus comes from writing a lot of film music. If you are mainly a film composer (like John Williams or young Elliot Goldenthal), you are typed by critics as a Hollywood type and not taken seriously in the concert hall. Critics love to put people into compartments and that compartment is one of their favorites. That compartment is a very easy one to get into if you do a lot of films.

Does that prejudice exist within the concert world itself? Or do symphony orchestras not commission original works from film composers because they'd be competing for their services against a Hollywood studio?

CORIGLIANO: No, I think the symphonies would be delighted to commission film composers because they write films and therefore they reach a population that doesn't go to the symphony. I don't think there's a barrier there, and certainly with young composers there's no barrier. They all look on film composing as something very exciting. I think the barrier comes from the critics. Basically their image of the film composer is that of (a) a sellout to his art, because he's composing for money in a sense and to someone else's order, and (b) a person who has no style, who therefore writes in lots of different vocabularies.

Style for me is the unconscious choices I make, not the conscious ones; the conscious decisions involve the use of techniques (harmonic, dodecaphonic, et cetera) in my concert music and film music, but in the end it is the unconscious choices (like a person's handwriting) that form one's style.

▶▶▶

LIFE IN TRANSFORMATION: PHILIP GLASS ON
KOYAANISQATSI AND *POWAQQATSI*

Premiering at the dawn of the music-video age, Godfrey Reggio's 1983 film *Koyaanisqatsi* (a title translated as "Life out of Balance") was a blend of artful, sometimes psychedelic visuals married to a pulsing score by Philip Glass. Devoid of plot as such, the film is a tone poem, a contemplation of the erosion and usurpation of the natural environment by an industrialized culture.

Though he had already distanced himself from the appellation "minimalist," Glass wrote a score—his first major film work—that in some respects recalls his earlier minimalist works, taking motifs or themes and repeating them in gradually changing forms, whether in slow, elegiac passages (featuring chorales in the Hopi Indian language), mesmerizing trumpet calls (over time-lapse footage of clouds bubbling over mountain ranges), or rush-hour-fast electronics (accompanying speeded-up film of urban life).

When discussing his participation in films in general and

this film in particular, Glass was humorously self-deprecating about his position, given the unconventional parameters under which he has typically written music for film. The fact that the films themselves—such as *Mishima* and *Kundun*—have been atypical of Hollywood commercial cinema actually makes his understanding of the process of relating music and image (whether for narrative purposes, documentary, or some hybrid of the two) all the more important.

▶

PHILIP GLASS: Actually, I don't know much about films. I almost never see them; I haven't been into a movie house in years. I'm not interested in films, and I don't particularly *like* the medium. I've written some music for films, but I basically don't know anything about it.

But that's hard to take as repudiation of your contributions to the form. A score like *Mishima* is certainly more valid as "film music" than much of what passes for film music nowadays.

GLASS: Well, maybe, because I don't know anything about what film composers *do*.

Maybe you come with an advantage, because you're not married to a conventional "film music" approach or process.

GLASS: I suppose, perhaps you can look at it that way. But I don't even *know* movies. When I talk to film directors and they quote films to me, I don't know what they're talking about. I have to pretend that I've seen movies that I haven't seen. And I

Philip Glass

don't then go and look at them. I don't do any homework at all, I'm not interested.

But perhaps what makes something like *Koyaanisqatsi* stand out is that it doesn't try to be like another film. It's a new film language.

GLASS: It's important to remember that Godfrey Reggio wasn't a filmmaker either. He chose film as a medium to work in as a vehicle for presenting ideas that he had about society, traditional ways of living, and the relationship of technology to individual freedom and choice and experience. He'd made two other movies before that were really student attempts to make *Koyaanisqatsi*; so he really had to learn the craft of filmmaking in order to make the first feature.

He came to see me in New York. He said he was making a movie and he had studied a lot of music and decided I was the right composer for it. And I said what I'd said to you: "I don't write film music, and I don't think you are calling the right person." And like you, he didn't listen to me!

And then a friend of his called me and said, "The guy came from Sante Fe and he's not going to leave New York until you look at his movie, so why don't you just look at it so he can go home?" So I agreed to do that.

I went down to see about the first thirty or forty minutes of the film, which was what he had; he didn't have that much shot.

So it was primarily the opening scenes of the desert and cloudscapes?

GLASS: Yes, and he was actually more clever at this than I had anticipated. He showed two versions of his demo reel, I should call it: One was with some Japanese electronic music, and then one was with *my* music. We looked at them both and he turned to me and said, "As you can see, your music works a lot better." And naturally I agreed! It was a sly maneuver, which forced me basically to agree that he had made the right decision, and then of course I agreed to do it.

It became clear then that I was working with a person with an unusual mission and a vision of films that was unique; basically it was someone who looked like a hippie from New Mexico with a bunch of pretty pictures and some very fancy ideas about them. And I liked him. I said (this was in 1978 or '79), "Look, if you get the money together I'll do it." But I never imagined that he would get the money together. He gradually got bits and pieces together and we began to work slowly, but I never thought he would finish it.

Did Reggio make specific requests about musical textures to match his visuals?

GLASS: No, never, no. It was my job to present things. For example the opening with the organ, when I thought of the film, I said, "Let me think of the theater as a huge cathedral, and the sound you would hear in a cathedral would be a pipe organ." So I used the pipe organ to cue people into what environment they should think of themselves in, but that was totally my idea. Godfrey didn't say, "I need an organ here, I need voices here."

But he did present you with the Hopi language text, which was sung.

GLASS: He did, and we were very careful with that. In fact there was some question whether some of those words are real words or not. I recorded the text and we sent my setting of it to the Hopi community, and my question for them was whether they could understand the words. I didn't ask them whether they *liked* it, just were the words comprehensible? And they said, "Yes, they are." And that was the only permission I needed.

During the process, did he show you those two earlier attempts to make *Koyaanisqatsi*, and did they differ much from the third?

GLASS: He never showed me the discarded attempts. He described them to me, and they were hilariously funny! He would construct things like buildings and blow them up! In fact, he discovered documentary footage which was available—NASA footage or footage that is routinely shot by construction companies doing demolitions. Theirs was much more powerful than anything he could fabricate. And he got involved with a very good cinematographer, Ron Fricke, and Alton Walpole, who was one of the editors, and he learned how to make the film.

What was the compositional process like during *Koyaanisqatsi*?

GLASS: Basically I'd fly out to Venice where Godfrey had some kind of setup there, and he'd gotten a young German composer, Michael Hoenig, to be his music director—which was a good idea because Michael got him set up with a music studio there next to the editing room. So I would go out there about once a month, we would look at film, and then I would go home and write music. We would do a demo track and I would take it out there and then we would put it up with the picture and look at it and Godfrey would either edit the picture or I would rewrite the music. I would guess it was more than a year we spent doing that.

There were a number of pieces that did not end up in the film, like "Facades," because he basically cut the scenes. Godfrey later made a short film in Italy in which he used "Facades," and I let him use it, though in fact my deal with him was that if he didn't use the music, the music rights came back to me. That's something I've told a number of filmmakers, it's just a little revenge I have! Someone like Errol Morris, you can write ten cues for Errol for one scene, and as I once pointed out to him, anything he didn't use belonged to me, which gave him a *slight* pause, but not much! And much of that discarded music, if any of it's useful it turns up in something else. I don't mind doing that.

But it was a long process on *Koyaanisqatsi*. We had lots of time because there was no release schedule, there was no production schedule, there was no money! And until the end Godfrey didn't have the money to complete it. Finally someone stepped in and gave him the completion money, but to do that (and this is the saddest thing) he had to give up any remaining ownership or financial stake in the film. He ended up owning nothing, except he got to finish the film. That's very common in that business, as you know; people wait around for these unfinished films and then with the last two hundred thousand dollars they get whatever rights remain. Quite sad, isn't it?

But that's how it worked in his case; he did finish the film ultimately. And then he had an introduction to Francis Coppola from someone, and he invited Francis to see the film. We were in a screening room in Los Angeles, there were only three of us there: Godfrey and myself and Francis. And I sat up in the front somewhere, and they were behind me, and I fully expected after a few minutes to hear some heavy footsteps and a door shutting. It never occurred to me that Francis would sit through the whole thing! In fact, at the end he was still there. He came up to me and shook my hand and said congratulations, and shook Godfrey's hand, said congratulations, and Godfrey and I looked at each other and thought that was the end of it. In fact, Francis said, "How can I help you?" And Godfrey said, "Could you help introduce me to people?" No one knew who Godfrey was; I was of course better known than Godfrey by then—this was four or five years after *Einstein on the Beach*. And Francis did something much better: He gave them this logo—it says "Presented by Francis Ford Coppola"—which of course doesn't *mean* anything. It's like introducing you to a girl, you know, "This is a really great girl, go out with her, you'll have a really good time." That's basically what he did, he didn't *do* anything, but in fact he did a *tremendous* thing, because on the basis of that, *Koyaanisqatsi* was put into the New York Film Festival. For some reason (I have no idea why they did this, another piece of good luck), it was shown at Radio City Music Hall. And they *filled* the place!

These films have always had a small, passionate following. But when they were first released, everyone thought Reggio was some kind of weird hippie, ranting on about ecology. A few oil spills later, with a bit more depletion of the ozone layer and global warming, they're saying, "Wait a minute, it isn't so crackpot after all." It's about the world we're living in. Suddenly, what was part of a counterculture has become mainstream—and urgent.

Powaqqatsi, which was in a similar form to Koyaanisqatsi, was concerned more with the third world and how it was being compromised by the industrial world. Did third-world music influence your score dramatically?

GLASS: I said to [Godfrey], it's no good just imitating an African band. It's like bringing back an ashtray. I can only write my own music. In the Andes, for example, I heard a sort of marching

(Above) Life out of balance: the psychedelic *Koyaanisqatsi*.
(Below) the Serra Pelada mines of Brazil to the tune of the
children's chorus in *Powaqqatsi*.

band playing in a Festival of the Saints miles away from anywhere. Their instruments had broken valves, the cymbal was cracked. It was difficult to work out what the hell they were doing. The noise was cacophanous, amazing. I went back to New York and wrote what I thought they might have sounded like if they had had proper instruments and known how to play them. It was an act of the imagination, but the music couldn't have been written without them.

On your later films with Reggio, including *Powaqqatsi* and *Anima Mundi*, did the process change much for you?

GLASS: *Powaqqatsi* he did in New York; he was on the West Side, so I basically just had to walk ten blocks to his studio, and the same things went on, working with the editors, Alton and Miroslav Janek. I spent a lot of time sitting with the editors looking at the music. It was routine to have a screening at the end of the day, and what would happen is we would put up any music or any film that was in some kind of shape.

Like musical dailies in a sense?

GLASS: Yes, combos of music and image. These are the kinds of things that industry films simply don't do, it never even occurs to them to do it. Because as you know it's done in quite a different way; the film is completed and then it's just dressed up with a little music at the end. Shocking, isn't it? Completely shocking that they do it that way.

Yeah, we pushed the process a little bit further. Not only did I go to the shooting, but I took the music to the shooting. For example, the Serra Pelada mines in Brazil, which is the opening sequence of *Powaqqatsi*: it's been documented, footage and photographs existed, so I knew what it looked like. So basically I wrote a ten-minute piece based on the Serra Pelada mines of what I'd seen.

I'm interested in how you chose a very bright, bubbly dance piece with children singing to go with images of men toiling in the mine.

GLASS: I think it was just an inspiration, really. In fact, they hadn't shot it yet, but the producer, Mel Lawrence, was surprised; he heard the music and he said, "Is this the right music?" And I said, "Well, Mel, I guess I could have [*sings dirge*] yo-ho-heave-ho! Is *that* what you want?" And he kind of gave me a sheepish smile and never said another word about it again!

In fact, what I found out is it was a better choice than even I had imagined. We recorded the music and we took it there, and the cameraman listened to the music while he was filming it. And we played it for the people in the mines. The day we got there Godfrey and I walked down to the bottom of the pit, it's half a kilometer down, and we sat down and I began talking to the guys there, and I said, "What are you doing here, what's it like?" And they said, "Well, we're finding gold."

And I said, "Did you find any yet?"

"No, didn't find any yet. But this guy over here got a big nugget yesterday."

People look at this place and say, "Oh, are these people in prison? What's going on here?" These guys would show me a piece of land that was six foot by three foot and they'd say, "This is *our* piece. Everything in this six-by-three-foot area belongs to us. You can dig as far as you can go—down to China—but it's ours." I became aware that I had never been around so many capitalists in my life! Sixteen thousand capitalists! People thought this was slavery; yeah, it's slavery, but it's the slavery of the mind. They were there because they *wanted* to be. In the morning there's a line of guys carrying gold dust into the bank. Not all of that got into the movie.

And I became aware that I was talking to very young people, there was no one in the pit over the age of twenty-five and many eighteen, nineteen, twenty years old. And suddenly it hit me like a ton of bricks that we were double their age. They *were* children! I realized that it was a much luckier choice [for the music] than I had imagined.

So they said, "What are you listening to?" And I said, "This music is *from here*. You want to hear it?" And I would hand them the tape. And the same guys that were in the film minutes later or minutes before were actually listening to the music. Isn't that amazing? So we went way beyond the point where people add music to the end of the film. We were using the film in a formative environmental dynamic relationship. And a composer who enters into a dynamic relationship with the material and the director has the possibility of creating an organic film/image experience. And if you don't do it, it will never, never, never happen.

THE DRIVING FORCE: ELIA CMIRAL ON *RONIN*

Take a mysterious package which some powerful people with deep pockets want very badly; add some terse, back-stabbing mercenaries who don't know who's fronting their paychecks, plenty of ammunition, and several nail-biting, high-speed car chases through the streets and tunnels of France, presented in a stripped-down, efficient manner, and you have an entertaining thriller of the classic variety. What is particularly unusual for a Hollywood action movie, however, is the rhythm of the music in *Ronin*.

The lessons of *The French Connection*'s legendary car/subway train chase notwithstanding, the majority of car chases today are scored at tempos that range from fast to faster to even *faster*. The composer of *Ronin*, Elia Cmiral, took a different road. He used a mixture of percussion, synthesizers, brutal strings, and low brass playing in a rhythmically anxious way—skittering, bumping, almost at odds with each other—creating tempos that are stilted, not uncomfortable, but wary, suspicious. Rather than being propulsive, the music of *Ronin*'s chase scenes sounds like it could go out of control, which heightens the audience's tension. The darkness of the orchestration also underlines the fact that there is nothing victorious or honorable about the characters' situation, or its outcome; it is desperate, and (for many of them) a losing proposition.

Topping off the score is a theme written for Robert De Niro's mercenary, a modern-day evocation of the *ronin* (a masterless samurai), performed on a *duduk*, a double-reed instrument from Armenia. The Eastern sound of the instrument vaguely suggests Japan and its legends without pegging the story as being specifically Japanese. In fact, the sound (and the character it represents) could be anywhere, lost in the world.

▶

ELIA CMIRAL: *Ronin* was my big step to the big world. Jerry Goldsmith was attached to the production but he walked away because of a conflict with his schedule, and Michael Sandoval, who is executive VP of MGM's music department, was asked to put together a list of composers suitable to score *Ronin*. And Michael knew my music. Even though at that time I hadn't scored any big studio movies, he had guts and he believed in my music, so he included me on the list. And I have to say that for this I'll be thankful to him for the rest of my life!

Then I met director John Frankenheimer. I saw the movie without temp, and we discussed ideas about the main title. I asked him how he would describe the main title, and he did it in three words: loneliness, sadness, heroism. We agreed that I would do a whole opening sequence, six or seven minutes long with the main title, as an audition. I got a tape and I went home to my studio to write the theme. And this is actually the theme that you hear in the final version, except it's now with orchestra.

The idea of using the Armenian *duduk* for the main theme came directly from Frankenheimer's description. I wanted to write something unusual and timeless. I also knew that I could not use any instruments, any elements, representing the sound of France—*Ronin* is a story that is Japanese, so I saw that it must be some sound which would be able to connect these things together.

So as not to limit the atmosphere of the film to its French locations.

CMIRAL: But not Japanese either. Because if I'd used a Japanese *shakuhachi* it would be kind of weird. I needed something which had this quality of sadness, and the *duduk* is an unbelievably sad instrument. So the instrument gave me the quality I was looking for. Also, I understood that this was my big opportunity, my first studio movie, so I wanted to write something which was really unique and sounded different.

Thematic ideas of the main title, the main scenes, everything was demoed for Frankenheimer. I played one instrument in time to my sequencer, and of course it's a rather slow process, but a great advantage in that I was able to immediately play it for Frankenheimer—we had regular demo sessions in my studio—and it sounded already like an orchestra, so I could get feedback from him. You spent more time playing it, then writing it, so it was very slow in one way, but in one way also fast. I could make changes, whatever needed to be done, then send the tape directly to the orchestrator.

John Frankenheimer is really a true director, a true music lover. He understands perfectly how it works, musically, in the movie. He was very articulate about what he wanted. He gave me great freedom in what to write, but he was very clear about when to start a cue, what kind of quality of emotions he wanted from every cue, and when we go out, when we let play sound effects, when I play a theme. He didn't care whether I used trumpets or snare drums; he was not this kind of picky producer-director who goes, "I don't *like* trumpets!" Nothing like that. Very open-minded.

He accepted my ideas and was very collaborative, but at the same time demanding to follow directions, to make sure we didn't go in different directions. We recorded all conversations—what was said at the spotting session with the film editor, music editor, and sound designer—so I had all documentation. I didn't have any problem understanding what was going on.

De Niro's character had this haunting quality in his theme. Did you also write themes for the other characters, his adversaries, who were even more mysterious in their origins?

CMIRAL: I don't have so many themes usually in my movies. I don't like the idea to write a theme for every character. I don't like to tell people what they should hear and what they should understand; I like to be a little bit more open for them. On the other hand, I believe that film today is like Wagner's *Gesamtkunstwerk*, it's a total art, and music is a part of the whole complex of the movie—with acting, with sets, with sound effects. So I believe I am kind of completing underneath something that *maybe* we want to feel, what we want to hear. I don't need to really say, "Oh, this is he, this is she . . ." You don't *need* it. So basically there's no melodic line or themes other than the De Niro theme in the main title. I did use fragments of the theme here and there; I like to play the theme when I have an opportunity to mention to the audience, underneath, emotionally, "This is the connection."

One of the most notable sequences was an extended chase through a Paris tunnel *against traffic*; it has a halting, almost *obstructive* rhythm.

CMIRAL: The music called "Wrong Way," when they enter the tunnel starting with the sign that reads "Wrong Way," was very interesting because the whole sequence is like a nine-minute-long car chase. It was actually my suggestion to let play loud sound effects beforehand and then start music on the sign, because nine minutes is really long. What can you do with nine minutes? You start to repeat yourself. And I felt I needed another gear to shift up to when they enter the tunnel. So we go into the chase, start with a huge, big sound on the sign—"Wrong way!"—and then go from there.

I also saw that instead of playing fast motifs in strings, it was actually a lot of fast tempo in the percussion and I played much longer notes on *top* of it. I didn't want to really have the same result as in some suspense movies where you have *da-da-da-da-da-da-da-da-da-da* strings again and again, it's not really interesting for me. The big car chases, with big shooting and action, they were scored separately from themes. There is no mention of the main theme in these sequences.

Of course I expected conflict with the music and sound effects later on final mix. That's kind of natural how film is done, because on the tape of the film I got to work with, they had some sounds but of course not *all* of the sounds. And when I see exploding cars I could guess, *Oh, that's going to be really loud!* But I think I really didn't ride the music as if I should go around the sound effects. I was very careful to write for dialogue and under dialogue, of course. I planned it so musically I had a concept for the big sequences but not really based on avoiding an explosion here or there.

The final mix we did in Los Angeles, and John Franken-heimer asked me to stay on the stage during the whole mix.

Even the sound editor was a really, really good one. Of course there were a couple of times we got into situations where we didn't agree with each other about the balance between sound and music; that's the nature of the business. So we decided that we would do two different mixes—his mix and my mix—and then we played it for John when he came in the afternoon, not telling him which was whose mix. I let him decide which he liked, and I have to say most of the time he chose my mix! The reason was not that I played music louder, it just was really subtle, small differences—not to lose, for example, the beginning of the melodic line in a car chase, because I felt if the audience loses the first couple of notes then they cannot *catch* it. So to have music in this moment—just a couple of seconds a little bit louder so we can catch it—then we follow it *unconsciously*. If you don't catch it then you just hear music as a wall of sound, but you cannot really follow the theme, because it's fast and there's a lot of action and sound effects on top of it. So these kinds of small things are important to me.

I wanted to find another way to score action sequences and, again, I wanted it to be unique. I am here in Los Angeles five years so I am not affected by growing up in front of TV and cartoons. I'm not saying this is bad, but I write music another way, I score it another way, and I think it's very important for me to keep this way. And I think it fit very well with *Ronin* because it has a flavor of Europe.

Is it characteristic of Hollywood films to have more music than European films?

CMIRAL: European movies usually have much less music; it is just something we have a little here, a little there, there's a theme here. If I go to extremes, like *Star Wars*, a big, huge symphonic one and a half hours of music in a one-and-a-half-hour movie, I don't remember even one European movie that has such a massive score like we can produce here. And, of course, as a composer it's a dream to have an orchestra instead of three lone musicians sitting in a studio playing piano, flute, and percussion.

Is the fact that there is less music in a European film because European filmmakers trust not needing as much music?

CMIRAL: Whether it's that they understand that they don't need so much music or if it's just they don't have money to record it, I don't know! In my experience in Stockholm, to just mention ten, fifteen musicians is like a big deal. I was fighting every time for one more musician. So maybe it's just because of the economy.

I think *Ronin* has seventy minutes of music for a two-hour film—it's just right. And we don't have so much source music, which is my next annoying thing in movies, that we use too much source music. And I hear again and again every day people talking about, "We want to use hip songs or hip contemporary music to be accessible for young audiences." Is it going to be accessible and hip and contemporary two years from now? How about in January?

Is there a big difference between the way film music is created in Europe and in the U.S.?

CMIRAL: How we score in Europe, it's a big difference. Somehow we never make the technical way of synchronizing music to film, through click track like in the old days or SMPTE code. What we do is we just write a piece of music and try to fit it on the editing table.

That suggests that European film music would tend to be more atmospheric, or mood music, rather than music tied to action.

CMIRAL: Yes, I think you are right, because it can't really hit action exactly, there is no way. If you hit one mark, the other one is out of sync; then you hit another one, the third is out of sync. There is no way in a two- or three-minute sequence to hit everything you want because tempo is fluctuating pretty strongly, and you don't have a music editor who would help you, it's basically the film editor who does it.

The effect of scoring *Ronin* for me was pretty large. I received a lot of publicity, a lot of reviews, I got first prize from *Movieline* magazine for the soundtrack. I also made a difficult decision to change my representation—I felt that this was an opportunity to move where most of the best are. All these things took time, so actually I didn't respond to the first projects offered; none of them were really on the same level as *Ronin* anyway. So I took my time, I redesigned my studio. I actually started a supernatural thriller, *Stigmata,* pretty soon after *Ronin* was done. It was very pleasant that after the success of *Ronin* and the attention the music got, there were no more questions about my quality. It was much easier! After *Stigmata,* I got an offer from Paris from a French director, Alan Barbérian, to write music for a film called *Six-Pack* starring Chiara Mastroianni, basically because he loves *Ronin*! So I did three studio movies in one year—*Six-Pack* is also a studio movie, even if it's a French production.

When I see my life from last September until today I made a great improvement of writing and demoing cues. I can also make extensive recordings in my studio with great control. I also feel that I found myself, my style, my voice, and my way of writing and creating music—that's what I can see after three studio movies.

To tell you the truth, to score *Ronin* was like all my dreams became true. I was very fortunate to get where I always wanted to be and work with such a director and crew and musicians. To think here I am coming from Eastern Europe and here I am with all these people helping me make my music sound great. It's very emotional and I feel very fortunate. And I don't have anything that I am disappointed in. What can I say? Maybe I sound kind of naive in this moment, but I'm writing for a big orchestra, I'm getting publicity, people talk about me, I'm getting awards for my music, what else can a writer wish for?

■

PERIOD PIECES

When you do a period film, do you do much research to make the score historically accurate, or do you take a more impressionistic approach—your impression of what the period would sound like?

BASIL POLEDOURIS: I suspect it's a little bit of both. I mean, I think I'm pretty well grounded in music history and the various techniques, but I'm sure a musicologist would rip their hair out in utter horror to think that it was an accurate representation of a period, but like everything else in film and fantasy, it *sounds* like it! For instance, in *The Hunt for Red October*, I didn't really study or go into any great research into Russian music, but I am certainly familiar with Stravinsky, with Prokofiev, and with Russian choral music, enough so that [what I wrote] feels right. I must tell you what I don't like to do, particularly in a historical situation—and I don't think I've ever done it yet—is to take a nineties approach to a seventeen-hundreds movie. I find that revisionist. And so far I haven't had a film where I had to do that. It might be interesting, it might be fascinating; I *could* have scored *Les Misérables* with synthesizers and a rock group, but I don't think it would have been much more effective than, say, *Ladyhawke,* was.*

That's an example where it sounded like it was done to make the film more accessible to a teenage audience.

POLEDOURIS: I think that's incredibly insulting to the teenage audience! It's like, look 'em straight in the eye and talk *down* to them!

I have no rules [about historical accuracy]. I guess that's my one rule: that I have no rules.

---

*Richard Donner's 1985 medieval romance, which sported an anachronistic pop music score.

STEEPING YOURSELF IN THE CULTURE:
CARTER BURWELL ON *ROB ROY*

Rob Roy, Michael Caton-Jones's romantic epic of the eighteenth-century Scottish warrior, opens with a stark, almost forbidding view of the Highlands as a posse tracks a band of cattle rustlers. The static opening frame is accompanied by a rippling drum riff punctuated by a wailing female voice, in the tradition of Celtic *port a beul*, or "mouth music," in which bagpipe pieces are vocalized.

▶

You did your first true period score for *Rob Roy*. How did you decide upon the concepts and instrumentation of the music?

CARTER BURWELL: Knowing Michael, I knew that, even though he's Scottish and he was shooting a Scottish movie, he was in a way also shooting a John Ford film, because that's the period of film that he really loves. He would *love* to shoot a John Ford film! If you look at the way the opening is shot, you realize this could just as easily be a western and those would be Indian tribes sneaking up on settlers or something. Those are Scottish and Irish drums [used in the opening scene], but those drums are just as much about Red-Indians-on-the-warpath footage as they are about a Scottish man tracking cattle thieves, which is what is actually going on.

The research was wonderful; it was so much fun to listen to gobs of Scottish music and learn about the history of it, such as what instruments existed back then and what didn't. For instance there were no accordions back then, so I couldn't use accordion. But what in fact I tried to do was give the music a very primitive quality. It's not like twentieth-century Celtic music. I relied a lot on percussion and voice; in that first scene, it gives it a very primitive feeling not having a lot of instruments.

I've been interested in Celtic music for years, so I already knew a lot about the general approach, but when Michael was shooting I went over and visited Scotland, and he'd gotten to know a band based in Glasgow called Capercaillie. Although they're a contemporary band they often sing old pieces. In fact the singer, Karen Matheson, like a lot of Scottish musicians, her parents entered her in competitions when she was a kid. (A lot of Celtic music is based around competitions—if you're a singer you go to singing competitions, if you're a piper you go to piping competitions.) She's sung the whole of Scottish traditional music that all those musicians carry around in their heads. So they were actually a source for me. I sat and talked to them about the history of the music and they pointed out interesting things: I learned there was a period when bagpipes were outlawed by the British, when people would do bagpipe imitations with their voices, and that became a whole genre of Scottish music. And they gave me leads on where to find records and tapes.

In the end, I didn't use traditional melodies for the score—those are my tunes, hopefully they *sound* Scottish; and for the drumming I used Gaelic drums, but it's not strictly the drum patterns that they would use. So it's hard to say exactly what the result of that research is on the score or how it pays off, except that just by steeping yourself in the culture you assume that [what you've written] is relevant.

I love *Rob Roy,* I think it turned out very well. And because the film's basically a romantic epic, those have to be the most fun things for composers to work on—you just have this gigantic canvas to paint on. In some ways I wonder whether doing a big orchestral score for something like that isn't maybe a little schmaltzy. That's my one misgiving about it. I don't know what the alternative would have been except to dry it out a little bit.

MYTHMAKER:
BASIL POLEDOURIS ON *CONAN THE BARBARIAN*

John Milius's adaptation of *Conan the Barbarian* brought Robert E. Howard's pulp hero to the screen in the ample guise of Arnold Schwarzenegger, as he battles the cult leader Thulsa Doom and his hordes. Basil Poledouris's music from *Conan*—hard, brisk, and brutal, like its eponymous hero—relies heavily on percussion, brass, and an effective use of chorus that painted a vivid soundscape of precivilization.

Despite this primitive sound, there are lilting romantic melodies woven into the score in an orchestra arrangement betraying Eastern influences, and a mesmerizing string waltz played during a pagan ritual, punctuated by horns and a gong.

The music helped make *Conan* a film that cried out for a stereo release, but in fact it was—notoriously—one of the last mono films from a major studio. The proliferation of stereo theater sound systems like Dolby, Vistasonic, Ultra Stereo, and, later, Dolby Digital, DTS, and SDDS has helped make stereo soundtracks on release prints not only commonplace but mandatory—though not in time for *Conan*'s 1982 premiere.

In addition to talking about the development of *Conan*'s score, Poledouris speaks of the chances of revising *Conan*'s soundtrack two decades after the fact for a DVD release so that the music would be allowed to play out like never before.

▶

What were John Milius's earliest discussions with you about what he wanted for *Conan*, which really got the sword-and-sorcery genre going?

BASIL POLEDOURIS: He wanted it to be prehistoric, so it went way beyond Rome as depicted in the great movie epics, very much like what Miklos Rozsa did to create the sound of Rome— nobody really knows what the hell any of *that* music sounded like. Milius wanted a very strong theme, and for it to sound mythological, [to have] that sense that this was a name that was known throughout time—as if Conan were as real as Ulysses.

He knew he wanted it to be an opera, because he had so few lines of dialogue in the film that he thought the music would really need to carry a lot of the scenes and help the audience understand what it was about. The main thing was to plant this idea of the mythological. There's a scene where Conan is in a cave with the skulls and the treasure, when he discovers the Atlantean sword. And I said, "What exactly is going on here?" And John said, "This is a ritual that's been waiting ten thousand years to happen—just make it sound like that." Oh, okay, that's really clear!

Basil Poledouris

But those are the kinds of directions he would give me: strong, powerful. It was about the strongest man on earth at that time. The romantic aspects of it I suspect just sort of snuck in because that's my personality. But John's very romantic as well. We just got on the same wavelength, and I always do with his scripts, because I understand them.

John loves melody. He and I share a great admiration for Ennio Morricone's scores for the Sergio Leone films. I think those were a model that he liked, because they were operatic in a way with their use of voices and leitmotif. But he also knew that *Conan* needed to be ancient-sounding.

I did a lot of piano work before he started shooting. I'd play him themes, and then he took a couple of them on location and it sort of grew as he was shooting, and I would continue to write. I did the same thing on *The Blue Lagoon* with Randal Kleiser. That's why I say when he wanted an opera, it wasn't so much the fact that we used the voices but it was really more the *idea* behind the music, using music as a storytelling device.

And having a vocal presence in the film?

POLEDOURIS: Yes, whereas *The Blue Lagoon* was really a ballet; it certainly had as many nondialogue scenes as *Conan*, but somehow they were lighter, they were lighter on their feet, it was more of a dance piece. Just the sparkle of the water, just a different world, different color and attitude.

What language did the chorus sing in *Conan*?

POLEDOURIS: Latin. Originally John wanted German, but I just thought that was too *young*. Latin seemed to have a more formal antiquity to it for me.

What served as the text?

POLEDOURIS: I wrote it. I don't even remember what it says: "Steel, we seek things of steel," basically they're Thulsa Doom's cheering section, the choir that sings at the beginning, in the "Riders of Doom" cue. "We are dying, we are dying for fated Doom," and then it continues, "Goodbye snow, goodbye sky, goodbye earth, goodbye life, we are dying, we are dying for fated Doom." It sounds *great* in Latin!

I don't speak Latin, and in cases where I need to have lyrics sung in a foreign language, I write them in English first and then bring in an expert so that linguistically it makes sense. The syntax in *Conan* was a little less than correct, because I was really more concerned about the way the Latin words sounded than with the sense they actually made. *The Hunt for Red October* was another matter; that's grammatically very correct.

You can take more artistic license with something that happened ten thousand years ago.

POLEDOURIS: Not only that, they're words that are shouted much like in a battle. There are no complete sentences when you're in the middle of chaos. I wanted that feeling—they just puncture the air. There's actually one instance in which I used some Greek words, when the dogs attack Conan's father.

You used the notion of "prehistory" as a jumping-off point. Did you first develop a melodic line or a lyrical framework, extrapolated from early music, or did you first choose what your instrumentation might be to define what the music would *sound* like?

POLEDOURIS: The very first thing was the melodic line. I actually sat down with a guitar and came up with a song about Conan, this guy who was a king of his tribe, as if I were the bard who would be passing on a Homeric kind of heroic poem about this warrior. And for that reason I actually wrote lyrics for the main theme of *Conan* because I wanted it to be communicative. I wanted the phrases of the melody to be singable, conversation-like, so that future generations *could* remember them easily. That's really where I started. When it came time to harmonize it, the main model was Gregorian chant—my *idea* of what Gregorian chant is. I didn't study Gregorian chant beyond school. But there's a fact that in primitive music the first interval was the octave and then historically what'll happen next is you have people singing in unison, some of them will be singing in fifths

171

and they won't realize it because they think they're singing the same note, so the next most primitive interval would be the fifth, and *Conan* utilizes a *lot* of that in the harmonic structure. So the film starts off very sparsely harmonically, and primitively (the sort of thing you'd flunk a harmony class in music school with if you turned it in as an example of your work). As the story line progresses, the characters move geographically southward from the Russian steppes toward the Mediterranean, so I started introducing intervals of thirds and sixths to warm the music and give it a more sophisticated harmonization, to represent Conan's accruing worldliness and maturation. I tried to keep an arc of the film *warming* until Conan's final realization, after he destroys the Temple of Doom, that he is king now, he has a responsibility—he's not just a warrior, a slayer bent on revenge. And that was supposed to set up the second in the series of three films, where the next one was going to be *Conan the King*. That of course never happened.

Conan the Destroyer was not originally part of Milius's planned trilogy?

POLEDOURIS: No! I call it *Conan the Pretender*.

I understand they are considering releasing Conan on DVD with a new stereo mix.

POLEDOURIS: I hope so, because I watched the video of Conan the other day and it just sounds hideous—like it was recorded right after *King Kong,* being in mono. We have been talking about this, and what we've discovered in the last couple of weeks is no one knows where the twenty-four-tracks are. Really what I wanted to do was the DVD 5.1—three across the front and stereo surrounds—and the only way I could really facilitate that is off the twenty-four-tracks, but if the only thing that exists are the three tracks—which is left-center-right—I don't know if I could do what I want to do with it.

I thought they were going to do the whole movie DVD, and that's when I got really excited about it, because the movie deserves it; it looks stunning, it's an amazingly visual experience. But then it was just going to be the music—not integrated with the sound effects or the dialogue, but as a stand-alone DVD mix of the music. Mixing down each one of those pieces of music and then putting it into sync would probably facilitate some recutting of the music. It's kind of a daunting task, although I've got a studio here in Venice where we were all prepared to do it—my engineer's excited, my music editor's excited about it—but now if we can't find the material, the only other option really would be to rerecord it. Which is something I've been thinking about doing.

To do that you'd have to match it to picture.

POLEDOURIS: That's right, and I would have to rerecord *all* of it, which would be quite costly. All I can tell you is, if they find the twenty-four-tracks I'd definitely proceed with it, but if it's just an enhanced version of what's on there right now I'm not interested.

Conan is dear to my heart and I think it deserves to be presented as best as possible. Because the original intent, believe me, was to do this in stereo. We begged Verna Fields (who was studio liaison) and Rafaella DiLaurentiis (the producer) to mix it in stereo but they just wouldn't do it: It was too costly. In fact, we mixed one of the reels in stereo and played it for Rafaella and Verna when they came to see the final dub and they got really angry! That'll be interesting to find that reel, I don't know if anybody's ever done that. There's a 35mm reel of the first ten minutes of *Conan* mixed in stereo.

How much more would it have cost to do a stereo mix (being 1982)?

POLEDOURIS: Thirty thousand dollars.

Plus the cost of distributing stereo prints.

POLEDOURIS: More than that was the fact that there were so few theaters that were willing to play it [in stereo]. It's kind of the same thing we came across with *Starship Troopers*. We mixed down in SDDS,* which is a wonderful format, it's five across the front and stereo surround. For a large orchestral film score, certainly for a film with that many sound effects, it's a great medium to work in, but they had advertised I think thirty-five hundred theaters worldwide could play it, and quite frankly I never saw it *anywhere* in SDDS—maybe the premiere, but then again, I'm not sure. SDDS is a wonderful format for action films, not unlike the old Cinerama where you had five speakers and surrounds (mono nonetheless) in the back.

They found the half-inch masters of *Conan,* but those are really left-center-right. I guess my concept of what's possible with DVD goes a lot beyond just rechanneling. I really want to get into choreographing space, particularly with the choir. I wanted to have it coming at the audience from several different speakers.

*Sony Dynamic Digital Sound, introduced in 1993, utilizes an eight-channel sound mix.

The chorus and orchestra were recorded separately?

POLEDOURIS: Yes they were, so that potential may exist if it's on its own separate L-C-R. But I think I did three or four choir over-dubs. I think the potential for choreographing space that the listener is in hasn't even been tapped. We're still, "Okay, violins on the left, cellos on the right." *Come on, guys!* We started to get into that with *Starship Troopers,* where I actually orchestrated for antiphonal trumpets, antiphonal timpani, but it was just starting to scratch the surface. And now I want to get into more things with overdubbing so you could discreetly place instruments in the sound picture.

■

THE SHAPE OF THE SOUND: ORCHESTRATION

The act of orchestrating a score can be a somewhat mechanical process—David Shire admits to orchestrating his scores while watching ball games on TV—but the makeup of the players sets the tone for the entire score, and the picture. A score's distinct musical signature—the jabbing cellos of *Jaws*, the theremin of *The Day the Earth Stood Still*, or the zither of *The Third Man*—can be only as distinct as the decisions on what instruments to feature are inspired.

A sidebar to the issue of what instruments become the musical "star" of a film score is the growing use of electronics. There has been a real change in the acceptance of—and dependence upon—synthesizers that can mimic (to a degree) any traditional instrument, in addition to creating sounds not otherwise possible. Electronics have become more prevalent as complementary pieces in an orchestra. But from a film music standpoint, their real influence has been behind the scenes, when the music is being written in the first place.

Synthesizers, and the software that marries them to computers, offer an immediacy and flexibility in the compositional process that nonetheless takes music from being a purely organic art into one that is more technical. Their use in composition, orchestration, and recording (which is particularly helpful in film work, given the crushing deadlines) makes the process seem—outwardly, at least—far removed from the traditional, romantic notion of a composer scribbling on staffed paper.

One may argue about financial savings from replacing session players with a synethesist (Vangelis nonetheless draws a hefty paycheck for performing the scores to *Chariots of Fire* or *Blade Runner* himself). Producers will see electronics as a means to trim the music budget, and directors may ask to "audition" music cues so that they will face no surprises on the scoring stage—thus giving them even more influence during the writing phase. A composer must therefore become fluent (or at least respectfully affable) with the technical demands of computers; the danger facing a composer is that the music may become less original in the process.

▶

JERRY GOLDSMITH: The area of electronics is so vast, the whole degree of sounds you can get is really unlimited. [But] you don't spend the whole time creating new sounds instead of writing music. So [at the beginning] I more or less get certain parameters in colors and say, "This is the library I'll use in this picture." I get a certain number of sounds in a vocabulary and I move on from there, and then I try to integrate it with the orchestra, too.

It's like when you're writing for an orchestra, you know that you've got a woodwind section, a brass section, strings, and percussion, and that's it. Within those sections there are certain variations, but it's been that way for three hundred years. But how you blend them together is still up in the air; there are still infinite combinations.

Sometimes you get an overall orchestral concept immediately on seeing the picture: With *Chinatown* I straight away saw strings, four pianos, four harps, percussion, and trumpet. I don't know where the hell I came up with that, but I thought immediately of that combination. I had no actual music to go along with it, though, at that stage. I don't believe in all this talk about orchestration—it's really quite subservient to what the *music* is, the actual notes. Anyone with any kind of technique can make an orchestra sound marvelous for two hours even without any musical content. There has to be this content, whether a motif or a simple line, or whatever.

So I guess I really think in terms of line: The color comes later—*with* the music, because I can't write something without knowing what instrument's going to play it. Even, you know, with effects. So often people ask me, "Gee, how did you do that?" Well, it's the *notes* that give the color. Very occasionally there are a-musical effects, of course, which don't have this genesis: In *Planet of the Apes* the French hornists blow air through their instruments [without their mouthpieces], but this effect immediately becomes musical when placed in a musical context—spaced and with rhythm.

The electronics in *Gremlins*, which are the "voice" of those creatures, mix well with the standard orchestra, and in a sense work as a counterpoint to the "serious" traditional instruments.

GOLDSMITH: I wanted sort of an animalistic sound to them. It's comical, and musical. Joe Dante's a fun person to work with. He enjoys music, and he wants a lot of music in his films. It turned out the crazier I got, the more he liked it. When I played for him the "Gremlin Rag," this funky way-out tune, he practically fell on the floor. Because it was just what he wanted, something totally out of left field.

Do you have a favorite instrument to write for?

ELMER BERNSTEIN: Well, as you can tell if you know my work, I'm very fond of woodwind instruments, primarily the flute and oboe, which you hear a great deal. In spite of the fact people think of the big things like *Magnificent Seven*, I'm much happier when I'm in that *Rambling Rose* mode, *Birdmen of Alcatraz*, *To Kill a Mockingbird*—that is more of my favorite mode. I enjoy the energy you can generate with a huge orchestra, but if somebody asked me to name the favorite things of mine to listen to, they'd be things like *Rambling Rose*.

People have never associated me with electronics, yet I was one of the first composers to use them, in two films in 1953: *Robot Monster* (very well known because it's probably the worst picture I made!) and *Cat Women of the Moon*. The major instruments in those two scores were primarily the old Hammond B3 organ and an instrument called the Novachord, which doesn't exist anymore.

For a film I did about mentally ill people, whose title I no longer remember, I used a Wurlitzer electric piano. The first thing you hear in the film *Hawaii* is a Moog synthesizer. So I have always used these instruments, but always as instruments, never as the "big electronic score." And now, of course, electronics have become a way of life, they've become considerably more present.

I think my recent interest in electronic music started with a seminar on film music I was doing circa 1981. Richard Rodney

Bennett talked about the Ondes-Martenot, a very ancient electronic instrument of which I knew very little, and my orchestrator Christopher Palmer (we were working on a film called *Heavy Metal*) said, "This Ondes-Martenot thing would be very good for this film." So we got the queen of the instrument, Jeanne Loriod, over from Paris to play this instrument and I absolutely fell over, it was the most wonderful sound I'd ever heard in my life. And I used it in a Broadway show I did called *Merlin*, so that reinterested me in electronically powered instruments.

There's a lot of electronics in *The Grifters*. You wouldn't call it an electronic score exactly, but there's a great electronic presence in it, much more than most people realize—and there is, by the way, in *A Rage in Harlem* and as well in *Rambling Rose,* only I don't use them in a way which says, "Oh wow, that's an electronic score," but as instruments, because they can do things that certain other instruments can't.

Do you ever get a suggestion for a director about a particular orchestral makeup?

GOLDSMITH: On one film I did, *The Blue Max*, I was told "The director wants to use a hundred-piece orchestra." And it was rather arbitrary: "A hundred-piece orchestra," there you go.

So you're stuck with trying to give one hundred pieces something to do?

GOLDSMITH: Well, that's not a problem; it's more difficult to write for *five* instruments than it is for a hundred. But on that picture, when I put the orchestra together, I came up with ninety-eight men. And I'm thinking, *I'm going to be a big hero, I'm going to save some money!* And the director looked at me with this sad look, like "Only ninety-eight? Sure you can't get a hundred?" It was this ego thing. He wanted to go into the studio and say, "There's a hundred-man orchestra there." I frankly feel it's a waste of money and time and effort, because there is [only] so much you can get on the soundtrack of a film. If you have seventy-five or a hundred pieces, I don't think it'll make much difference. There's so much degradation of sound that, when you mix in the sound effects and the dialogue, so many subtleties are lost; you're really writing more for a soundtrack album than for a picture.

That's the one thing that is always a disappointment when you're scoring a film. You get a lot of subtleties in the music that are completely eviscerated by the effects and dialogue and just general transferring from pure music reproduction into secondary reproduction which is a film soundtrack. So subtleties are something that can really get lost, even with electronics. You can work with interesting sounds, fine overtone, definition, great subtleties you put in there—they're *gone*.

And another thing: A lot of the subtleties with the electronics are eaten up by the orchestra! We're getting into a whole different world of acoustics with electronics, especially when you're applying them to the film medium.

Years ago, we would all pride ourselves with using these strange orchestras; Bernard Herrmann especially was a master of very unusual combinations of instruments. And it'd sound wonderful on paper, and it sounded rather interesting on the scoring stage. But by the time you get to the picture, nobody's going to know you're using six clarinets and six bassoons and *no* flutes and oboes, or using twelve harps or something. It just doesn't come across that way, unless the music has a chance to really play off on its own, which is very rare if not unheard of in motion pictures.

▶▶

What score of yours that was particularly experimental for you in an instrumental sense was the most pleasantly surprising?

CARTER BURWELL: Well, the one that immediately comes to mind is an odd example, but I'll give it to you anyway. There was a movie called *Kiss the Girls*, and the score which was released with it was Mark Isham's, but I actually did an entire score which they ended up not using. Originally all they wanted was a synthesizer score, one person playing a synthesizer—they had a very small budget—and I got them to broaden it to be enough for a string quintet and a few other players. So it ended up being a string quintet, piano, heavily processed electric guitar, Bulgarian bagpipes, Bulgarian flute, and percussion. And it actually came together really well. I was really proud, and I guess in the end it was just a little too strange for Paramount Pictures, or for the director. And the director had liked it all; when we were recording it, he was present and was enjoying it, but a few weeks after we recorded it he came by and asked me if I could do a more conventional score for him.

Did he give you a specific reason why?

BURWELL: Well, I think he felt the movie as made and with that music was just going to appeal to a smaller audience; it was going to be looked on as a kind of arty psychological thriller. Whether it was him or Paramount Pictures, I could never say who was driving a decision like this, but I think he felt that he needed a movie that would more openly appeal to an audience who would watch it and be *into* the movie rather than be discomfited by an odd-sounding score. In fact, the way I read it, the movie's *supposed* to be uncomfortable—it's about a man who kidnaps women, keeps them in a dungeon, drugs them, and rapes them. So I thought that a somewhat uncomfortable score would be appropriate! Anyway, it's an example of an interesting mélange of instruments that really did come off very well, but in that case, it's tempting to say it's *ironic* that one of my favorite scores did not end up actually appearing in the film, but in fact there's something very *reasonable* about it, it's not ironic at all. I'm actually kind of *proud* of the fact that it didn't end up in the film. Now, it took me months to get over the disappointment, of course, but now I listened back to it recently and thought, it's all worked out right because it first of all confirms for myself that I am still one to take risks—I guess a lot of people at some studios aren't, but I'm glad that after all these years in the business I'm still able to take risks; that I don't compromise what I'm doing to try to bring it down to the level of what the studio might want; and the music's clearly good, very interesting, I guess just a little *too* interesting for the film, so all these things are *good*. Of course it's a disappointment that it's not *in* the movie.

Can you do something else with it now?

BURWELL: Well, of course Paramount bought it when they paid for it. I'm not going to put it in *another* movie, but the people who played on it are really eager to see it released, and I may be able to buy it back from Paramount in some way if I can find a record company that would put it out.

One way of making a score stand out is to employ an unusual or rare instrument—*Under Fire*'s pan flute, or *Titanic*'s uilleann pipes. But what if the instrument is not native to the story or characters?

ELIA CMIRAL: I really hate using ethnic instruments or elements just to spice it up and make it attractive. Absolutely. That's what I really hate. I understand film scoring is not about musicology, so you are free to use anything, but sometimes I feel like, *Oh my God, I've heard this kind of sound already, the percussion, I've heard this flute,* and it's annoying.

On *Stigmata,* I wanted to connect the concept to the story. I used three themes: One is three tones on the piano, next is played by a ney flute, which is a two-thousand-year-old instrument—the story is connected to the first century—and the third theme is written for female voice singing lyrics in Aramaic, which is Jesus Christ's language. So all these three things are absolutely right where they are. Composers should always think: Concept is the key, the concept must be right. So if I have to think about what instrument to use, I have to ask, is it right for this concept?

CARNIVAL OF THE ANIMALS: MARK ISHAM ON
NEVER CRY WOLF AND *FLY AWAY HOME*

It seemed natural that filmmakers such as Carroll Ballard and Alan Rudolph, whose works are long on atmosphere, would be attracted to the work of Mark Isham, who played with several San Francisco Bay Area bands before producing the acclaimed electronic album *Vapor Drawings*. He has been a regular collaborator with them, producing such insinuating scores as *Trouble in Mind*, *The Moderns*, and *Afterglow*.

Isham's first score, for Ballard's *Never Cry Wolf*, was remarkable as much for what it wasn't as for what it was: It avoided the clichés of children's nature films that anthropomorphize animals to give them character and engender pathos. His music created a tonal palette that at once painted a daunting picture of the bleak and inhospitable Alaskan wilderness (while emphasizing biologist Charles Martin Smith's lonely scientific quest), and suggested a mythic musical color for the wolves that are the subject of Smith's observations.

By using synthesizers and unusual ethnic instruments, Isham mixed a score much like a recipe that was certainly reactive to the images on screen but never overstated or obvious. For example, in the opening, working the sounds of a plane's propeller into the music mix accentuated the meaning behind the images: as a tiny plane heads farther and farther north, we sense destitution, grandeur, isolation, fear.

In addition, there were suggestions of native Inuit music that underlined the movie's message of protecting nature (in this case from hunters and entrepreneurs raping the environment).

▶

MARK ISHAM: Carroll Ballard had heard a tape of synthesizers and Oriental flutes that I had made with a friend who was an Oriental flutist—we'd been writing this music to try to get a record deal. And it didn't go where we wanted it to go, but it made its way into Carroll's hands somehow. He heard it, and he said, "That's what I want in my film."

It turns out he had known the flute player, who had done some flute playing on *The Black Stallion* for him, and he tracked him down and said, "Well, who's the guy that does all the other stuff here?" So he met me.

Basically he offered me a weekend in a studio and taught me how to run the machine that had film on it. He put three scenes on there and said, "Write the music for these three scenes, and we'll see how it goes," and came back on Monday to listen to what I had written.

He took a very big risk. It was an eighteen-million-dollar film, not a cheap film, and he basically hired me with no experi-

Mark Isham

ence and set me up with a pretty good team of people to back me up: music editors and arrangers, orchestrators.

He'd had a couple of orchestral scores written and he didn't like them, and so he decided to try me. I dove in, worked for about four months, night and day, and finally sort of taught myself how to score a film. On-the-job training! He was very, very involved, I mean he knew that he'd chosen somebody who had no experience, so he would come by every day and go through everything and we'd talk about where things were going. I have to hand it to him, he really did put in the time to get what he wanted from me for the score, which took a lot more effort than it might have normally, because of my lack of experience. But it worked out pretty well.

And it was, you know, such an *odd* choice to do a 60 percent electronic score for a Disney nature film. But it caught the mood of what he wanted, and I looked at it the other day actually, I think it holds up pretty well.

One of the stand-out scenes was when a pack of wolves attacks a herd of caribou, which contained some powerful percussive effects.

ISHAM: Yeah, Carroll had been working on the film for a long time, so he knew a lot of the problem areas. And in the caribou scene you have these hooves of charging animals, and he wanted basically a drum track to score it, but they had tried several different things and he couldn't get any drums that would actually cut through the sound effects without being swallowed up. They had done this research before I got there, so I was quite amused when he said, "Look, what I want you to write for are these Tahitian war drums." They're made out of petrified wood, so it's almost like you're hitting stones or something—they have this *tremendous* impact, they do cut through everything sonically. He had to go down to the Tahitian embassy and get permission from the cultural attaché to borrow their only set in America and it was quite a thing.

You were lucky; most directors aren't quite as specific about the sound they want!

ISHAM: Yeah, he'd been through this for two years working on the score, so he knew where his problem areas were, and I was more than willing to learn from the mistakes he'd made!
[In the caribou scene,] that's literally taking about four or five wild elements and ideas and just collaging and montaging a couple of drum tracks, and we had taken the big Chinese bamboo flutes to sort of be the wild element of the wolf, and this big

chordal vastness of the elements and the environment, and we just painted with sound. It was a masterful mixing job by Todd Boekelheide. It really is musique concrète—I wouldn't have the faintest idea of how to notate something like that. Very improvisational—all the keyboard, electronic things are improvised, all the drum parts are taken from very rough ideas, improvised by a wonderful drummer, George Marsh.

One thing that concerned Carroll was that the wolves in the film not just come across as big dogs. He had lots of stories about working with them on the set, trying to get them to act fiercer. He'd say, "You gotta nuts 'em up!" And if you had the wrong music they could wind up looking quite tame and playful on screen. With the music he wanted to show a fear of wolves *progressing* toward the film's portrait of them as family-oriented animals, nonthreatening to man.

What was the Disney studio's reaction to the score, since as you say it was not characteristic of their nature films?

ISHAM: Well, I believe in the early days when he still hadn't really hired anybody and was throwing out scores left and right, they had said, "Just hire John Williams, you know, we'll *pay* for it, it'll be fine," and he just refused. And I think the only reason that they put up with him hiring *me* was that I was so cheap. They must have thought, "Well, if it doesn't work out, it hasn't really cost us any money." Although the time factor was ridiculous—I mean, he'd been in postproduction for over two years. That's one of Carroll's remarkable talents: he's very tenacious, he gets his way; he just stands his ground and doesn't let the studio walk all over him. I say that especially considering he's not what you'd call a commercial director, a director with those billion-dollar successes behind him.

THEY WANT THAT *ONE* RECORD

Isham's next collaboration with Ballard was on the 1996 film *Fly Away Home*, loosely based on the true story of a Canadian artist who led a flock of geese south with an ultralight plane to imprint safe migration patterns.

Curiously, the origins of this film—a segment of the ABC newsmagazine *20/20* which aired in 1993—revealed an exceptionally distasteful *overuse* of music, a loud, sugary, and unnecessarily "uplifting" musical accompaniment, a practice that unfortunately has been increasing over time among many television documentaries and news programs. It is therefore an appropriate and pleasant surprise to hear Isham's music bring the tale back down to earth, as it were, by focusing on the emotional state of a young girl, shaken and withdrawn because of the death of her mother, as she slowly reenters the world through her foster care of a clutch of baby geese.

I was very impressed by the violin solos, which characterized both the idea of flight and the spirit of the young girl played by Anna Paquin. In an instance like that, does the choice of instrument come first or does the melody?

ISHAM: It happens both ways. I think the orchestration was actually decided upon later. To communicate the idea of flight I was working basically on just the piece of music; the orchestration for that came about more from thinking about the dynamics of the story.

I played around with a folk rhythm section and guitars, but

it didn't really work. Neither did having it in a pop music genre, although we did have the Mary Chapin Carpenter song "10,000 Miles," and I used vocals slightly within the score that recalled that—Carpenter provided those as well.

I think on *The Moderns* I was introduced to this musician named Sid Page who's a wonderful violinist, and he became sort of the centerpoint for the whole score for *The Moderns*. While I had been aware of jazz violin—that sort of sound in other contexts—in other classical contexts I'd never really done much with it; and after meeting Sid and seeing what he was capable of, Sid has become a sort of standard in my vocabulary. He's actually in my band, he plays live with me, so I think there's an example of the "sound" of the instrument helping to direct the music.

For *Fly Away Home,* the solo violin gave us a chance to get very intimate. At points in the film, like when the little girl finds the eggs and has the eggs in the drawer in the barn and hatches them, it has very, very intimate moments, and I wanted to keep that intimacy. In addition, it's a story that in some ways starts very small and then broadens way out, becoming bigger and connecting to things much bigger than itself—just as the girl, who's withdrawn following the death of her mother, learns to extend herself outward into the world and into friendships, and her relationship with her estranged father. And yet, there's something sort of off-kilter about the whole thing because these are *geese*, it's not like it's a group of kids or something.

Well, I was always a big fan of the Penguin Cafe Orchestra, this little band out of England that Simon Jeffes founded, playing kind of a folk/classical music with an eclectic group of instruments—things like violin, accordion, spinet, ukelele, telephone, rubber band. They've done a lot of really great stuff, and I always wanted to try something like that. And I thought, what a great idea of having a small, slightly quirky mixture of instruments that would play the intimate scenes with the girl and the geese, and then as she breaks out of her shell and extends herself into the world, expands herself, the music extends itself as well, becoming larger and fuller.

All of a sudden the basic structure emerged, which was that this little core of instruments featuring Sid on violin was actually surrounded by an orchestra, and they played on their own and with the orchestra, and the orchestra accompanied them.

What was the breakdown of the ensemble?

ISHAM: I think it was solo violin, solo cello, clarinet, bass clarinet, accordion, electric bass, piano, electric piano, mandolin, harp, and marimba.

Fly Away Home **is probably one of the best scores never released commercially on record or CD. What dictates a decision like that?**

ISHAM: Well, it seems to be based on enthusiasm from record labels more than anything. If the studio gets a call from a record label that says, "We want that score and here's our offer," and they feel it's an okay offer, then it happens. The more legally complex something is to put together from a deal point of view, the harder it gets, and I think that's what happened with *Fly Away Home*. In spite of the fact that it's a Columbia picture and I'm a Columbia artist and Mary Chapin Carpenter was a Columbia artist, the fact that the soundtrack guy at Columbia had had a very bad year and had lost a lot of money made him shy about picking up any scores that he didn't really feel were going to be huge hits. And even though Carpenter was signed to a part of Columbia, Columbia is just a *huge* company, so it's almost worse than if it were separate companies, because they're supposedly all able to talk to each other but they have no idea where Chapin's A&R department was or my A&R department on the film, I mean it just didn't work. We never got the rights to Chapin's song, to Chapin's performance for a record, so that's pretty much it. In spite of the best-laid plans on my part, putting everybody in the same company together, it didn't happen. But basically I think it was just Columbia's lack of enthusiasm, and then by the time they expressed that, it was too late.

For anyone else to release it?

ISHAM: Yeah. It's an expensive score, an orchestral score with a major artist singing on it, so with the reuse fees and the deals you have to make it's probably going to be a fifty-thousand-to-sixty-thousand-dollar proposition. That's a lot of money for something that the studio isn't promoting as their summer blockbuster.

It always struck me that they just sort of threw that film away, because it got tremendously good reviews, but I think they got scared off by the fact that that girl got killed in a little plane a few months beforehand,* and everybody just started backpedaling. I still don't look at it as something that I totally understand, but it was just an odd coincidence of circumstances that led to the film not doing nearly as well as I thought it should have and then the record not even coming out.

The problem is by the time the reviews have come out, if you're not already in boxes ready to ship it's too late. You'll never get it made in time to get it out to catch that first two or three weekends when people go see the film and want—then and

---

*Jessica Dubroff, a seven-year-old pilot accompanied by her father, died in spring 1996 when her Cessna crashed during her attempt to fly across the United States.

there—to buy the soundtrack album. So you've got to get every-one's commitment to make and release the record simultaneously with the film. I've certainly had people come by and release scores of mine a year later, but the only ones that that happens with are those where the actual production costs are very, very low; then they just figure, you know, an Isham score in the cat-alog, that makes fifteen to twenty-five thousand copies over a few years, if they can keep their costs to the point where that will recoup, they'll do it. But a sale of fifteen thousand to twenty-five thousand copies will never recoup a sixty-thou-sand-dollar investment.

When it comes to film scores, you have no permanent rela-tionship for recording film scores for any one particular label. Most record companies are looking for the one-shot wonder.

■

IT'S "THE FRANCIE BRADY SHOW": ELLIOT GOLDENTHAL ON *THE BUTCHER BOY*

A bright, percolating melody seems to carry Francie Brady down the street of his impoverished Irish town before melting into mordant blues, spunky jazz riffs, and echoey evocations of classical music. In fact, music is about all ten-year-old Francie has to fall back on—that and his own uncompromising grit, which helps him survive a suicidal mother, a drunken father, hateful neighbors, a lecherous priest, and his own outbursts of startling violence.

This 1998 black comedy, based on the novel by Patrick McCabe, lacked easily lovable characters, as it basked in the unreality of Francie's view of the world and his place in it. The music of *The Butcher Boy* revels in this same exuberance and unwillingness to compromise one's identity or fantastical vision of life. Since the score consistently depicts Francie's point of view, the most horrific aspects of the story are told through a filter of naive optimism that is nonetheless as unstable as Francie's own sanity. Like in a fever dream, music comes into and out of consciousness in a jumble of conflicting melodies, melting from Dion & the Belmonts to "Mack the Knife," "Ave Maria," and Frank Sinatra's "Where Are You," which accompanies a mesmerizing Apocalyptic vision of nuclear destruction.

At the center is Goldenthal's original score, played by a combination of keyboards, accordion, hammer dulcimer, dobro, saxophone, trumpet, and drums, that together succeed at sounding just a little bit off—and, like Francie, entirely winning.

▶

You had worked with director Neil Jordan twice previously. How was this project different for you?

ELLIOT GOLDENTHAL: By the time we got up to *Butcher Boy* we had done two *big* movies—*Interview with the Vampire* and *Michael Collins*. For *Butcher Boy*, I told him it needed a much quirkier, almost homemade-sounding approach to it. There are some comparisons to the approach to scoring *Drugstore Cowboy*, which is a very early score of mine, but the material is not unrelated, where you have action, you have segments of magical realism, semifantasy sequences, and then you have a running narration. So I was revisiting that *Drugstore Cowboy* way of composing which was much more iconoclastic.

For example, in *Drugstore Cowboy* there was a scene of just people sitting around a room and talking about drugs. It was a very dull conversation and a very dull scene. And Gus Van Sant originally had some pop song (which is always a director's first choice in films like this). I love pop music, don't get me wrong, but we're talking about *film scoring*. So we had a pop song and the scene was even *duller*. So I said, "Why don't we try a choir of didgeridoos,* and then introduce a sort of low pulse to these didgeridoos?" And he thought I was nuts—totally *Why did I hire this guy* kind of thing. Until you saw the scene. Then you felt like you're part of some primeval rejoicing of these drugs which are going to take you for a ride. That's an example of taking something that seemed not only radical but almost Dadaistic at the outset without knowing that there's a method to a specific madness to make a scene work. And *Butcher Boy* was the same way.

I got the feeling that Neil came to me because [on our previous films] I had brought him into areas that were unexpected, and that he liked being taken there. And for him it was, "Don't even listen to the temp music. Don't even *think* about it."

For *Butcher Boy* it must have been hard knowing what point of view the music should take, for the central character is a very hard character to take on board—he's fun but also troubled, violent—and on top of that is his own narration as an older, wiser version of himself telling his life story. Yet the music does get into the head of the character in a fascinating way.

GOLDENTHAL: That was the revelation. I'd started the film two or three times. And Neil said, "No, you can't do this movie, I don't think you're getting it, you don't *know* it." Not until I woke up one morning and said, "Well, if Francie Brady wrote this score, what would it be?"

He was the star of his own life, as if life were *The Francie Brady Show*.

*An Australian aboriginal instrument.

GOLDENTHAL: This is *The Francie Brady Show*, and this is *his* theme. And once I did that, things came along pretty easily. *Relatively* easily! But there were two or three starts where I wasn't getting anywhere. I was scoring it as if I were the composer, as opposed to if *Francie Brady* were the composer! In this particular film, that character had that much of a pull.

I really had to go *into* the world of nonreality that the boy was living in. I had to even deconstruct the Beethoven *Für Elise*—I called it "Pig Für Elise"—taking that and grinding it down until it morphed into klezmer music, and then into this strange Chicago, 1960s free jazz, until it finally left a vestige of Apache drums playing.

That sort of stream-of-consciousness scoring, switching from one style to another within a cue, was it written that way or did you experiment in the studio, mixing one musical piece into another?

GOLDENTHAL: No, it was written out. It had to be performed at Abbey Road with an orchestra. Even the chamber things were all written out because you've got to get musicians to play it.

Beethoven entered the picture because a neighbor was practicing *Für Elise*. So as long as music entered Francie's consciousness it became allowable, even if it seemed anachronistic?

GOLDENTHAL: There was nothing anachronistic in a sense that it was the artists—Patrick McCabe and Neil, myself, and the performers—looking back and having an opinion about a time, in the same way that Shakespeare might look back to the Roman or Greek periods. There are anachronisms in Shakespeare but it's

Elliot Goldenthal

not "anachronistic" because it's *him* looking back, and so it's a valid recording of an opinion of a person displaced by a few hundred years—in our case with *Butcher Boy*, displaced by forty years.

Apart from getting inside Francie's head, how did the film's setting inspire you?

GOLDENTHAL: This was taking place during the Cuban missile crisis, and there was this scene of a spiffy kitchen with all modern appliances, and this boy goes into a rage and destroys this kitchen, and then he defecates in this woman's living room. And you look at this scene: it's horrific in a sense, it makes you smile for a second, and then you see a TV set with shots of atomic bomb tests and children having to duck-and-cover under their seats at the same time this boy is smearing cake all over the wall, destroying this person's house.

So I took all sorts of sound clichés of that period—really sort of cheeseball sounding Farfisa-type organ, pizzicato strings, cheeseball-bubblegum-sounding backbeat on the drums—and created this hyperpop, super-bubblegum early-1960s music that had a great *joy* to it while the boy is destroying this house. And Patrick McCabe said, "My God, this music looks exactly like that kitchen!"

There was also a tune, "Butcher Boy," a sort of old Irish standard, semiboring ballad about a butcher boy and a girl in love with him; that's where Patrick McCabe got the title for the book. And they dredged out the old ballad and had Sinead O'Connor sing it. Fine!

Also there was this super-sentimentality related to how Francie's father felt about how he'd fucked up his life, his alcoholism, et cetera. I had to write a theme that was really, *really* that sentimental. It had some notes, some pitches that had some dissonance and elbow to it, but in general it had to have *There's nothing for me to do today except get drunk and think about how I messed up* type of music.

Your music is notable for the use of dissonance, for unusual sounds that could almost be considered sound effects. That's probably expected in a film like *Alien³*, but you've also been able to employ them in more "normal" films.

GOLDENTHAL: John Corigliano's work in *Altered States* was a very, very powerful model for what you can do with an orchestra. And I've taken that opportunity to take that baton and run with it in projects that weren't necessarily about altered states or changes in the psyche. I've worked with alternative-type orchestration even in movies like *Cobb* about a baseball player, whereas

I think twenty years ago the use of experimental orchestration in a baseball movie would have been thought of as *insane*. And even in *Michael Collins*, there was a lot of unusual orchestration. Using Irish pipes played in the manner of John Coltrane with two click tracks going at different tempos, and sort of Penderecki-esque orchestration behind it in an Irish revolutionary movie would have been unheard of. Putting skewed, big band jazz in a Shakespeare movie would have been unheard of. So I think almost like taking my pencil as a musical Trojan horse into certain areas, I've made some inroads—almost unnoticeable!

I think I am drawn toward stuff that's big and mythic, that has the possibility of surrealism involved: *The Butcher Boy*, *Drugstore Cowboy*. *In Dreams* had a special quality. Even *Batman* was mythic, comic-book fun. It wasn't as much fun for me to do *A Time to Kill*, which is a very serious courtroom drama.

Does that present a greater artistic challenge to you, to try to do a courtroom drama in a way that hasn't been done a million times before?

GOLDENTHAL: Certain things can't handle that much experimentation, and when I got into it, that was my thought, that I could experiment with a kind of Japanese/Asian approach to this American Southern setting—very minimal pennywhistle and percussion. And I thought I could use this really dissonant orchestral music to display racial violence. But in the end it wasn't a form for me to be really special with. Others can argue, but if you listen to *Batman Forever* that's much more exciting! It had much more of a wild canvas to it.

ADAPTATION

You wrote music for a stage play, *The Winter Guest*, and later adapted that music for the film version. Can you describe that process?

MICHAEL KAMEN: I love the stark reality of theater. The music that I made for *Winter Guest* was very minimal, unlike most of my bombastic and "maximal" music—it was very gentle and very unobtrusive, which was its goal. The music in the film was more fully rounded because it was a much more literal treatment of something; there was no abstraction in the film. If you were looking at a frozen sea, you were looking at a frozen sea. If they were walking across a field, it was covered with snow—everything was frozen. There were wide spaces, there was an ocean, there were hills and fields and a town; all of that reality that you cannot do in a theater is present in the film and you tell the complete story musically.

The thematic device that was used in the theater was completely reconfigured for the film, so the theme would show up in varying guises, and quite literally in the film *became* a character. (There was a boy next door who played the piano—you never saw him but you heard him play, and the characters comment on him—and the theme came from him playing.) Alan Rickman and I worked very closely on the score to the film, and in fact it's entirely performed on the piano.

It's a very simple melody which in fact I borrowed from myself, from a saxophone concerto that I wrote, and funnily enough got more attention for its sixteen bars of music as part of a theatrical play than two and a half hours of score for *Robin Hood: Prince of Thieves* got, in terms of recognition by critics. There were four paragraphs in the *London Times* about the music for *The Winter Guest*, the theater critic paid a lot of attention to the music; movie critics almost never do.

EVERYTHING OLD IS NEW AGAIN:
ELMER BERNSTEIN ON REINVENTING *CAPE FEAR*

During more than three decades of scoring films in all genres (but becoming best known for his suspense scores for Alfred Hitchcock), Bernard Herrmann fiercely protected the integrity of his craft, often vociferously combating studio executives, directors, and other inferiors intent upon getting a pop-sounding, highly commercial score from his labors. They were usually disappointed—they got art instead.

The composer of *Vertigo*, *Citizen Kane*, and *The Day the Earth Stood Still* was frustrated by what he deemed the execrable level of musical appreciation in Hollywood, and so he spent much of his later life working on obscure European productions. Perhaps to his surprise, in the early 1970s he was recruited by the younger generation of filmmakers (including Brian de Palma and Martin Scorsese) who accepted their elder's temper as the price for his musical grace on such films as *Obsession* and *Taxi Driver*. It was tragic that, succumbing to a heart attack following the recording sessions for *Taxi Driver*, Herrmann didn't live long enough to cash in on his reborn currency.

In 1991, Scorsese embarked on a remake of the J. Lee Thompson thriller *Cape Fear*, which had been scored by Herrmann. The piercing music of the original reflected the black-and-white schematics of the tale about an ex-con seeking revenge; shrieking violins matched the fury of Robert Mitchum in his attempts to brutalize Gregory Peck and his family.

Scorsese, who very often incorporates preexisting music in his films, knew early in the shooting that his remake would retain the original score (an experiment that was later duplicated even more exactly in the Gus Van Sant remake of *Psycho*). While Scorsese did not shoot to playback (as he had with sequences of *GoodFellas*), he spoke on the set of how Herrmann's music for *Psycho* and other classics seemed to color the air during the filming. "*Psycho* of course is fantastic," he said. "*The Ghost and Mrs. Muir* is very sad, beautiful. His music really got to me after *Vertigo* and *Marnie*. I think [that] was when I realized the sense of ruin, sadness, melancholy, fear and anxiety—and that was really *terrific*!"

This was not the first time Herrmann's music had been adapted to other purposes; his score for an otherwise forgettable 1974 horror film, *It's Alive*, was posthumously used in a sequel, reorchestrated by Laurie Johnson. Scorsese's *Cape Fear*, however, really puts the Herrmann sound to good use, as it reinforces this remake's interpretation of Max Cady as a spiritual figure. Cady tries to teach his unenlightened prey a lesson about the true horrors of life; the music therefore emphasizes how easily Cady insinuates himself into the Bowden family, upsetting the very fragile relationships among parents and daughter.

Following his relatively sunny score for *Rambling Rose*, Elmer Bernstein, enlisted to adapt the music, spent three weeks composing forty-nine cues, many shorter than a minute each given the rapid pacing of the film. "This film has very little relationship to the first *Cape Fear*," Bernstein said. "The only reason the Herrmann thing worked is, in a curious way—don't ask me why—the score that Bennie wrote is much more appropriate for *this* film. I think he was the best creator on that [earlier] project, and he saw something in the film that wasn't there—but it's there *now*!"

In the more sensuous, foreboding atmosphere of Scorsese's remake, the music takes on an eerier tone. Herrmann's four-note theme, meant to represent Cady, is used sparingly to introduce images of the ex-con's psyche—for example, photos on his cell wall of a religious martyr, along with Nietzsche and Stalin. Otherwise, the score slowly intimates a sense of foreboding, matching Scorsese's tilted camera angles. Rising chords played on wind instruments instead *descend*, as if the weight of the Bowdens' situation is sucking them down into the mire, represented by swirling, nervous violins.

On the recording stage, a cavernous studio near Manhattan's Times Square, the chilling airs of vintage Herrmann manifest from his typically unorthodox orchestral arrangement: four flutes, eight horns, and about five dozen strings. On the screen above is projected the Bowdens' flight from the scene of Max Cady's latest atrocity. As French horns trumpet Cady lurking just out of view, trembling violins cascade over the listener like the deceptively calm waters of the Cape Fear River. Later, Bernstein conducts the cellos as they underline Sam Bowden's soul-searching chat with the private detective Kersek, who remarks on the South's long tradition of fear. The scene is short, sedate, quiet—the music, unnerving. By now the score seems to have grabbed hold of the film and stuck to it, leaving the air freely susceptible to Bernstein's jokes.

For the picture's climax, Bernstein appropriated music from Herrmann's discarded score for Hitchcock's *Torn Curtain*, originally created (ironically) to accompany a desperate, prolonged attempt to kill a human being. "I felt by the time we get to the latter part of the film, it would be good to have some different color," Bernstein says, so he augmented the orchestra with additional brass and timpani. The music for which Bernstein takes the most credit plays under the opening titles, designed by Saul and Elaine Bass; images of water turning blood red are matched with dissonant wind instruments, pierced by string and brass variations of Herrmann's Max Cady motif. This opening is more ominous than in the original *Cape Fear*, where the evil of Cady was presented in a more straightforward fashion.

This blissful dive into horror is crassly interrupted by a rudely boorish *thump! thump! thump!* sound leaching through the recording studio's supposedly soundproofed walls, from a record label's promotion party being held three stories above—as invasive a presence as Cady himself. When word is passed down that the music cannot be halted until the resident pop artist's new release is played through, a good twenty minutes off, Bernstein explodes.

However his talents may match those of his mentor, though, Bernstein's temper is nowhere near that of the incendiary Herrmann, whose fiery anger and fierce pride were legendary. "He'd probably be horrified to know what we're doing!" laughs Bernstein of the new and improved *Cape Fear* score. "I said to Scorsese, 'I think maybe this is all right with Herrmann, because if it weren't we'd probably both be *dead* by now!'"

▶

ELMER BERNSTEIN: When I met Scorsese I really liked him and I liked his producer, Barbara De Fina, and we had a really nice time with *The Grifters*. And when I saw *GoodFellas* again—I had a private Scorsese festival, I ran all his early films—I thought, my God, this man is such an incredible filmmaker that I would really just like the experience of working with him. Now, I had heard that he was doing *Cape Fear* and that he was going to use Bernard Herrmann's score. Well, I was a great admirer of Herrmann, who was a great help to me when I was younger; he had recommended me for a picture that they wanted him to do that he wouldn't or couldn't do, called *The View from Pompey's Head* [1955]. And of course we were great friends.

Had you worked with Herrmann?

BERNSTEIN: Nobody worked *with* Benny! He never had orchestrators, are you kidding? He was a solo act, and he worked in the most extraordinary way. Once they agreed on where the music was going, he sat down and—very often in ink—started to write the main title, right into the score, started from the beginning and just wrote the thing all the way through to the end. Very unusual.

Basically I called Barbara and said, "I know you want to adapt the Herrmann score, you don't want an original score here, but I would really love to do it, just for the opportunity of working with Marty," and that's how that came about. Just wanting to be part of a cinematic effort of that kind. And it lived up to all my best expectations.

We had a nutty schedule. We had our first meetings in late July and had a second set of meetings at the end of August. So actually I had about three to four weeks to write the score. That's all. Marty and Thelma Schoonmaker [the editor] had been working on it a couple of months, so by the time I saw it, it was certainly structurally the way it is now. But of course they fine-cut, fine-cut, fine-cut.

One of the things that worried me turned out not to be a worry at all. When I first saw the film in July they had some temp music in it already; they used the old Herrmann score. There were some things that we both liked right away that Marty had chosen, and they seemed very appropriate, and in those places generally speaking I followed his plan.

I was concerned because they were cutting to temp tracks and I felt that, in order to do a really good job—in other words, to bring my scoring experience to bear on the project—I had to sort of cleanse my mind and say, "No, I'm going to look at this material and do what I think is appropriate, the best thing to do for this film." And I realized there would be differences to what they had done on their temp scoring.

We had no trouble with that whatsoever. Marty Scorsese, when he looks at what we do and what's going on, looks at it totally objectively in terms of what works for the film, and I have a feeling every time we did another piece he wasn't really a prisoner of some preconceived notion he has, and that was very refreshing. I was very pleasantly surprised to find that was true.

The Herrmann material I used was very much altered in the sense that I sometimes combined two cues that might be both Herrmann and neither of them would be pure Herrmann because the construction was different. In some instances there are things that are purely me, because things had to be written which didn't exist in the 1962 score. The main title, for instance, is totally different from the original main title; that is mostly me. But I must say from Scorsese's point of view it didn't make any difference; what counted as far as he was concerned was whether a thing worked, whether it was dramatically correct. I don't think he analyzed it or was wondering which part is Herrmann and which part is Bernstein's.

We did use the original Herrmann parts; there were some

really fairly good sketches of the original score, and we used the exact orchestra that he used—four flutes, eight horns, and strings—so that maintained the integrity of the Herrmann sound. In the case of the main title, which I wrote primarily, I did add two trumpets, two trombones, and tuba and timpani. There were no trumpets at all in the original score.

Also, we used material from Herrmann's abandoned *Torn Curtain* score as well.* That was an extraordinary orchestra: also without trumpets, but [consisting] of twelve flutes, sixteen French horns, nine trombones, two tubas, celli bass, and two sets of timpani.

The Scorsese film is texturally a much richer film than the original *Cape Fear*. The way Scorsese shoots film is much more interesting. And Scorsese doesn't come across to you as the great director he certainly is, but that's not what's going on when you're working; what's going on is you have two people working, and the work is more important than the egos involved. That's wonderful when you find that—particularly wonderful when you find it with a great director. It was all coming to him fresh while we did it.

He never talked in purely musical terms; his concerns were purely dramatic, as they *should* be, and it was left to me to figure out mostly how to get it done. So he would listen to something and it would either be fine, or he would say, "I don't know, could we do more at this point to heighten things?" That sort of thing. He's a man who has reached a point in life where he has a good, healthy trust in his instincts, and therefore he can make those kinds of decisions with music—which is a medium with

---

*Herrmann's final collaboration with Alfred Hitchcock, who had—at the behest of studio executives—demanded a commercial-sounding score for the 1966 thriller, only to be met on the scoring stage by Herrmann's eclectic ensemble playing pulsating, almost brutal music. Herrmann was fired on the spot, replaced by John Addison (*Tom Jones*).

which he seems to be very comfortable—and he seems to be able to come to conclusions about musical problems rather easily, quite quickly. And luckily with the musical experience I have it was relatively easy for me to make adjustments on the stand, and solve problems right then and there on the scoring stage. There were about five or six instances where it was just necessary to rewrite things that couldn't be done on the stand, where we tried things that didn't work for one reason or another, or that either one or both of us thought could work better.

There was a piece yesterday which I recorded and which was the very last piece in the film and Scorsese said fine, and I said that I thought that we could do something better at this point, and it was me at that time changing things.

Getting back to our original question about the best uses of film music, I think the score for *Cape Fear* certainly plays the tensions that are unseen (or even unrecognized) by the Bowden family.

BERNSTEIN: Curiously enough, I think that the score for *Cape Fear* does that, not in terms of the characters so much, but the overall feeling of the music to me tends to be not on top of the film but somehow *inside* the film, in a very effective way. And I don't know whether Marty felt that, whether it was intuitive or instinctive, what his motivation was for adapting the Herrmann score, but there's no question that it's totally appropriate to this film.

DREAM STATE:
JOCELYN POOK ON *EYES WIDE SHUT*

When Jocelyn Pook's 1994 CD *Deluge* (recently released in the United States as *Flood*) came to the attention of Stanley Kubrick during production of *Eyes Wide Shut*, he enlisted her to write cues for selected sequences of his film, to be heard alongside music by Dmitri Shostakovich, György Ligeti, Franz Liszt, Chris Isaak, and the Oscar Peterson Trio.

A disturbing dream fugue involving the sexual fantasies and distrust threatening the status quo of the marriage of Bill and Alice Harford (played by Tom Cruise and Nicole Kidman), *Eyes Wide Shut* is a fitting testament to the late director's perfectionism and unwillingness to compromise—and in the music, an example of his customary eclecticism.

▶

JOCELYN POOK: Most of my music in film has been used in a very "foreground" sort of way, which is maybe more unusual. Perhaps it's because of where I came from—writing for theater, experimental visual theater—my music was always very much used as a strong voice. I mean, I never did what's termed "incidental" music, but having said that, the stuff I did under Nicole Kidman's monologue in *Eyes Wide Shut* I suppose is what is called "incidental." It certainly had to be very delicate, and that was quite a new experience for me; I hadn't done much of that kind of writing, under dialogue, in the background.

I understand Kubrick came to know your music when a choreographer played it during rehearsals of the ritual scene.

POOK: He hired me before he even shot that bit. He heard the music in a rehearsal and eventually the piece that he first heard—the cue "Masked Ball" on the soundtrack, which was originally called "Backwards Priest"—was the piece he shot to for that particular scene. It was slightly adapted for the film. Then for the orgy scene he edited an already-existing piece of music to that.

I started off trying to write new stuff for these scenes—I didn't imagine that this old piece that he'd first heard was going to be the finished product. Since these scenes hadn't been shot, he told me in detail what was happening and what was going to happen, the kind of atmosphere he wanted. He wanted me to try other stuff [than what was in "Backwards Priest"], and I did lots of sketches and different ideas for that whole ritual section, the orgy scene as well. But he ended up going back to those original pieces, and I think he was right to do that.

Jocelyn Pook

Did he go into great discussion about the rest of the film?

POOK: Just the particular scenes. That section of the film with the orgy is fairly self-contained, so it didn't matter too much not knowing what happened later. It *did* matter when I was trying to score my other scenes [Alice's monologues, and the dream sequences where Bill is fantasizing about his wife and her lover] and I didn't know how loaded things that were being said were. (I was writing to the finished footage.) And I just said, "Look, I've got to see the *whole* film, I've got to know the whole story." Because I was trying to work without knowing too much, and it was impossible. It was quite interesting actually, that exercise of trying to do that, because then you really don't know how to pitch the music. You don't know the gist and the ideas.

Film scores often develop thematically along the lines of the characters; does not knowing what happens to the characters make it more difficult to write?

POOK: Yes, as you say, you just don't know how to pitch it unless you know what's what. That process taught me a lot, actually. I'm learning that you have to infuse yourself into the film and the *ideas* of the film—whether the scene already exists or whether it's still to be shot. From there you try out ideas and see how you respond musically. You really need to be able to do that.

Your music very slowly unveils to reveal the inner life of the characters that had heretofore been concealed, from themselves as well as each other.

POOK: Yes, I think it was my response musically to the kind of complexities of that inner world. Also, you're bringing out dreamlike qualities; the way it's shot is kind of strange and dreamlike. I wanted it to have a mesmeric quality, [but] that music's coming in there to be a new dimension that's very revealing of an increasingly turbulent inner world, both their emotional states—Bill's getting blacker and blacker!

Did Kubrick make specific requests regarding musical qualities, orchestrations, electronics?

POOK: At the beginning he was very open to suggestions, actually. At one point he said, "I think it should be quite choral, that sort of weirdness" is the word he used! At the beginning of something you're usually both searching for the right thing. It's very rare that you can say, "Right, I think it should be an orchestra with French horns." Usually you are grappling with what the right thing *is*. It's a journey you're both taking to find the right thing.

The orgy scene, that's a funny one because it was very difficult to know what the right music was. And he'd tried so many different things before I came along—baroque music, all sorts. I didn't have much of a brief for that, he just said, "Look, I want *sexy* music!" And how do you *define* that? Actually, some of my early sketches are nothing like the final result, they could not be more opposite to "Migrations." I tried other things which were more feminine, these backward-singing female vocals, quite ethereal and strange. But he just heard that and felt that was the right thing.

Often I'm surprised by the process. One film I did called *Blight* was commissioned by a BBC series called *Sound on Film* for a composer and a filmmaker to collaborate and to make a kind of music-film, whatever that would be. That was a really interesting experience in that where we started and where we ended were very surprising, like the fact that's when I first started using voices. That film was about the building of a motorway where the filmmaker and I had both lived, and our houses were being demolished and we moved out, along with hundreds and hundreds of other people. We ended up interviewing people and I was using their voices in the soundtrack and I really didn't expect to do that. I've gone on to use that quite a lot in my work since then—in answering-machine phone messages and stuff. It's quite enjoyable when things lead you down unexpected paths.

When you saw the complete film of *Eyes Wide Shut*, had it been temped with the other composers' music already?

POOK: Yes, but not the scenes I was doing music for.

Did those pieces you composed undergo much revision during editing?

POOK: He cut the orgy scene to "Migrations," but the music for "Masked Ball" was edited to footage; it's kind of a mixture of both, really. He'd shot to "Masked Ball" [which is important because the blindfolded pianist is miming to it], but then the second half of it was changed, just lengthened; I did a bit of work on that. Certainly the first bit was exactly in sync when he shot it.

Your cue for the orgy scene, "Migrations," opens and closes with what sounds like the Ligeti two-note piano piece "Musica Ricercata, II" that's heard elsewhere in the film.

POOK: It's funny because that's a complete coincidence. Dominic Harlan, the pianist who played the Ligeti, noticed that as well. When I had my first meeting with Stanley he was really excited by some Liszt piano music ["Grey Clouds," heard during the morgue scene], and that opens with these very atonal few notes. I remember him playing it for me and saying, "What do you think this is?" You just don't think it's Liszt because it does sound very modern. He was quite excited about it. Anyway I started doing some sketches using those first few notes. It really is a complete coincidence that it sounds like the Ligeti.

What is the text of the backward vocals heard in "Masked Ball"?

POOK: It's a backward Romanian priest. Some people think I altered the pitch but in fact it's actually the same. It's one of those very Russian cantor types.

And in "Migrations," what was the text for that?

POOK: It's got a bit of a story, that piece. Originally when I did it for the dance company O Vertigo in 1994, I'd actually used the Koran—I didn't *realize* it was the Koran, I'd gotten this tape of singing and I used some bits of that—and I didn't want to use it when I put my album out. So I changed it, and got this singer, a yogi, who chose to sing some text from the *Bhagavad Gita* (he was improvising around that in fact). It sounds really atonal, it sounds really *wrong* what I've done—it doesn't sort of fit in the Indian scales—but it was what I wanted to hear. Anyway, I used the vocals he sang and that's what's on the album. But it offended people that the *Bhagavad Gita* was used in the orgy scene. It's singing used more as atmosphere—the text wasn't crucially important—and Stanley knew nothing about the text. So we changed it to some very simple words.

The controversy started in America, it was the Hindu organization there,* and then they alerted people in England. The controversy was a bit heavier in England, so all the prints in England were changed before it went out.

Has it been changed in America as well?

POOK: I don't think so, no.

Although you were offered specific scenes to score, did you have any discussions with Kubrick about scoring other parts of the film? Did you suggest that you write for other scenes?

---

*After the film premiered in the U.S., the American Hindu Anti-Defamation Coalition and other groups protested to Warner Bros., demanding the lyrics be cut from the film and the CD.

POOK: It was too late, because, sadly, he'd died when I actually thought of a couple of other things I would have liked to have done. I would have suggested that, but it was too late by then. He'd already long, long, long before chosen the Shostakovich and that Liszt, and I can't really argue about that! But there were a couple of other sections later on I would have suggested.

Sections without music that you thought could have used music?

POOK: Not particularly, no. I'm a real one for advocating *less* music in a film, I think it's often so overused. I think it was a slight overuse of the Ligeti.

How has your career been affected by the release of *Eyes Wide Shut*? Have you been asked to score other films since?

POOK: I have had near misses! Projects I'd either decided not to do at all or I didn't have time. So far I've been approached about projects for fairly sensible reasons; I've been asked to do things that would seem appropriate for me. But I just want to be quite careful, I'm not intending to do lots and lots of film work. But it's been wonderful to have the exposure I've had with this film; that's a big change for me. It's a wonderful thing to have worked on. And that's the other thing—it's quite a hard act to follow!

LIKE A DUET:
PATRICK DOYLE ON *LOVE'S LABOUR'S LOST*

At a time when one of the most successful recent Shake-spearean adaptations was a contemporary, pop-filled *Romeo and Juliet* set amidst the gangs of Miami, director Kenneth Branagh's *Love's Labour's Lost* sets the bar even higher by introducing the Bard's amorous tale within the framework of classic Hollywood musicals, interspersing the sacred text of Shakespeare with the sacred standards of Cole Porter, Irving Berlin, George Gershwin, and other stalwarts of Tin Pan Alley.

Just as his score for *Henry V* marked new territory for Patrick Doyle, *Love's Labour's Lost* was similarly challenging, being his first foray into the blithely artificial world of a 1930s singing-and-dancing musical film.

▶

PATRICK DOYLE: It's set just before the outbreak of the Second World War. Although the costumes are nodding toward that period—Ken is giving a very strong flavor of that period—one isn't being absolutely precise and exact and saying, "Well, that hair wouldn't be precisely in that kind of bun, or the costumes and the dress may be an inch too short or too long," or whatever. In general, as in *Henry V*, there's a general *impression* of the period, but one isn't being absolutely fixated with that particular year or decade.

Was the motive to introduce period songs into Shakespeare to jar one's perception of the work as a dated piece?

DOYLE: I think the goal was to experiment, which I think has come out brilliantly. The idea was these songs had became arias as in the operatic sense: you get to a particular point, you've said, "I love you," so let me just tell you I love you in fifty-five different ways. This is what the song was doing; we're taking a given point, a song was then more or less extolling the thought that had just been transmitted.

I had done a musical for the stage, been involved in pantomimes, which are almost like the Broadway/West End musical, but none of us had done a musical for the cinema. So nobody was there to say, "Well, *this* is what we do." Everyone was learning as we went along.

He uses a number of songs which are Cole Porter, Irving Berlin, Gershwin songs, where I find your standard four-bar, eight-bar, sixteen-bar, whatever-bar intro to them didn't work because it was Shakespeare, and to have a song in the middle of Shakespeare just seemed to *surprise* me. I mean, you're surprised when you watch an MGM musical and see the song come out of the action, but you somehow accept that genre; with the added thing of Shakespeare it just seemed a bit *too* unusual.

So I found eventually, after lots of to-ing and fro-ing, that what was needed were much longer introductions: i.e., the underscore became almost like an albatross taking a 150-yard takeoff, as opposed to a sparrow taking two feet before it's in flight. The audience had to be guided into the moment when the song appeared, but it still had to remain very natural. One of the introductions in particular, it's almost a full minute and a half before the lyrics begin, and when the song happens it seems totally natural.

After the first song you totally accept it. I think it's one of the best things Ken's ever done; it's one of the most exciting things I've ever been involved in.

With songs coming from different composers, did you have difficulty maintaining a stylistic consistency in the underscore?

DOYLE: Ken chose the songs to sum up the appropriate piece of action; the underscore inhabited another world. It still on occasion very often reflected the film's period, but because of the story itself, it's a very strong, classical symphonic underscore. It's very lush, romantic, and very bold, because the colors are very bold and the performances are bold and the *idea* is very bold. But the score inhabits its own world [apart from the songs].

I mean, one *could* have evoked the songs in the underscore. The other day I watched *South Pacific* for the first time in many years, and I noticed that the scorer took the theme of "Bali Ha'i" and in another scene totally removed from that song, one of the characters who had sung "Bali Ha'i" was involved and I heard all these variations on that particular song being tossed around to create the moment at that particular point. In fact I never, ever did that in *Love's Labour's Lost* because I created my own

Brush up your Shakepeare: Kenneth Branagh leading rehearsals for *Love's Labour's Lost.*

melodies (and there were many of them) to drive Shakespeare, and the songs became their own thing, so it was like a duet between the underscore and these songs—two different singers, as it were. And I think they both complement each other.

Did you involve yourself in researching thirties music or orchestration?

DOYLE: It's funny, it's something I grew up with. When I was a boy, they showed lots of old movies on television, so I was brought up on all the *Road* movies with Hope and Crosby and all those MGM musicals with Fred Astaire and Gene Kelly. One of my earliest memories, preschool, was watching *Singing in the Rain*, and being amazed at this man, Gene Kelly, and transfixed by the music, dance, movement, and the whole collaborative process. So when it came to writing that style of music (and the same on *Dead Again*), it was indelibly imprinted on my brain, all those sounds, the type of chromatic writing that took place which is very different from now.

I specifically listened to some marches that they featured behind the Pathé newsreels as a reminder of the style. Apart from the songs, all the music is original.

How much work was involved prior to shooting because of having to shoot to playback?

DOYLE: Oh my God, it was endless! None of us had ever been through the process of a musical before—the work which one had to do in terms of helping to supervise the recording, the artists. I mean, I could not have done it without my agent and music producer, Maggie Rodford. At one point she had to produce 250 CDs for the first day of rehearsal for all the performers, the sound men, myself, editors, they all received a CD of songs with click tracks and *without* click tracks in the vocals and *just* vocals and *just* orchestra . . .

The whole rehearsal process was just people everywhere, rooms everywhere, some with a singing tutor constantly there, choreographer constantly, and the lighting man was there all the time and I was there popping in and out making suggestions. My job was to musically direct and oversee this mammoth operation, but my real job didn't begin until obviously the underscore had to be written. I would brief the arrangers for the songs and say, "I feel the orchestration should be bigger, I feel it should be bolder." There were sometimes two or three passes to the songs, and I would pass on Ken's suggestions—"It's got to be this, it's got to be that"—and I would suggest they kick down an octave here, an octave there, make it more accessible here, it's too fast or slow, they have to up-tempo this or change the key. The crew was fantastic, and as the operation was huge it needed a very big team.

Did you work with the actors to prepare them?

DOYLE: No, a terrific gentleman called Ian Adam, who's a very experienced and talented singing tutor, who taught Michael Crawford and various people in the West End, another fellow Scot. He is particularly gifted with actors. He really instills enormous confidence in these people, and elicits terrific performances. He would vocalize with them and take them through the songs and help them to overcome various changes in voices and registers, the usual breaks; he would help them vowelize and consonantize; he would discuss the key with them and decide, rather than drop a key now, keep going, because the voice wasn't warmed up—"You'll find this key would be easier"—whatever. Ian has worked a lot more than I have with singers, although I have performed similar work in the past, more in the theater than anything. I worked with Kate Winslet a little in *Sense and Sensibility*. But he is vastly more experienced, so it was like, "Thank you, *you* get on with that!"

RECORDING

CARTER BURWELL: Since around *Rob Roy*, I have been conducting. I think that was one of the last movies in which I conducted some parts but not all, and since then I've been conducting all of them. It's a trade-off. It has to do with the complexity of what's going on during a film score recording, so we might as well get into that.

In one room the conductor is standing in front of the orchestra and there's usually a video monitor, or the film's being projected onto a screen; then in the control room sits the engineer who's making sure it's all working right, and the director, probably the producer, and who knows who else. And the question is, which of those rooms is the best room for the composer to be in? Being in the control room is good because the director is there and we can talk; I'll know moment by moment if the director or producer doesn't like what they're hearing or something like that, and I'm free to explain to them, "Oh, you're not hearing this particular instrument because that's going to be overdubbed later." We can have an ongoing conversation while the music is being recorded. The advantage of being with the musicians is I wrote the music, and a score for a piece of music does not contain all of the information required for a performance of a piece of music. In other words, if we could hear what it sounded like having Beethoven conduct one of his pieces, we would know a lot more about his music than we know from what we have now, which are his scores. There's information inevitably that just doesn't make its way onto the page; you can't put all the subtleties of tempo and things like that on a score. So there are good reasons for composers to conduct their work, even if they're not good conductors, and I'm not a great conductor. Someone might be able to conduct it better than I could, almost certainly that's true, but there is information that I like to get out of the musicians that isn't going to come easily in any other way. I could sit in the control room and pass my suggestions to the conductor, and I often have done that, but there's just nothing faster really than my standing up there and waving a stick and talking to the musicians. So that's the advantage of being in the room conducting. It's a trade-off.

To be quite honest, one of the reasons I've been conducting recently has nothing to do with either of those two things, but more to do with the question which was brought up earlier: Why do I do this at all? It's because I like to try to find new things to do. And at a certain point once I'd become comfortable with writing music for film, comfortable with orchestras, my next question was, "What can I still find that will give me discomfort?" Because it's only really in discomfort that you are alert and, you know, *learning*. Conducting seemed really scary, like the scariest next thing that's possible. So I thought, *That will be the thing to do*. I tried conducting one thing just off-the-cuff and realized, "No, this is *not* something you can do without a little training." So I took a class at Juilliard and started conducting. I'm still learning a lot; like anything else, you only learn from practice, and it's not that easy to get practice at conducting because you need an orchestra to do it! To be perfectly honest,

Basil Poledouris conducting the chorus for his score from
For Love of the Game.

the main reason I'm conducting is just because it's scary and it's
something I'm learning about, and I just enjoy the learning
process.

BASIL POLEDOURIS: *Conan* I wanted to conduct because it was
all free-timing. There were a couple of cues where I used clicks,
but for the most part I really wanted it to breathe, I really
wanted it to have a sense of being very natural. I think there was
time to record—I was in Rome for three weeks—so we had a
very comfortable recording session. When we recorded that, we
didn't record every day, and because of that I could hear play-
backs and really listen to try to find out what it was we were
doing, but everything was fine.

Because you had breathing room in the recording schedule, did you rewrite cues after hearing them performed?

POLEDOURIS: I could have, but no, I didn't. That's another issue, the jury's out on that one for me: whether a score should be recorded all at once or over a period of time. I think when you're writing and if you're on the right track, it's probably better to record everything in the same sitting, because it's a different process. Writing and conducting for me are two completely different processes; as a conductor by definition you need to be gregarious, you need to be instructive, you need to be a director, to get the dramatic concepts of the music across. Being a writer you *know* what those things are and you don't have to communicate with anybody, and I much prefer not to. The only people I talk to really are my music editor and my orchestrator and that's it—I really do shut myself off from the rest of the world as much as I can. And I think when one stops the writing process to conduct, even if you conduct the first twenty, thirty minutes of the score, then you go *back* to write, it makes it more difficult. I start to second-guess myself: like, "Gee, is this going to be as good as that thing I just recorded? I really liked that so maybe I should use some of that here instead of this new bit." It feels like it's coming from the outside instead of the inside. It's done, unfortunately, because of the schedules, particularly if you're chasing a dub and reels one through four need to be written and then you've got a week to finish five through six, and it's kind of a concession to a scheduling issue. But I would very much like the writing to be finished and then really concentrate on conducting, because conducting is a serious art form.

You see, I believe in magic. I believe that there is a moment that occurs in the writing and in the performance, and if you can capture that thing on paper or on tape, that's what makes it different from an arranger coming in and taking a great piece of [existing] music and making it sound like a great piece of film score.

When you're recording the score, do you record all of the music at one time?

MARK ISHAM: I remember on *Timecop* there was a lot of action music in that, and I broke up the schedule into two bits because I had this feeling that I might not get it on the first pass, the way director Peter Hyams works. He is very exacting but I wasn't trusting that we were totally duplicating each other.

So I split it up and it was a smart thing to have done, because in fact during that first pass we spent a lot of time rewriting on the stage, and in fact I think there were a couple of cues I just put aside. Once he heard it with a real orchestra he was much more able to be specific as to what he wanted, so by the time we went back into the second set of sessions, everything went flawlessly. There was not a single rewrite or major correction to be done on the stage.

MYCHAEL DANNA: Certainly in the mixing stage of *8mm*, suddenly all of the interesting Moroccan stuff disappeared because the mixers thought it was too weird. They just went, "What the hell's this? It's interfering with the rain sound. Your drums are distorted, man."

"No, those are snares on bendirs."

"Oh. Well, they don't sound good with rain so we're dropping them." Whatever, it's on the CD!

Are you generally invited to the mixing stage?

ELLIOT GOLDENTHAL: That really depends on the director. Julie Taymor and Neil Jordan have a degree of influence; other directors have just said, "You're welcome to come but it might be worthless for you, or painful!"

Do sound effects people hold sway in that situation?

GOLDENTHAL: Well, you have ninety tracks of sound effects but like two tracks of music! You not only have sound effects and ADR and foleys (all those little scritchy-scratchy things whenever somebody moves their arm against the side of their body), so when you've written this beautiful love theme and the beautiful girl in the Edwardian dress sits down on a settee, you hear all this scritchy-scratchy stuff that's so damn noisy you've already cut through half the score.

I'm not averse to sound effects; I'm averse to directors thinking that they can balance everything out instead of just having "That's sound effects, great; that's music, great." But when you try to stuff it all into one bag, it might give you the *feeling* that it's right, but if you really had selected either one you'd be much more happy. It would give you much more of a sense of clarity.

■

CODA

SEQUELS

It is almost de rigueur that a film sequel would incorporate the recognizable music from a successful original. John Williams's follow-up scores to *Star Wars*, *Raiders of the Lost Ark*, and *Jaws* all feature the original signature themes, even though an abundance of new (and, in the case of *The Empire Strikes Back*, superior) material is present.

The challenge is always to make a sequel sound fresh and new, which is sometimes at odds with the filmmakers' intentions—which are usually to avoid risk by *repeating* whatever worked the first time around.

▶

CARTER BURWELL: Apparently when they wanted Tony Perkins to do *Psycho III*, his price for doing it was that he be allowed to direct it, and he's the one who selected me. He knew full well that I was a strange choice, that I had never worked in Holly-wood, I'd only done one movie. But he liked *Blood Simple* a lot, he liked the music for it, and he really went way out of his way to hire me, which was *amazing* to me. Because after *Blood Simple* it's not as though I anticipated having a career doing music for films, not at all. I thought, "Well, *that* was fun," and I was just going on doing the things I was doing at that time. It just so happens I'm a big Tony Perkins fan, so when I got this call out of the blue that he wanted me to work on his film I was amazed. And he just pretty much asked me to do what I wanted to do.

He had no particular interest in the music having any rela-tionship to the previous *Psycho* scores; he hadn't liked the score to *Psycho II*, he thought it was not dark enough I guess, or *strange* enough. He never gave me any guidance of any sort—his never having directed before might have been part of it—but it was an unusual experience. Of course, at that time I had so little experience myself I didn't know *how* unusual it was; I didn't know at that time how unusual Joel and Ethan Coen are to work with, because I just had no other experiences to compare it to.

At one point Universal wanted to do a song to go on the movie—yes, the *Psycho III* song! Tony didn't want to just slap some piece of pop music in there that had nothing to do with the movie, but what he wanted them to do was have me collaborate with a songwriter or take one of my themes and turn it into a pop song. At one point they put me together with Danny Elf-man, who at that time had just done, I think, one film score also, *Pee-wee's Big Adventure*—this was when he was still active in Oingo Boingo—and Danny and I talked about what we might do. He had an idea about sampling the shower scene from *Psy-cho* and slowing down the *"Eeeeee! Eeeeee! Eeeeee!"* strings and making a rhythm out of it, so we worked on that a little bit, but it was obviously kind of off-the-wall, and Universal pulled the plug on that pretty quickly! But that's the closest we ever got to giving any consideration to the previous scores, because there was no way that I was going to compete with Bernard Herrmann or Jerry Goldsmith. I didn't want to face that challenge. Honestly I felt the only thing I could safely do that I could do well was just write my own piece of music. I can't do a worthy homage to them, so I didn't try.

BRING OUT YOUR UNDEAD

In 1999, Philip Glass was hired by Universal to write a new score for Tod Browning's 1931 film version of *Dracula*, starring Bela Lugosi. Since the original film's soundtrack had hardly any music to speak of, the commission could be viewed both as a belated gesture at finishing an "unfinished" film and an attempt to re-view the horror classic through a more contemporary sensibility, namely a postmodern composer's music performed by the Kronos Quartet. The film was issued on video and DVD with the Glass score, which was also performed live in sync to a screening of the film.

▶

PHILIP GLASS: I viewed *Dracula* actually as a play that had been filmed, which is what it was. You can see that the actors learned their lines and they put up the camera and they shot it. I can well imagine that they went through the editing process in weeks, if not days! You see a lot of long shots. There may have been two cameras, but I doubt whether there were a lot of editing choices to be made. So the whole process we have today— maybe fourteen weeks of shooting and nine months of editing— that wasn't the way they did it then, so you can't even talk about *Dracula* in terms of contemporary film.

Furthermore, *Dracula* was much closer to the style of melodrama, a form of theater common in the late nineteenth and early twentieth century, in which actors speak over music. I had done a melodrama before with David Henry Hwang called *1,000 Airplanes on the Roof*. It's a form not common these days, but it's a wonderful music theater form. And I looked at *Dracula* and said, "Oh, this is a melodrama, which for some quirk of fate had never been completed"—the quirk of fate being that theaters of the time didn't have the equipment to play back big sound-tracks, so they didn't need them. But once you saw that that's what it was, I saw that I was completing a work which belonged to another genre entirely. It was basically a piece of music theater.

So from that point of view I was totally free of the industry approach to filmmaking, I didn't have to think of it at all, and there was no one around to think about it with. All I had to do is keep the people at Universal happy, and they were; they liked the idea, and they liked what I did and I didn't have any trouble with them at all.

■

THE ORGANIC SCORE

It is not being flippant to suggest that if some film scores can be called "organic," others cannot. Too often music has been slapped onto a film's soundtrack without much thought as to its dramatic or aesthetic relevance; this is especially true when the tie-in marketing of pop records is brought into the mix.

An organic score can be defined as one which grows parallel to the growth of the entire film, which was the case with such projects as *Kundun* and (because music is an integral part of its narrative) *The Red Violin*. It is nonetheless rare for a composer to be on the production from the very beginning, or—given increasingly shortened postproduction schedules—that he would have an amount of time to contribute to the project roughly comparable to the time devoted by a cinematographer or costume designer. If a composer is brought onto the project eight weeks before the release date, after the film has been shot and roughly edited, his contribution *could* be characterized as an afterthought, a finishing touch to a project pretty much wrapped up before he even came into the picture. So how might a composer's musical contribution change if he were more involved with the film from its very inception?

Is it truly useful for a composer to be on the shooting stage as opposed to simply viewing the film cold when it's edited together, approaching it as an audience would?

DAVID SHIRE: I think mostly from viewing it when it's done, but if they've invited you to the shooting—it means you're in on the project that early and you've read the script—then your subconscious can start germinating themes. *The Conversation*'s score evolved over a long time; I was at the first read-through before they even started shooting. Francis Coppola wanted me around to soak up the atmosphere. There's time to do it when you're working with a great director who's very responsive to music and its values, and so you have six months to evolve. But more and more assignments get handed out at the last minute, [where] you have ten days to do a score.

You have to come up with your basic material, which is the name of the game for me. If you have great basic material, the cues almost take care of themselves. You need what I call "throwaway time": the time to write a theme, put it away for two days or a week, come back to it, and say, "That sucks!" Then you can go, "Oh, I see what I *should* do." That's the process. That's one of the reasons I like writing musicals for the theater; it can take a year or two or three to write a musical, during which a score evolves and builds on itself, and makes rich connections—and you throw away!

A REFLECTION, LIKE THE MOON ON WATER: PHILIP GLASS ON *KUNDUN*

Philip Glass's music for Martin Scorsese's biography of the early life of the Dalai Lama was as picturesque as the film's cinematography and design. While the music in places did not correspond to specific characters or actions, it very effectively evoked a sense of place and a time seemingly—and tragically—lost to history.

▶

PHILIP GLASS: Marty Scorsese and I worked together on the script before he was shooting. I told him the only way for music to become an organic part of the film was to begin with the script before the shooting.

You have to remember that this is the way that operas are written. I basically adapted my theater and opera approach to film. I've done fifteen operas, I've done lots of ballets and plays, and basically what you do is you look at the written script—the libretto of an opera becomes the basis of the opera. You don't *see* the opera when you write it, you're working from a text, and it's actually quite easy to do. Most scripts are a hundred to 110 pages long and the movie is 110 minutes long so roughly speaking it goes by at the rate of a page a minute. You don't have to know more than that to write the music; [the script] gives you the general scale of the piece. It's helpful to know who the actors are, to know the art director and to get as much visual input as you can, but if you wait for the assemblage to happen you're too late. Then what's happened is that the editor begins editing and they have no music, or they put in *other* music, which is a disaster. With Marty, he was getting music from me when he was in Morocco shooting.

The thing is, he picked a subject that I happen to know top to bottom. I had been in touch with the Tibetan community for thirty years, I've known personally the Dalai Lama since 1972. I knew people in the movie, I knew the actors. It was easy for me to connect to the material. He didn't have to show me what a Tibetan costume looked like or what a Tibetan village looked like; I knew what a sand mandala [sand painting] looked like. I have books and books of pictures of Tibet right here in my library. Reading the script was easy for me to see [what was necessary], the story was one that I knew well, so there was no prep time for me.

What were your goals for the score?

GLASS: It was very simple. I told Marty the score has to do two things: One is to create unmistakably the sense of place—the music would transport you immediately from the very first notes to an exotic (by Western standards) environment, filled with images that were totally unfamiliar, and the music was the magic carpet that was going to take you there. As you know, he didn't film it in Tibet—basically it's a virtual film with the mountains painted in, they built everything in Morocco and they put in second-unit shots with the Himalayas afterward—and my concern was that the feeling of place could have been compromised. Now, it turned out *not* to be the case; in fact, Dante Ferretti is a fabulous art director; it looked excellent.

Secondly, I felt the music was a bridge between the audience and a culture, and it's important to remember that the Tibet of that film simply doesn't exist anymore. The costumes don't exist, the clothes don't exist, the environment is gone, it's completely *gone*, so basically we had to create a virtual Tibet that's no longer existing—and then we had to create a doorway into that world so that people could look at it and have *some* familiarity with it. In my view the images and the story are so exotic by our familiar standards, so I thought of someone who went to the film—an ordinary German or Italian or American—and I wanted to provide them with a bridge, even if it's one of those little swaying bamboo bridges that you see up in the Himalayas: it's not much of a bridge, but it's *enough*, and with it you can get from one place to another. And Marty liked that idea. He said, "Great, send me some music."

The great thing about working with Marty is that he is very, very open. He's a great collaborator because he wants people to generate materials—he doesn't tell you what it's supposed to sound like, he wants what *you* know. Of course, the difficulty comes when you get into the editing and he wants the trombone right when *this* horse comes on the stage, and you get into this kind of stuff.

Once he heard the music, what feedback did he give you?

GLASS: Not much about the music itself; everything after that was about sychronizing the editing with the music. He accepted almost totally all of the music I had written, with the exception of one scene which he asked me to rewrite because he said it wasn't sad enough. It was the scene of the Dalai Lama going to the Dungkhar monastery the first time he leaves Lhasa [prior to the Chinese takeover of Tibet]. And he said the music should be a little sadder. The director without any question prevails, but that's the only disagreement we had, and that's not much of a disagreement. I just said, "Well, I don't think this is right," and he said, "No, I want this." And I then gave him basically what he wanted. I said to him, "You have the movie, I have the record." And he said, "Fine." And that [original] piece I later put on the record.

My favorite interplay between the score and the images was the test of the little boy, where he picks out the objects he remembers from his previous incarnation.

GLASS: That was edited fourteen, fifteen, sixteen times. That was painful! All of the elements were there, but as he continued to change it, as you can see, certain elements of the music cue certain events that happen; in other words, when he picks the right object you hear the bells. The music is set up that way, and that has to happen that way. And Marty edits like a sculptor walking around a piece of stone; he'll take a chip here off, a chip there, and he *keeps* walking around it. So literally he would reedit something by taking out five frames. Well, five frames is not a rational musical length of time, it's like *nothing*, it's like *part* of an eighth note. So that went on and on and on—I remember I would get calls from the editor, Thelma Schoonmaker, late, late in the process. The editing process took nine months, from January till the end of August, September, right up until when they were mixing.

Did you go back to the studio to rerecord?

GLASS: No, I do everything on work tapes until the final cut is done; nothing is actually recorded. And while this is happening Michael Riesman, a guy who works with me, reedits the scores as we're reediting the tapes, so basically ten days before the mix, when I actually know what the piece *is*, we go into the studio and record everything. We only have to make the recording once. The advantage of this, of course, is you only have to spend the recording money once.

I am set up with my own studio and I can make work tapes. I would bring in some Tibetan musician friends of mine and we'd make samples, and some of those tracks ended up on the final film. That often happens; elements of the work tape will end up on the final tracks of the film. But the real money is saved for when you bring in the session players: the *real* trumpets and trombones, string players. That's where the real money comes in, and I only have that budget once, so I don't rerecord.

There were many Tibetan instruments used; did you also incorporate native Tibetan music for thematic material?

GLASS: There is some source music there. There's some nomadic singing in the background when the young boy's mother goes to make some offerings outside before they leave their home for the trip to Lhasa. There was some source of that kind.

The trickier part was to get some music for the Chinese Red Army, and we had to be very careful to not use anything that originated from China itself or the picture company would have been all over us for that—the Chinese would have gone crazy. (They were going crazy anyway!) Marty and Thelma had found some Chinese piece for temp music, and they showed me what they wanted, and then we gave it to a Chinese guy from New

Jersey we met through contacts in Chinatown to arrange that music, and we were able to do an "authentic" Chinese piece. As it is, there were no grounds for complaint; the Chinese music we used was created in New York. It's only a few minutes, but it has a certain place in the film; you have to have it. Apart from that, and a little bit of nomadic singing source music, everything else was the original score.

And when the Dalai Lama visits Mao Tse-tung and is greeted by the children's chorus?

GLASS: That was American, a Chinese children's choir in New York. If you look at it carefully I don't know if you actually *see* them singing. Basically we dubbed that in.

I was impressed by how the filmmakers didn't try to *explain* everything in the film, such as the scene where the body is taken out to be fed to vultures. No one says, "Well, we're doing this because our religion teaches us such and such" or "This is a punishment."

GLASS: Marty didn't feel compelled to elucidate all the details. He said that you can't explain everything, you just have to take it the way it is.

PLAYING WITH PARADOXES:
MYCHAEL DANNA ON *THE SWEET HEREAFTER*

The cinema of Canadian director Atom Egoyan plays greatly on paradox: the gulf between what is known and not known, what is hidden and what is palpable. His most successful film, *The Sweet Hereafter*, is a thoughtful character study that is not limited to the flaws or dreams of its protagonists, who wrestle with the aftermath of an accident that costs the lives of a small town's schoolchildren. The film reflects an omniscient point of view that reveals the sadness, hope, and longing of those who are lost, putting the audience in a position to ruminate on the potency and fallacy of memory.

Composer Mychael Danna's long relationship with Egoyan led to a unique folkloric-sounding score that recalls the fable of the Pied Piper of Hamelin (which is a recurring theme in the story). Performed by an early music ensemble, the Toronto Consort, and featuring an Iranian ney flute played by Hossein Omoumi, the almost medieval-sounding music, in its simplicity, builds to an emotional intensity without resorting to cheap tugs at the listener's heartstrings.

▶

You've worked with Atom Egoyan since the very beginning of both your careers. How did you meet up?

MYCHAEL DANNA: We both were at the University of Toronto at the same time. I think he was doing poli-sci and I was doing music, and he was involved in theater there. As it happens so was I, in that I knew a bunch of people in theater, and I ended up doing sound for a lot of the productions. So we met through that world, although we never worked on a play together. He was getting his first film together [*Family Viewing*, 1987], and I played him some of the things that I'd been working on. The first meeting we had was this real enjoyable session where we just played each other things that we liked, and we both *knew* each other's favorite stuff—medieval things that he was playing me, and Middle Eastern things that I was playing—so right from the beginning we recognized our tastes were pretty close.

Neither of us really [knew or were interested] in films—Atom especially is extremely naive of film and film history. I don't think he'd seen *Star Wars* or anything in the seventies. He made this big discovery around 1980 of this band called Led Zeppelin, he was telling me about—"It's a really cool band, you should hear it!" He was a *little* disconnected that way, and I think you can see that. I was maybe not quite as extreme an example, but I had no interest in films, I actually didn't even really *like* films. I had no interest at all in being a film composer, and the John Williams/Jerry Goldsmith school of film music made me vomit—you know, it was the last possible thing I'd ever want to spend my life doing. So I never

Mychael Danna

considered film as a career at all. So when I approach film (and Atom approaches filmmaking the same), it's as *play*. And it's just such a different kind of approach than a studio film where it's all business first and art second. We're very lucky here in Canada to have the funding agencies the way they are;* they basically encourage you to play and have fun and enjoy what you're doing and explore the things that gave you the reasons you became a musician or a filmmaker in the first place.

---

*To promote production and distribution of indigenous films, federal and provincial government funding agencies typically subsidize Canadian film-makers.

What sort of conversations do you have with Atom on his films? Does he speak a musical language or do his discussions emphasize drama and it's up to you to come up with the musical aspect?

DANNA: Well, with Atom they're probably as sophisticated discussions as I have with anybody. He is quite accomplished musically; he's a classical guitar player, in fact that's why he originally came to Toronto from Victoria, to study guitar. So he can actually get into musical terminology. He's got a very wide-ranging knowledge of different styles and different emotional contents of different kinds of music, so it's really very much a collaboration.

I start out usually reading very early drafts of the script, which is also kind of unusual. We just talk about the story at that point and what it's about, what the different layers are (which is something his work deals with a lot). It's really just a matter of taking a lot of time to really understand intimately what the film is and what it's about and what it's saying, and what the ramifications of the different themes are on the music. We'll start early on theorizing about different possible musical routes, but we're very open to those things changing drastically, and they usually do. In fact, with *Felicia's Journey* it took a violent about-face three weeks from the mix.

How did you decide on a structure for the score for *Sweet Hereafter*, given the fragmented nature of the story with flashbacks within flashbacks?

DANNA: That is another role for music, how it can on a deeper level set up this ambience which the entire film lives in. That is something that's kind of hard to describe, but it's one of the most important aspects of film scoring, or at least I think it *could* be; I don't think it is very often, perhaps, because in most films we get the same old ambience, which is late-nineteenth-century grandeur.

But most films have straightforward storylines which perhaps don't allow for a deeper ambience.

DANNA: That's true, there's a lot of films where that is the appropriate tack to take; when I watch films sometimes I would be at a total loss to know what I could do that would be interesting from my point of view. But for the sort of ambient world of *The Sweet Hereafter,* the goal was to not give those things away, given the fragmented structure of the story; i.e., you don't want to hit story points in a structure like that. You want to set up an understanding of the overall theme of the film, which is the Pied Piper, which has its symbolism within the film—it's this very magnetic, attractive, but yet somewhat slightly dangerous and dark and exotic presence—and also to set up the ambience of the town. I wanted to portray the town in a medieval way, as kind of a self-enclosed world where things usually don't come in or go out. It's a little world unto itself. So just making those aural choices of an Iranian flute player and a medieval band—and of course picking the right notes for them to play, which is harder to do!—means that you're saying those things, hopefully [on a musical level].

What led to your instrument choices? An Iranian flute isn't typical of a frozen Canadian town. Did the idea come from seeking a particular sound within this narrative context, or did it have a personal meaning for you?

DANNA: Neither of those, really. Basically that film score (except for the band music that Sarah Polley sings, that's a whole other thing) has nothing to do with *The Sweet Hereafter*, it's not scoring *The Sweet Hereafter*—it's scoring the Pied Piper's story. And that right there is what all the music is about. It doesn't have anything to do with this frozen Canadian tundra town except inasmuch as a little town like that has something in common with a thirteenth-century Flemish village, and the idea of the Iranian flute player is just that somebody from Iran would have been an exotic Pied Piper to a European in the Middle Ages.

I think once you build a concept that really works on those several levels, where it tells a story that's certainly there already—you can't just throw something in that doesn't exist, but when you're reflecting a story that's within a story—and you stay true to that sonic world, then everything you do will make sense with the story. Atom had already chosen the Pied Piper story as his analogy, so that was kind of an easy choice, we never really spent a lot of time worrying about that, that seemed pretty obvious almost from the beginning. And we were very excited about it because we were thinking, "Finally we can use these medieval instruments that we've both been talking about and waiting till we can use!"

The band that Sarah played in was a little more up in the air as to what kind of a band that would be; that was really fun to do as well.

Did you consciously have the songs relate to the characters in a way the underscore didn't?

DANNA: I guess the important point of that is sometimes in a film, not that there's flaws in a film, but you want to rebalance what's there, and you can do a little bit of that with the music. And one of the things that Atom was concerned with was that people understood that Nicole (Sarah's character) had this blossoming life which was taken away from her. If you don't understand that then it's less affecting what happens to her. So we wanted to really establish that she had this band that was kind of cool, that really sounded pretty good, it still had an amateur quality to it but it had a certain magic going on there. We did the one song that's on camera, then later we made a decision to do four or five more songs and scatter them throughout the piece just so that people would recall, "Oh yeah, Nicole's a singer"—or, "She *was* a singer," depending upon where you are in the film.

To hear her singing *after* you recognize her career is over makes it more heartrending.

DANNA: Right, that was exactly why we did that. And as far as choices of the band makeup, I just thought, well here's this little village, it's just whoever happens to be in the town. There's a cello player, a guitar player, there's a guy who plays harmonium—God knows *why*, but there he is (which is *me*!). So it's just this weird pickup band that's really kind of eccentric, it had this slightly unreal quality to it, and the fact that the songs are all so sort of slow. The whole style of it seems a little dreamy. That was the thinking behind that.

It's always just so important before you write a note to really spend a lot of time thinking clearly about what you're trying to *say* with the music, and find the most elegant way of expressing the scene in the most interesting way. If I do anything differently than other people, it's that right there—that I spend a *lot* of time thinking before I start, and talking with the director and trying to understand every possible "themelet" within the film.

The point you brought up before is absolutely correct, that there's a huge genre of films where there isn't any hidden undercurrent or theme, there is no ambience, and that's fine too, but you should probably look for one first anyway.

Polley is a fine actress with years of film and TV experience, but she doesn't come across as a polished singer. Was that something that was purposefully taken into account when devising the songs?

DANNA: The very first time I met Sarah she was about twelve and we worked on this animated Christmas show where she ended up having to sing, so it was very funny that several years later we were singing together. She would be the first to tell you that she is an absolute amateur singer, so really what you're hearing is what she is. Hers is a totally untrained, young voice with a certain kind of appeal, a natural attractiveness to it. In a sense it's very realistic. It all made sense. That was something that when Atom cast her he didn't know how that was going to work out, and so there was originally just this one on-camera song appearance (when her band rehearses at a local fair), but everyone seemed very happy with what they heard so that's when we decided to do more of it.

Thirty or forty years ago they would have brought in Patti Page or somebody to dub the lead actress's voice.

DANNA: In India it would have been Lata Mangeshkar! We were wondering at the beginning whether this was going to work at all or whether we would just use three seconds and cut away before she sang—just get her breathing in and . . . *cut!* I think it worked out as well as we could have hoped in that way.

On an earlier film with Egoyan, *Exotica,* you traveled to India to record "found" sounds and music to incorporate into your score. How did that come about?

DANNA: The theme of *Exotica* was this whole idea of not knowing what's inside another person, and why they are where they are now, what the history of that person is, and how we project our own thoughts about that onto other people. It's also about obsession, and it just seemed for me if I wanted to do a really fine score about those subjects that I should do something that *I'm* obsessed about, which is the Far East and Middle East. And so in a sense I projected myself into the film.

I basically walked around South Asia with a DAT recorder, taping all kinds of things, and then there was one instance where I actually wrote a part for the violinist Rivka Golani and I to play and we recorded that in Bombay. A lot of the dance music was completed before the shoot so that the dancers could actually wriggle to the correct beat, then it was perfected over the next six months, while the score was just a matter of me playing and having fun with those sounds. Basically it was random sampling of things that were going on.

Right from the beginning of that film (more than on any of the ones I've done with Atom) it was very clear to me what I wanted to do, and when I explained it to him he was very supportive. When I said I'm going to India to record a bunch of stuff, he thought that was a great idea, and my whole idea of setting that whole film in a kind of Middle Eastern/Eastern sonic world made a lot of sense to the theme of that film.

I guess in a way you and Egoyan are at an advantage working away from the Hollywood studio system in that you are freer to experiment, both musically and filmically.

DANNA: When those kinds of films work, I just don't think there's anything that can beat that system. It's true, we're very fortunate to have that sort of funding system in place here, still sort of barely hanging on here. There's never a producer calling and saying, "I don't get what you're doing" or "I want to cry more in this scene." We didn't get any phone calls like that at all, nobody bothered us, and so we just did what we felt like and what we were interested in, and did it until it looked right to us, and that's really the end of the story there.

I have a studio at home and I played twelve, fourteen hours a day with it for six months, that's really how we've approached it. I've learned about scoring films on the job, really, and I think Atom learned how to make films on the job, and perhaps if we've done things that are unusual, that's really why.

What is an example of a musical concept that was found to be not workable and had to be reworked?

DANNA: In *Felicia's Journey*, Atom and I talked about Hilditch (Bob Hoskins's character) who's kind of a psychotic mass murderer, but it's a side of his character he's very much hidden from himself; he's built up this self-image of a man who's very warm and helpful in a cushy, 1950s English sort of way—cardigans and all that. That was where we started out with the musical idea (and in fact some of those elements remain) of a Mantovani-style theme which gets a little twisted here and there but it's basically very smooth, it's supposed to be very soothing—it's the masking side of his character. But the idea was to have the entire score like that and it really just wasn't working. So we had this crisis where we were just both pulling our hair out.

How did you gauge it wasn't working, from preview screenings?

DANNA: No, I was really having trouble writing it, to be honest; I was totally blocked. That's never actually happened. It's kind of funny, after all these years it was like the worst moment that we've ever had. I just didn't feel that this was the right route and yet I couldn't think of *another* one. So finally we went to the other total extreme and I ended up writing a very brittle, serial-ist—not to pun the serial killer thing—twelve-tone score for string quartet and snare drum. It's a really new music-y, quite nasty-sounding score in a way, and I think it's one of the most fun things I've ever done in my opinion. It was one of the most enjoyable experiences, even though I've never worked in that school since school.

Was it fun because you played against the smooth fifties sound?

DANNA: Yeah, and that's something I love doing and so does Atom: the paradox of image and music, and cultural paradoxes and sonic paradoxes. It seemed to work on so many levels, because the string quartet gives it this English tea party sound and yet what it's saying is something very different; and the whole idea of the hidden code of twelve-tone music and the unveiling of this tone row seems to work with his character, so that by the end, the very last scene, as he makes a self-realiza-tion of what he really is, the tone row becomes completely revealed almost as a very nondissonant row, so it fools you in a sense that it starts out very chaotic and unclear as to what it really is, and it becomes revealed at the end. And the snare drum adds a piquancy and also has the connotations of his military background. So yeah, satisfying to watch now, but it was really quite a hellish experience in a way.

Can you compare this symbiotic relationship you've had with Egoyan with the experiences you've had on more mainstream Hollywood films like *The Ice Storm* and *8mm*, and whether you felt protected by the director from outside sources saying, "Well, music is something that can be marketed and therefore we have something to say about it"?

DANNA: Well, that's certainly what happens, absolutely. And I think if I hadn't had the upbringing and education in the film business here in Canada it would have been very difficult for me to come up with an original idea when people are questioning you at every moment, especially early on when you don't have the confidence. If someone had come and seen our early work on *Exotica* and just gone, "What the hell are you guys doing, man? Get an orchestra!" I probably would have thought about it and gone, "Oh yeah, he's right," and then thrown it away and that would have been the end of that.

Now working with Ang Lee, it's very close to working with Atom in the sense that he's extremely sensitive and very, very knowledgeable about music, and very insightful; I learn a great deal about music and film when I work with Ang. But yes, those phone calls *do* come from producers and studios. Working on *Ice Storm* they did, and working on *Ride with the Devil* they were even more intense, and in fact I kind of caved on that one. They got what they wanted, which was a big, overblown orchestral score. It wasn't what I wanted to do for the film originally, but the pressure was extremely intense (as a lot of other composers would attest) and I did start questioning my concept and ultimately I trusted Ang, and I think Ang was convinced of that by other powers as well. There are some folk music, Civil War elements in the score, but it's certainly the most conservative (in the film scoring sense) score that I've probably ever done. I don't know, maybe it's less conservative than I think, but it's certainly a lot closer to that model.

I think the score does what it's supposed to do, but it's certainly not anything I'm wildly proud of, and the score doesn't enlighten you in any interesting way, I don't think. I don't *know* what I think of that score, actually. I guess what happens is you just get confused when you get people sending you CDs of other scores saying, "Make it sound like this." I literally got phone calls like that every day. And I kept some of those messages, they're pretty hilarious: "Make it *big, bigger!*" After a while you just go, "All right, all right, leave me alone! You want big? *Here!*"

What size orchestra did you use?

DANNA: It was in London and it was probably eighty-five pieces. And it's gorgeous sounding in that physical sense, it really is. So it was a really interesting experience, but I don't think it's an interesting score, and I would not be that interested in doing very many scores like that, except that film was so brilliant; I do trust Ang's taste, so I gave myself up to him in that way.

Joel Schumacher was wonderful to work with on *8mm* in that he really did protect me from those phone calls. I didn't get a single interference from Sony at all. Joel's directions to me were "Be bold." So I said, "Okay, I'm going to Morocco for two weeks to record stuff," and he went, "Great!" That was a really great experience in that sense. It was like working on an independent film more than any other bigger film that I've worked on. The film I'm working on now again is a Sony film, it's James Mangold's *Girl, Interrupted*, and it's the same thing. Certainly there's the shadow in the background of what producers will think and so on, but I'm just working with James, and it's pretty much one-on-one.

I think because of the résumé I've built up, I don't get calls to do James Bond films or anything like that—I'm just not going to get those calls. So people understand what they're getting; they're not going to be shocked or anything. For *Girl, Interrupted* [about a young woman's detention in a psychiatric hospital], I'm using a glass orchestra mixed with a regular Western orchestra. At first there was a lot of stress about that choice, and it got really scaled back at the beginning, but then people got more used to the sound in the temp versions I was sending down, and they started asking for some of it *back*. So it's ended up pretty well where I would want it.

The thing about working on independent films [compared to] working with the big studios is, there's just no respect. Atom and I have a great relationship but every other part of that experience is pretty ragged.

Just trying to get the film released, let alone finished.

DANNA: All those things, every other thing about the whole working experience. When I'm at the studio I can really see why people want to spend their entire working experience on the lot: They're taken care of, they enjoy it, and in a sense don't really worry about what they're churning out here and there, because you're treated really quite wonderfully, you're treated with *respect*. There's something very seductive about that whole end of things. They lavish you with all kinds of support, financially and morally—whether it's sincere or not I don't know, but it doesn't make the hotel room any less real! And working with the best orchestras, the best this and that, whereas before I would lose money on films because I would spend my own money getting scores made, flying to India and so on. I mean, they would say, "Sure, go ahead—we're not paying for it, but go ahead!" So that certainly comes into the equation as well. Ultimately I live in Toronto because, while I am seduced by that, I'm not about to move in. My priority is still pretty much the same as it's always been. Hopefully it will stay that way.

PROVENANCE:
JOHN CORIGLIANO ON *THE RED VIOLIN*

The Red Violin is an ambitious—musically and narratively—moral fable centered on a remarkable three-hundred-year-old instrument. Told in flashbacks interwoven with a late-twentieth-century auction at which the violin is the prize attraction, the omnibus film follows the provenance of the instrument as it passes from owner to owner, from Italy through Europe and England and then to China and ultimately Montreal. The influence the violin has on its owners mysteriously reflects the prognostications of a seventeenth-century tarot-card reader who (as the film's framing device) is ostensibly predicting the life path of the violin maker's progeny.

"The movie is about the passion and love for music and the many ways music is used and abused and thought of," said John Corigliano, who composed not only a central theme but also a chaconne* centered on the violin, as well as a series of related études that are performed live, on camera, in succeeding centuries. The result is a virtuoso musical odyssey in which the intimacy of the violin (as backed by the film soundtrack's string-only orchestra) is made all the more potent by the persistent inability of the characters to truly *own* the instrument. The violin becomes a taunting, challenging, and unforgiving muse.

▶

JOHN CORIGLIANO: The story basically deals with this woman, Anna, who was the violin maker's wife, and him building this violin for their anticipated son (she was pregnant). And this tarot-fortune-teller through the whole film tells her this history of what her son will do. What she's *really* telling is what the *violin* will do.

The film went through three centuries and five different countries and five different languages, and the only thing that stayed the same was the violin. The cast would change, everything would change, so you needed a very strong musical thread to bind it together. Part of my decision to do this film was the fact that music was *necessary* to make it a cohesive whole.

I wanted a structure on which I could build everything; because the piece is so varied, I felt it needed a unity to make coherent the fact that this is an unbroken line from 1690 to 1990. And so the chaconne was to give a sense of order to the diffuseness. It had seven episodes of this tarot dealer, so I used seven chords to build everything for the whole film. The seven chords represented those seven episodes right through to the present, the twentieth century, where these flashbacks would happen.

*A composition comprised of variations on a harmonic idea.

Importing order is very important, and I used that as an organizational process.

"Anna's Theme" plays against the chaconne as a counterpoint, so therefore it comes out of it, and so do all the other themes of the film. But that means that it's organic, and hence the variations that the violinist plays during the film all derive from "Anna's Theme," too, even though they're in the eighteenth- or nineteenth-century worlds. Plus the fact that the chaconne was underscored in variations in its own style. It gives a quality of unity which I felt otherwise would be sorely lacking. So that was really the problem I had dealing with the film, the diffuseness of it and yet the obsessiveness of it—I had to make that unity clear.

But when you got into live music, you had to get into the style of the period. You still had the same material, disguised. The director did not want to hit you in the face with it, he wanted to be very subtle about it, so he made me make it subtler and subtler every time. He said, "I can still hear it, in a sense," but I wanted to have it there as the foundation.

Originally the director, François Girard, had asked you to write around other composers' violin pieces that would have been performed on camera.

CORIGLIANO: I said, "There's no point in having you play Bach and Paganini and Mozart and me do a background score. First of all, why call me? What's in it for me?" We talked out the business of the original theme being the basis of the études and that I had to write them, and if he had said no to that, I wouldn't have written the score. And second, I think using the violin repertoire is a bad idea because it's not organic—pieces are all over the place. And I can write music in those other periods, [so] I said that's the only way I would do the film. And he said, "Well, I understand that. As long as it isn't too obvious, that makes sense to me." And then I mentioned only using strings for the background score because it's an obsessive movie about a violin, and he loved that. So what I like about François is he is very musical—he plays the piano, he reads, he's listened to every violin piece ever written, he's done his homework—and you can talk to him. So there were times where he did things that I wasn't crazy about and some times when he was *right*, but at least he was someone I could talk to. And that's a big difference, a very big difference between that and the kind of film director that says no and just takes your music and throws out this, keeps that, plays something else here. He never did that. I always felt a collaborative aspect, and I respect him for that. And he respects me a lot, and I think that was part of it, because he came to me wanting something very special, not a traditional film composer thing but something a bit more unusual.

The film—and the score—is capped by an episode following the death during childbirth of Anna, in which the grieving violin maker finishes his instrument. It was one of the strangest love scenes one could imagine, but the music seems stripped to its very thematic essence there—back to the beginning—rather than a climax.

CORIGLIANO: Anna's blood was mixed in with the varnish with which he painted the violin—a few drops of blood were put into it, which colored it—and in fact it was painted with a brush that he cut from her hair. So it's a very mystical scene. That was a scene in which I tried very hard to write super-romantic music. I took "Anna's Theme" and played the first and second violins against each other with these low, rich chords as if to say, this is the most romantic thing he could do, the most loving thing he could do, but it's not the *craziest* thing! There I specifically set out to romanticize this and make it believable, that it really

The stuff that dreams are made of: *The Red Violin*.

could happen—because it *is* kind of crazy, of course, that you mix the blood and then paint the violin. The music could have tottered off into almost-horror and made it ludicrous.

How did you get involved with the production to begin with, since you hadn't done a film score in over a decade?

CORIGLIANO: Sony was in on this before I was. Sony had worked with Rhombus Media with a lot of Yo-Yo Ma projects, like the "Inspired by Bach" series of cello suites. Peter Gelb, the president of Sony Classical, loved the *Red Violin* script. I was speaking to Peter about Yo-Yo and Emanuel Ax doing a record of stuff of mine they'd played, and he said, "That's all very good, but actually I know that chamber music isn't going to sell very much, but there is something I am really interested in, and it's this movie because I think it's a great script and it could really go places. Take it home and read it." And I said I don't really feel like doing films anymore because my last experience was not the best, and I don't need to financially. And he just said, "Well, take it home." And I did. The script was damn good, and I called him back and said I wouldn't mind doing this. He then set up a meeting with me and François.

So I met with the director and we had to get to know each other—we were kind of wary of each other at first. I was *very* wary of directors, so I had to decide whether this was a director I wanted to work with.

Had you seen Girard's *Thirty-two Short Films About Glenn Gould*?

CORIGLIANO: Yes, and I liked it, but I thought this script was much better. *Thirty-two Short Films* was a little arty; I liked it, but there were things I didn't like about it. I felt this script represented a growth because it keeps this elevated attitude but it doesn't go into what I would call an "art-film-only" atmosphere, which the other one did. I didn't want to just do an art film, and this I think can reach out. It is limited because it doesn't have Leonardo DiCaprio in it and there's no single character, nobody has a major role, so it's not the same kind of film as *Shine*, for example, where you have this creature that everybody sympathizes with. I mean, *Shine* could be a baseball story, it just happened to be a music story, but it involved a kind of crazy person and *could he surmount his craziness?* That's what it was about, and the music was just incidental in a sense, it wasn't integral—whereas in *The Red Violin* the music *is* the story.

When did you decide to do a concert piece based on the film's music?

CORIGLIANO: The decision was done by Peter Gelb—Sony had an agreement with Rhombus to produce the music, so they paid for the music production and of course the soundtrack CD, and they own the publishing to that. I had mixed feelings about [doing a concert version], I wasn't sure I wanted to do it. I'm really happy now I did because it turned out well, but I didn't know if I could make it into a concert piece and I kept telling him that, and the next thing I know he scheduled it with the San Francisco Symphony and a tour with the Boston Symphony in Carnegie Hall, the Kennedy Center with Seiji Ozawa and Cleveland and Toronto . . . ! And I said, "I didn't agree to do this yet!" So then we had to negotiate a contract and go through all that and I had the summer to write it.

I wasn't sure that I could do a concert piece that flat-out romantic. But when I heard it, I felt very glad that he forced me into the position of writing it! I wouldn't have done it; I would have procrastinated and just said, "Well, I don't know if this is the right subject for that," but he wanted to do it and he arranged it, because Peter can call any orchestra and conductor and say, "Put this on," and they will! He got Esa-Pekka Salonen to conduct the Philharmonia with Joshua Bell in the recordings. Peter can do that. And I really hand it to him, he puts really good things together sometimes; the result is pretty staggering. I listen to the performance we did at Abbey Road studios, and the recording quality and the excitement of that, it's just a fabulous concert piece. I'm saying this braggardly, but partly because the production values were so high and it sounds so damn good that I'm really glad I wrote it!

What I'm going to do is add two more movements, since this is eighteen minutes long, all I need is two more movements and I've got a thirty-minute concerto, which I will do in a few years—which gets complicated legally because Sony will own the first movement and Schirmer, my publisher, will own the other two!

In fact, the order of events of *The Red Violin* is unique to me because of the live playing. Obviously I had to write these caprices (which were performed on camera) beforehand, and in order to write those I had to derive the seven-chord chaconne and "Anna's Theme" (as well as the funeral music and a few other things). So first I had to derive this, then I had to compose these pieces that were played on-screen. Then when they went and filmed it, Joshua Bell (who recorded the solos) went on some of the shoots to help the players' fingering when they were done to playback. While they were doing that, I was composing the "Chaconne for Violin and Orchestra," based on the materials that I had: the études, the chaconne, and "Anna's Theme." That was written for full orchestra. And on the week that that was premiered, I was given the tape of the film to score.

Unlike the concert piece, the film's score was written for strings only. Was that limiting to you in any way, not having the other sections to bring in?

CORIGLIANO: Strings are far less limited than you can imagine. The string section can sound like an orchestra, but the winds and brass [alone] cannot. The fact that we don't use them doesn't take away from the orchestral sound, because strings really are the basis of the orchestra. And a trumpet can make like two or three different sounds—if you put a mute on it, it sounds *slightly* different, but it's still just a trumpet—but a string section makes so many different sounds that it's really an orchestra in itself, if you use it that way. And that's the way it was used. People don't miss it, they don't even know it's not a [complete] orchestra. But it gives a richness to it. I remember *Psycho*, [which was] only strings. So this is probably the second score like that. It does give it a special quality if you limit yourself that way.

What was very interesting was, in the building of the chaconne, the developmental things happened in "Anna's Theme" and the rest of the music which I could then incorporate *back* into the film. So again the cross-pollination happened: the original source material being used to make a violin and orchestra piece, and then the violin and orchestra piece used to go back to be added to the film score. So on the soundtrack CD, we first hear the string orchestra playing the whole film score—well, not all of it, but a representative amount—and then you hear the "Chaconne for Violin and Orchestra." I like that you can hear and identify how one piece grew from a series of shorter cues into an eighteen-minute entity.

Josh is a terrific violinist—he's immaculate, he's overly perfectionistic, which I *loved*. He came in knowing all the notes and everything. He was going to record it, he could have read it, but he knew it by heart, and was very quick to make changes. If you need a change he can make it immediately, super, super smart, he's a terrific violinist, and I have great admiration for him, and he listens to me—which he should, because I wrote it—but he comes up with interesting suggestions sometimes and I listen to him. I'd never worked with him before; he's played my violin sonata like fifty times and I'd never heard him play it! I didn't know whether he'd be difficult to work with or not, but he's fairly reasonable. On the other hand it's like François; it doesn't mean he's just an obedient servant, he also has a point of view and expresses it. I like that because we can talk it out and come to a better conclusion. What I don't like is rigidity or total submissiveness, because with either one you don't get really a point of view—if someone is rigid, they get their way, you can't make your points; and if they do everything you say then there's no personality.

I'LL SHOW THEE WONDROUS THINGS, THAT HIGHLY MAY ADVANTAGE THEE TO HEAR: ELLIOT GOLDENTHAL ON *TITUS*

Ritual blood sacrifice, beheadings, dismemberment, rape, murder, and a rather unsavory vengeance in the form of a meat pie containing a mother's own children—such are the hallowed ingredients of what is perhaps Shakespeare's least honored play, a tale of revenge and mocking treachery during the waning days of the Roman Empire. Nonetheless, *Titus Andronicus* proves, in Julie Taymor's rich film adaptation *Titus*, to be a monumental story of clashing cultures and generational power struggles. Filmed among ruins in Rome and Croatia, the production also features sumptuous sets that speak more of the twentieth century than of the fourth. Costumes run the gamut from Roman-era armor to dinner jackets to punk fashions. And props include microphones, pool tables, and champagne flutes.

Titus walks a dangerously fine line—it would be easy

for a period film in which Roman troops drive motorcycles and tanks and where a young prince plays video games, to be viewed as over-the-top. But the film keeps its balance throughout—its anachronisms enrich rather that detract— partly because of the support given by Elliot Goldenthal's music. His score sways from heart-stopping, percussive military airs to hyperactive dance music and electronica. And while it is keyed into the stark, often surreal visuals, the music's bold and sometimes jocular sound reinforces the humanity of the tale—thereby unscoring its timelessness.

▶

I was impressed by the boldness of mixing different, seemingly anachronistic designs in the film, and how the music was able to match these juxtapositions without being jarring.

ELLIOT GOLDENTHAL: There was one surviving print that was contemporary to Shakespeare of a performance of *Titus Andronicus*, and the print showed the costume design in Shakespeare's time; it had people in togas *and* Elizabethan garb, so even in its inception the costumes were both contemporary and ancient. So I think there is that built-in quality of telling an old story in a new time. In that respect, Julie Taymor is a twenty-first-century director telling a story written by a sixteenth- or seventeenth-century guy talking about a vague area of Roman history somewhere around A.D. 300 or 400, and with references to Christianity, that has a "no-timeness." And one can't have anachronisms in no-timeness. But in solving problems, like how do you dramatize two people (Saturninus and Bassianus) electioneering, how do you make that interesting for an audience? By having them in cars going through Roman streets!

All this stuff might seem unusual until you actually go to

Rome, where you see people in front of ancient Roman temples with boom boxes, people dressed up like ancient Etruscans taking snapshots of tourists, people with rings through their tongues and green hair, guys that look like they're out of *La Dolce Vita*, Lambourghinis from the 1950s, edifices built by Mussolini, you see *everything*. And then you see supermodern fashions that might resemble the toga more than they resemble a suit and a tie. There's no anachronism; that's exactly what Rome *is*!

The film originated from Taymor's New York stage production in 1995 for which you composed the music. Was much of that music retained for the movie?

GOLDENTHAL: Well, about thirty seconds of music from the stage production got into the film. The stage production was done with electronic tape and two trumpets, and it was very effective. There were transition scenes, but I did have underscoring for entire scenes as well. It was very soft, backstage, electronic stuff.

The advantage of working on the stage production was that I memorized the play before I did the movie, so it helped in terms of a deeper understanding of the web of plot that Shakespeare wrote.

Shakespeare is really difficult to compose for because you never really have a clear-cut, good/evil/funny guy like you do in *Batman* for example. I mean Bruce Wayne/Batman lives a double life but they're both basically heroic guys. Everybody is archetypal and very mythic, almost Wagnerian.

But in Shakespeare it's not that simple. Who's the villain in *Titus Andronicus*? Is it the guy that started out as a General Schwarzkopf–type who then baked people into pies? Is it the slave Aaron whose past we don't know—who knows *what* was done to him?—that's living in a world of treachery; why doesn't he just participate in that treachery and be the *most* treacherous, if he's going to be stomped on anyway? Is Tamora, the Goth Queen, evil after pleading for her son's life and calling out, "Cruel irreligious piety!" Is she evil? Who do you root for?

For the film, particularly because there were these blatant juxtapositions of style and fashion, were you forced to be more literal in terms of what music does dramatically? Or were you able to ignore the visuals and write more inside the characters' heads, as it were, evoking their state of mind?

GOLDENTHAL: The literature of Shakespeare, again, is such that there are so many meanings in one scene. So you look for certain constants in the structure of the drama. In one case, there seemed to be times when different characters find themselves in a similar position: the Goth Queen, Titus, and Aaron (the three major characters) beg for their children's lives to be saved. So you say, what if I write a theme, say, a "Compassion Theme" or "Pity Theme" and repeat that—would it work? So I wrote this one theme away from the film at the piano. I thought of it as a two-part partita—there are two people involved, one that's begging, one that can give reprieve—so it's in two-part counterpoint. And indeed it did work; it worked for Tamora, it worked for Titus, it worked for Aaron—*and* it worked for Lavinia [Titus's daughter, who is raped and mutilated]. It worked every time those characters were begging for their lives or pleading for their children.

Was this one theme orchestrated differently depending upon the character?

GOLDENTHAL: Very little difference, basically string orchestration.

Then there were generational differences, and I felt that for the older generation (Titus, Tamora, Aaron) the music tended to be a little more orchestral; for Saturninus and Bassianus, the younger electoral candidates, I thought they were more in a jazz age—certainly because they used jazzy automobiles and Mussolini's governmental palace, and you had these dance sequences for which music had to be precomposed (Julie wanted people to be swing dancing). It seems like the sophisticated thing to do if you were a sort of jazzy Roman king! And clearly Tamora's children were more in the age of punk rock. So the art direction and costumes were key in designing that.

In shifting from one musical style to another, did you maintain a melodic consistency?

GOLDENTHAL: Yes, for sure. It always helps to hang your hat on a theme. I think I do in every film—even in *Batman*. You have one theme and you manipulate it. It could be a heroic kind of thing or a campy dance sequence.

I liked how the saxophone was introduced when the newspaper flutters into the shot announcing Caesar's death— one seeming anachronism heralds another.

GOLDENTHAL: If you noticed, that melody was picked up from the English horns. There is an eight-note theme that the English horn did in the previous scene and then the saxophone picks up the exact notes.

I wanted the whole beginning of the film to feel like it was going to be an ancient period (even though you're seeing all these tanks and stuff). I wanted this chorus, which is, by the way, singing material cut, which was the original speech of Titus's entrance ("Romans, make way: the good Andronicus. Patron of virtue, Rome's best champion"). I had that translated into Latin and sung, so it is still Shakespeare! So we wanted this chorus and percussion, and then it got dark [in the tombs] and there are Tibetan bowls and still voices in Latin singing from Ovid.

Then for the first time the camera comes up and the whole screen is *filled* with light. Everything is bright, it's a sunny day, there's a child out there, there's a newspaper: "Caesar's Dead." And I wanted the audience to smile! If the audience smiled or even chuckled a bit, they would get what *Titus Andronicus* is all about, which is the juxtaposition between horror and comedy. And I thought that a saxophone would make people smile.

It made *me* smile!

GOLDENTHAL: Good! And then having Saturninus and Bassianus electioneering with this cool jazz. Otherwise, having to swallow the pill of exposition can be very, very tedious, you know?

Again, there was one theme in the beginning that's slightly warmer, when Titus is with his daughter and he says, "Lavinia, live." Funny, in the beginning of the movie he says, "Lavinia, live," and in the end he says "Die, die, Lavinia!"

Now, did you repeat that particular theme when he kills her at the end?

GOLDENTHAL: No, I didn't; I brought back the theme of compassion when the child, Young Lucius, walks into the shop of

Cultured clashes: *Titus.*

the woodcarver, the maker of the saints, and he sees all the carved hands and gets a pair of hands to bring to Lavinia. (It's not in Shakespeare, this is Julie.) I used that theme also when Marcus discovers Lavinia on the pedestal with her hands cut off, and also at the end when the father has compassion for her and performs euthenasia. It was directed in a very tender way; the daughter knew her father was going to do this mercy killing, and it wasn't a horrific, angry act. And Anthony Hopkins's performance wasn't rash; it certainly wasn't a spur-of-the-moment killing by a madman. So in that way I wanted the music to be noble, reaching for something that had a connotation of compassion.

In Titus's arrow attack on Saturninus's court, there was this repeated musical pattern that reminded me of the minimalism of John Adams.

GOLDENTHAL: As much as I love John Adams, there was nothing either specific or general I was thinking about [in terms of minimalism]. I was thinking about a repeated figure which to me sounded very martial—that Titus was maybe winning a little bit!—and the musical ideograph of this marcato kind of motif which might have been used by Vivaldi or Mendelssohn has a pointedness, an arrowlike quality to it. And then I subjected it to the Beethoven approach in the sense of using that motif and an inversion of the motif underneath that, just by pitting that inversion together created a very, very tight thing which might seem minimalist but is really being as stingy motivically as you can be.

Portraying madness through music is tricky in *Titus*, because the audience may be led to believe that Titus is

mad, as Tamora and the others think him. But he may be simply feigning madness to draw people closer to him so he can kill them. That may not be madness after all.

GOLDENTHAL: Yes, but you can also draw the theory that there are certain types of madness that are clarity.

Did you try to portray Titus's state of mind musically, whether you make an editorial judgment on his madness or not?

GOLDENTHAL: There's a device in the movie that Julie and I like to call "Penny Arcade Nightmares." These are images where the Shakespeare stops and there's a frozen suggestion of a certain connotation of feelings, like a tableau—they're sort of fissures or cracks in the character of Titus. You get a sense that his sense of well being on a day-to-day basis is being completely turned askew. Whether it's madness or not, that's still up to the audience. I wanted to keep that up to the audience.

So is madness clarity? I think we were after that, too—not necessarily the music getting more and more dissonant but more and more "extra-real." For example, when Titus is in the bathtub alone and clearly a little bit "out there," making pictures on pieces of paper with his own blood and planning his retribution, he hears Tamora putting on this play of *Rape, Revenge, and Murder.* It's very surreal, but as soon as he looks outside the window and actually sees her, he says, "Why from up and down you look like the dread queen Tamora." The madness stops—and there's nothing in the scoring that suggests it.

How did you decide on "Vivere," this jaunty Italian song played under the horrific final banquet scene?

GOLDENTHAL: I was thinking about that song since I was a boy almost. I was always terribly fascinated by the ghostly sound of that song; it sounded like people having themselves a real ball during the last moments of fascist Italy, sort of like showing up at a picnic with friends on a perfectly sunny day and hearing a rumble of thunder in the distance. So I was juxtaposing the fascist European era with the apparent gaiety of that song and the irony of the lyrics—something like "Live and enjoy life" in the 1930s, which is like the anacrusis to the crucifixion of civilization.

You see, for me a lot of these projects are almost about nonmusical issues. I really, really hate Wagner's approach to life, but yet I can understand why he was so obsessed with the nonmusical issues of the dramas he was doing.

Shakespeare does things in this play that idiots who think it's a bad play are way, way off. For example, in every production I've ever seen, Titus—in this hideously absurdist scene where the sons' heads are returned with his severed hand—tells his children to take the heads and he tells his [now handless] daughter to put his hand in her mouth so she can carry it back. And in every production that gets a laugh. You say, *What's going through Shakespeare's mind?* Here's a guy who's already written most of his sonnets—he's not some dumb young idiot writing a play. What did he do this for? Well, it's *genius!* Earlier in that scene, Marcus says, "Why are you laughing?" And Titus says, "Because I have no more tears to shed." He's laughing at the horror. So to draw the point home, three minutes later Shakespeare makes the audience laugh at the horror, puts you in the position Titus was in a second ago, as he's constantly putting you in the position of that person that might be capable of creating a horrific act.

■

LOST AND FOUND:
ROBERT TOWNSON ON ALEX NORTH, *2001,*
AND THE ART OF THE SOUNDTRACK ALBUM

Most always an offshoot of a film studio's marketing division, a commercially released recording of film music is a unique opportunity for a single element of a motion picture to be exploited outside of a cinema. While published scripts rarely sell in high numbers, and the work of costumers or set designers is generally ignored by licensors, soundtracks can sell due to a film's popularity while at the same time draw a composer's fans to a film which they might otherwise ignore. (It is a curious fact, for instance, that some collectors would readily purchase a favorite composer's score album without ever seeing the film it was written for, which means—for them—the music will always live outside of its purpose within the film.)

Often the score for a film that failed at the box office will get its due from a release on record or CD. For instance,

Somewhere in Time was not a big hit when first released, but sales of John Barry's soundtrack album took off when the film premiered on cable TV. But while studios will acknowledge the ability of a popular soundtrack to help sell a movie—whether it is a film score such as *Doctor Zhivago* or *Titanic*, or a song compilation like *Saturday Night Fever*—they rarely release film scores that (to them) show little promise of financial success, regardless of their intrinsic artistic value. Some scores by such recognized and popular masters as Bernard Herrmann, Jerry Goldsmith, and John Williams have never been released on disc, leaving the door open for bootleggers to satisfy a film buff or music student's curiosity. (Among the best scores that only exist on bootleg recordings is John Williams's masterful and hypnotic music for Robert Altman's *Images*, much of it performed on steel wire sculptures by percussionist Stomu Yamashta; clearly uncommercial, the atonal and sometimes violent music is one of the composer's very best works.)

Recordings can occasionally raise an important film score from the dead, even one that never had a proper birth. One of the more celebrated releases of classic film music in recent years was a recording of Alex North's previously unheard music for Stanley Kubrick's *2001: A Space Odyssey*. Having worked successfully with Kubrick on *Spartacus*, North was hired for the epic science fiction film, which in the editing stages was temp-tracked with music by composers as diverse as Johann and Richard Strauss, György Ligeti, and Aram Khachaturian. North brought his modernist sensibilities to bear on the project, producing a startling work as bold as Kubrick's ideas and images.

For the early "Dawn of Man" sequence, which Kubrick had left largely unscored, North matched the harsh, desert-like vistas and meager existence of the apes with percussion, bells, low brass, and woodwinds producing chords and thematic motifs that sounded embryonic, until the introduction of the monolith—then, amid the chaos of the apes' reaction to this extraterrestrial object, there emerged a stately anthem heralding the dawning of a new intelligence.

For the scenes of traveling from Earth to the moon, North created balletic music of the spheres, celebrating the freedom of space flight. He also incorporated a solo voice reminiscent of Shirley Verret's elegy over the battle dead in *Spartacus*.

None of it was used; the film was released with the original temp tracks preserved. While *Also Sprach Zarathustra* (which opened the film) entered the popular lexicon of music, North's opening fanfare for *2001* was consigned to a shelf in the composer's closet. Though North was rumored to have worked his musical ideas into a symphony, and indeed incorporated some pieces into scores for other films, his music was perhaps the most famous rejected score in Hollywood history, made all the more notorious by the audience's enthusiastic acceptance of the film's official soundtrack.

Robert Townson, a record producer for Varèse Sarabande—a label devoted to soundtracks and new recordings of classic film music—talked of the effort to resurrect North's music, and of the general difficulties facing the production and marketing of film music recordings.

▶

ROBERT TOWNSON: I always considered Alex North one of the really great composers of film music. In 1993, having known Alex for a few years—he and I had become friends working on reissues of some of his older scores—we started talking one day at lunch about some new recordings. Of course we talked about

Spartacus and *Cleopatra* and *A Streetcar Named Desire*, all the scores he's so famous for. And over the course of the discussions (which Alex was very excited about), I started brushing every now and then on his lost and unused score for *2001: A Space Odyssey* that no one had ever heard. The famous story was how he was commissioned to write the score and was never told it wasn't going to be used in the film. [The scoring] was done certainly under difficult conditions—Alex was writing around the clock at the time and ended up ill, not able to conduct; he was literally taken to the sessions in an ambulance. He discovered only when he went to the premiere in New York in 1968, expecting to hear his score, that there was Strauss and Ligeti and the rest of the temp track. The effect of that left him kind of scarred and demoralized and devastated. He had put so much work into it and had never been through anything like that, and it definitely had an effect on him and became a real sore spot for him. He did everything he could to just put it out of his mind.

The only person who'd ever heard the music aside from the musicians that performed the score—it had been recorded in London—was Jerry Goldsmith. He and Alex had been friends for many years and after dinner one night when Jerry was over at Alex's, he asked if Jerry wanted to hear a cassette of *2001*. Of course Jerry jumped at the chance. And then sometime thereafter the cassette was actually misplaced! So from that point on, Jerry was the first *and* the last to ever hear it.

So, never having heard it but based on an undying and blind confidence in Alex as a composer, I started lobbying him to let people hear what he did. Luckily he felt comfortable and trusted me to help facilitate that and do a recording that would show people the *2001* that Alex had in mind. So he asked, "Well, who would conduct?" And I'd always thought of Jerry as the conductor of it, because there is such a connection there musically between the composing styles of the two men, [plus] they were friends. And Jerry was obviously an incredible legend all by himself, so the concept of doing a recording of Alex's *2001* with Jerry Goldsmith conducting was just unbeatable. So I just had to come back to the office that day and give Jerry a call, and pitch the concept. I didn't even have to have the whole question out of my mouth before he enthusiastically committed himself.

Were there legal problems with MGM over ownership of the music?

TOWNSON: No, because, blessedly, Alex had a clause in his original contract that allowed the ownership of the music—not the original recordings but the music itself—to revert to him if it was not used in a film for a period of two years. MGM had no ownership or control over his compositions themselves, so no one could stand in our way.

Do the original session tapes still exist or are they lost?

TOWNSON: As far as the original master tapes, I don't believe they're lost; my hunch is they're either in the archives in MGM or that Kubrick has them.

It took us a couple of years to actually get everyone's schedule in place and have time with the National Philharmonic Orchestra in London available in the studio, with the main difficulty Goldsmith's own composing schedule being as unrelenting as it always is. And sadly in a devastating sort of way, in the interim Alex passed away. Ultimately, in January 1993, we all got ourselves off to London, in Studio One at Abbey Road, with a 105-piece orchestra, and performed this music for the first time since the original session recordings. (Ironically, Alex's wife, Anna, had found the cassette literally just a few days before we left for London, so we did actually get to hear the original ses-

Jerry Goldsmith directing the National Philharmonic
Orchestra for the premier recording of Alex North's *2001*.

sions before we recorded. I'm not sure if Jerry listened to it; he
may not have.)

The score is really just sizzlingly brilliant and far-reaching in
its style and how contemporary and groundbreaking it is. So it
was definitely a major event to finally release that CD and let the
world hear this music. The response was overwhelmingly positive. Jerry and I were both on CNN and the *Today* show, all sorts
of coverage, because even aside from its musical relevance, it's
just such a legendary Hollywood story, probably the most infa-
mous story of that sort. The music of *2001* has always been such
an integral element of what *2001* is, and so to all of a sudden
have the *alternate* version, the way it could have been (or,
depending upon the point of view you bring to it, the way it
should have been), it was really wonderful and inspiring and
heartening to see it embraced the way it ultimately was.

Did you get any feedback from Kubrick himself?

TOWNSON: There wasn't any direct feedback, more kind of indirect in that I heard he was not pleased that we did the recording. I know he was hearing about it from a variety of sources. When I finally got in copies of the finished CD, I took some to the recording session for *Schindler's List*, which John Williams was conducting; Spielberg was there. So after one of the takes I pulled a few CDs out of my bag and John was checking it out, and Steven was just kind of glaring at it in disbelief, like *I can't believe I'm holding this,* because he hadn't heard about us doing it. For something that legendary to all of a sudden be in your hand when you've got no idea to expect it, it was really a fun moment: Here we are after John conducted the first recording of the end title from *Schindler's List* and everyone is focusing on the *2001* CD, John and Steven included! Steven said he was going to listen to it as soon as he got home and then call Stanley, so you can imagine the conversation that took place! Because everybody pretty unanimously was just loving the recording, and Stanley had always over the years taken credit as being the great genius behind the music of *2001,* and all of a sudden that was being brought into question, like, *Well, is that the way it should have been? Could it have been even deeper with the score that Alex wrote?*

Jerry has always said Kubrick's use of music in the film just ruined it for him. The waltz sequence is a great example; the waltz that Alex wrote for the Space Station sequence basically is just so much more fitting and kind of fanciful and highlighted the balletic aspect of it. Inserting "The Blue Danube" into the film brought different baggage; everyone would have preconceived notions of what that piece is to them, where they heard it first and what it is, and those aren't ideas or thoughts that you *want* to have imported into a movie like *2001,* or *any* film, unless you actually make a conscious decision that those are the feelings you *want* there, which is difficult because everyone will have a different association with it.

Was it common knowledge in film music circles that North had used bits of *2001* in his score for *Dragonslayer*, whose Dark Ages setting suited the music very well?

TOWNSON: It was, without being much of an issue. Sure, there are parts of it there, but not exactly verbatim, and then there's just so much of *2001* that's not there at all. So *2001* at this point does stand up as its own piece, and it's been a great pleasure to see it looked upon as one of Alex North's great masterpiece scores, a real integral piece of the puzzle that makes up Alex North as a composer.

How ironic to have something come from out of a black hole and we have the discovery of this great work—not a footnote, or fragments or sketches for the first movement of a tenth symphony. It would be more like having never known Beethoven's Seventh Symphony, and then all of a sudden that materializes!

What are some of the factors in deciding which older scores are rerecorded?

TOWNSON: Largely it's a delicate balancing act, the factors being: scores that I feel strongly about; things that I want to record, which is a dominant factor; and (hopefully) coming up with some commercial angle or some degree of popular appeal where you're going to have an audience and sell enough copies to recoup your cost. Frankly, in some cases it doesn't work that way. Certainly some of them do pretty well, but some of them need the ones that are doing pretty well or better than expected to help cover their back end.

Something like Bernard Herrmann's *The Trouble with Harry* or even North's *Viva Zapata!* are frankly tougher sells because, as highly thought of and respected in the inner circle of film music as they are, they don't reach that broader audience that will really help pay for themselves. We're not going off to Germany and finding some nonunion orchestra; we're not using reduced-sized orchestras or synth-supplemented things. It's full-scale Royal Scottish National Orchestra or London Symphony Orchestra or National Philharmonic Orchestra with world-class composer/conductors on the podium. But in a great many cases these recordings are done because I feel they really *have* to be done.

There are to varying degrees other recordings of music from *To Kill a Mockingbird,* in suite form and a couple of old recordings, but to my mind there was never a really definitive *To Kill a Mockingbird,* [which] to me is on the very, very short list of the greatest film scores ever composed; so that kind of made the cut. Elmer Bernstein and I went off to Scotland with, luckily, Elmer on the podium with the Royal Scottish National Orchestra, in a really world-class, state-of-the-art, twenty-bit digital recording. After we were done his first comments were, "Well, that's the best *that* score's ever sounded."

And then across the series you see these resurrections of scores and in some cases first discoveries of scores. For *Who's Afraid of Virginia Woolf,* the original soundtrack album was covered with dialogue from the film, so to finally let that exist on its own—do a new recording and have it be just about the music, which is one of the most understated but powerfully dramatic and emotional scores ever composed—was definitely one of the things that Jerry Goldsmith and I both felt very strongly needed to be done.

Do composers come to you to suggest scores to rerecord, or are you the one who approaches them?

TOWNSON: With almost no exceptions they start off as my idea. There was a CD of *Patton* and after we'd already started working on the project Jerry Goldsmith said, "Well, what about adding *Tora! Tora! Tora!* onto this?" I didn't need much convincing! [It had never been commercially released before.] That might be the only exception.

With rerecordings, do you present the music as it was first written, without consideration as to how it may have been altered or revised to fit changes in the film?

TOWNSON: The unwritten law is that I try our best effort to present the score in the way that is best representative of the way the composer intended the score to be; in the cases where we don't have the composer to consult with, our best guess. So if there were changes made, if they were director-notated changes that when weighed against the way the composer originally wrote it we feel [worked] against the integrity of the music, we would not incorporate those changes into our recordings. If they were composer-instigated changes where we feel it was a revision or improvement based on musical ideas that the composer had after he'd already put his pen down, then we do try and incorporate those.

The albums are about the music; there's no nod to the film per se that I try to maintain. It's already done its service to the picture, so now this will be about the music. For example, Jerry, after going through the score of *Virginia Woolf* and watching the film, noticed Alex in his performance was chasing the film through a couple of cues; he was picking up tempo in order to keep everything in sync.

Another popular trend is releasing expanded versions of previously released soundtrack albums, containing most if not all of the score. What would get in the way of that happening to, say, Jerry Goldsmith's score for *Gremlins*, whose soundtrack album featured mostly rock and disco songs and little of his orchestral score?

TOWNSON: What makes that one tricky is that the album produced at the time, those few Goldsmith cuts on the Geffen album, those tracks are owned by Geffen—they're the main themes of the picture. Now, the tracks that *aren't* on the Geffen album are still owned by Warner Brothers (the producers of the film); you would need to pay reuse fees on all of those tracks. So to rebuild the score you end up with dual ownership and control over different parts of the music. It makes assembling a single CD a very difficult thing to arrange. And as far as re-creating it, the amount of electronics in that score makes a new recording of *Gremlins* very difficult if not impossible. Jerry and I did talk about that at one point; we just both kind of sighed in horror of what it would entail to try and do, and sadly moved on.

What can you expect to sell on a classic score rerecording?

TOWNSON: Obviously we're not talking in the hundreds of thousands [of units] and barely even into the tens of thousands. Hopefully, over time they build the numbers; and the numbers are all relative. The budgets over them vary quite a bit, but they are expensive projects, and certainly some of them because of their scale simply aren't covering themselves.

There are so many hurdles for these things, so many demons to conquer. One problem that's cropped up far more often than not, once we decide, "We're going to record *The Sand Pebbles*," is discovering that none of the music for *The Sand Pebbles* has survived all of these years. The orchestral parts for so many of the great scores have been discarded. In many cases we had to have the scores completely reorchestrated from composer sketches or from scratch by taking a take-down from some of the cue's original recordings. It's an often-proved horror story of Hollywood of the dilapidated state of the film music archives at the studios. It varies from studio to studio, but more often than not it's not a very pretty picture.

Do you think the growing popularity of classic film music has spurred preservation efforts?

TOWNSON: Yes, absolutely. It's definitely changing. I work with all of the studios on their new films, which kind of helps round out the relationship; they know they're going to get calls from me periodically where I need some older items. Sometimes not even that much older. We had a series called *Hollywood '94, Hollywood '95*, etc., where we'd record an overview of the summer's popular films. On one of them, we were going to record a theme from Joel McNeely's *Flipper*, and when we went to retrieve the parts from Universal those parts had been lost already—it had only been recorded two months earlier in London. Everyone was checking their archives, checking in London to see if they'd shipped, nobody had them there and Universal didn't have anything here. Finally, a couple of days before we left for the recording, long after we had admitted defeat and replaced that piece with something else, there was a call from Universal that someone had found the parts we were looking for just sitting in the corner of someone's office—it had been misdelivered. You could just picture it: a stack of orchestra parts built up as a little table with a telephone on top of it. So luckily we got the recording in after all, but it shows you how easy it is for something to be lost; all of a sudden there's one more gone.

Did parts exist for your rerecording of *Citizen Kane*?

TOWNSON: No, *Citizen Kane* was long gone, *Great Escape* was long gone, *Magnificent Seven*, *Patton*, *Sand Pebbles*, chunks of *Mockingbird*. *Vertigo* was in pretty good shape, *Psycho* was in pretty good shape. *Logan's Run* was gone, *Out of Africa* was gone, *Body Heat*. *Superman* was gone. *Viva Zapata!* was gone, *The Agony and the Ecstasy* was gone. *Somewhere in Time* had parts but no scores. *Streetcar Named Desire* existed, of all things. You can see that batting average would send you back to the minors pretty fast.

As grave as you think it is, after I have done this for so long, it's always worse than your worst nightmare. It's almost never a *pleasant* surprise.

■

END TITLES

What responses do you hear from people about how well music might have fit into a film?

MARK ISHAM: I guess you hear a lot of the time, "The music was too loud," which means that basically it didn't mesh with the film properly, but that it pulled you out and called attention to itself. But if you get comments like "Great score," it usually means that it brought attention to itself *just enough* but never pulled you out of the movie. That's probably the line you're always trying to find. I think producers always want that feeling: Guys walk out of the theater humming something, that they're *happy* to hum it, they don't feel that they've been assaulted by it or had it forced on them, it just sort of comes to them in a natural way.

What gives you the most satisfaction about your work right now?

MICHAEL KAMEN: The ability to pontificate about what I've done is very nice! Because I think I'm very prone to it. And the genuine regard that I think I'm being held in by my record label, which is affording me all sorts of freedoms, like writing a symphony and thinking about projects that I wouldn't normally be able to indulge myself in under the guise of being a "film composer." I've worked with some of the world's greatest artists, directors, actors, and I have been extraordinarily fortunate. I really don't have any more than a few dozen scars from glancing blows from the industry that are probably tantamount to awards; when you have battle scars, presumably the battle was worth fighting.

When you're not writing scores for films, do you work on nonfilm music?

JERRY GOLDSMITH: I have to keep writing. You want to keep in training. It's also what I enjoy most.

What composers are favorites of yours, in and out of the film world?

GOLDSMITH: Stravinsky, Bartók, Alban Berg, Debussy. Alex North. John Williams does some real nice things; David Shire does, too.

DAVID RAKSIN: I don't want to say, because I know too many composers and I'd leave somebody out. But I have to say that [among recent film scores] I have heard two masterpieces, and those are John Williams's *Schindler's List* and Ennio Morricone's *The Mission*.

ELMER BERNSTEIN: I'm fairly catholic; I'm very, very partial to Bach, to Brahms, to Chopin, to much of Tchaikovsky, Debussy, Bartók, some of Stravinsky (not all), Copland, some of Benjamin Britten. So I'd say that my tastes are fairly wide-ranging in that field.

In film music, Bernard Herrmann I'd say would be right at the top of the list; surely David Raksin has done some things which I think are extraordinary, as did Miklos Rozsa, Franz Waxman, certainly; some of Alex North's are absolutely outstanding, though I'm not an expert on all his scores. Of people more of my generation, I suppose I'd put Jerry Goldsmith on top of the list, obviously John Williams, certainly Henry Mancini (a different genre, but very effective), if you get younger than that, another generation down, certainly James Horner, and Bruce Broughton, who's a very, very interesting composer.

It's amazing how many composers have at one time written scores that one can admire, even if it wasn't consistent, people like Roy Webb—some of his scores are quite amazing!

ALAN MENKEN: The classics: Beethoven, Brahms, Schumann, Mahler, Stravinsky, Prokofiev, Bartók, Chopin, Debussy, Ravel, the impressionism of Copland, Bernstein . . . I'm sure there are others! Pop music: Certainly, like everyone else, the Beatles, Elton John, Randy Newman, Joni Mitchell. I never was consciously influenced by film scorers particularly, I just got into that fairly recently. I always enjoyed John Williams's scores and Jerry Goldsmith's scores; I think those were my favorites.

Is there any recent score you've heard that stands out in your mind as being truly different or special?

DAVID SHIRE: Almost everything of Thomas Newman's. He's a composer who always seems to find like a specific voice, a musical voice, for each film. There's never a generic score. He always finds something ear-catching in particular and I *love* that. I think he's one of the classiest out there. John Williams, I'm always thrilled by his music, but he's much more versatile than Hollywood lets him be most of the time. He can write anything, and he's written some very avant-garde things like *Images*, an astounding score. Or even *The Eiger Sanction*, stuff that wasn't necessarily a symphony orchestra pumping away.

I learn something from almost everybody I listen to: Jerry Goldsmith, Lalo Schifrin, Dave Grusin, Jerry Fielding (who did all the Clint Eastwood movies). And the constant nourishment of the classics—I mean, I never stop studying scores and trying to take apart music that I enjoy and thought was effective but didn't quite know how it was made, to get the scores and get the records and study them.

THE STATE OF THE ART

What do you think of the general state of film music today?

SHIRE: I think movies have become too inbred in many ways, where movies are about other movies or about the style and history of film. I got a slinger the other day for a symposium, and the subject of the panel was "Why do most movie scores sound the same these days?" It was a very good thing to discuss. It relates to safety. There's a lot of safe scoring going on in movies, where they get the flavor of the month: the Hans Zimmer sound, the James Horner sound. These are people who write very good scores and establish styles of their own, and they don't want to repeat themselves any more than anybody else does, but pictures are temped with them, and if they can't get Hans Zimmer they still want a "Hans Zimmer score." I was asked once to do a "Danny Elfman score," and I said, "Well, why don't you get Danny Elfman?" And they said, "Well, we can't *afford* him."

GOLDSMITH: Now is certainly not the greatest time for film music. There's a preponderance of dilettantes and sophomoric people in the business, but filmmaking is a cyclical thing. Those who have talent will grow regardless of the circumstances. And those who don't will ultimately fall by the wayside.

I think it's appalling, the state of film music. I've finally come to that conclusion, having watched enough. I mean, there's no bigger champion of electronic music than me; I've been involved with electronics since the early sixties. But I'm sort of appalled by the *mis*use of it now; it's dreadful. Forget about the lack of musicality; the nonrelationship of the music to the dramatic content of the film is what's shocking—it's nonsense. If I hear another set of drums on a picture I'm going to jump out of my skin.

Yet I love all those things—I love using the drums, and all the electronics. But music for films has descended to episodic television music, and even *that's* gotten pretty low. It had never been great, but at least it was somewhat imaginative. And now, as far as I'm concerned it's all interchangeable—one sounds like another. I keep praying that this is [merely] a trend.

It seems like film's becoming just a big video to sell compilation records: "Let's track a picture with pop songs, then let's see how many of these we can stick on an album and sell." You look at a picture today and at the end there are a zillion song credits.

Is buying preexisting music cheaper for a producer than hiring someone to write and record new music?

GOLDSMITH: It's not a matter of saving money on a score; it's a matter of *selling records*. It's tremendous, the clearance costs— the sync rights to these songs can end up [costing] hundreds of thousands of dollars by the time they total it up.

The record industry is the same as the film industry; they're always looking for hundred-million-dollar grosses on pictures, and they're looking for platinum and double platinum on albums. So there's not really a big desire on the part of record companies to put out [score] albums. Again, unless it was *Star Wars*, which was a freak, motion picture soundtracks just don't sell in the kind of numbers that record companies are used to.

A lot of instances they'll go to electronics to save money, but they've been trying to save money on music since films first started being made. There are ways of doing pictures economically, musically. But that doesn't mean that the quality of the music has to degenerate so much. God only knows, I've done enough low-budget pictures in my time; hopefully, the music was valid. But now in so many instances the music doesn't make sense in a film.

When you're watching some of these pictures, do you just grate your teeth, knowing you would have done something differently?

GOLDSMITH: Not that I wish I had done it. Most of the pictures I would be glad I *didn't* do! I just don't understand—forget what the composer's doing, what the *filmmaker* was thinking. And I've always been so impressed with the younger filmmakers, their awareness of music. I've taught and I've lectured enough at film schools and universities, and I've worked with enough of the younger directors, to know they're so keen on music and what it can do. And yet so many of them sit back through this nonmusical music, nothing much more than sound effects. Sound effects would be better!

As I've said, a big rock video. And I thought I had seen all these trends. Pop music in pictures, whether it was jazz or early pop or rock 'n' roll, I've seen it come and go. But this seems to be the longest period. I haven't lost work because of it, it isn't that. I just hate to see what was developing into a twentieth-century art form sort of falling apart. I see this sort of constant quality of mediocrity. I never thought I'd live to see the day I'd start saying things like this, but God, I'd love to hear something really special in the music, and I don't.

I'm just judging the *relationship* of film to music, that's all I'm judging really. But this isn't what I was taught; this isn't the way music is *supposed* to work in films. I have to take a class in how to sell records!

It's not *all* blues as far as I'm concerned. I really think that, as long as there are filmmakers (and there always will be) that are sensitive and understand drama, there will always be a use, a *need* for good music. I must say as sort of a disclaimer for what I've been saying, perhaps this kind of pop music is also influenced by the pop style and pop influence in film itself—and, I suppose, in our culture, the whole pop invasion of our social mores. It's there, where we eat, what we wear. Films are more or less crafted to reflect the influence of the pop music and pop culture of our country, so that's why so much of it is used. Take *Ladyhawke*; their attempt to do rock 'n' roll I think was a bit around the bend. But *Risky Business should* be like that. And if you're going to approach it that way then fine, but do it with at least *some* skill!

What would your advice be to young composers who want to write for film?

RAKSIN: The first thing they have to learn is to be composers. And there are a lot of guys who are not, who have coteries of young guys on the way up who will work for them; they'll write some little piece of material and make a cassette of it, and give it to somebody else who *really* writes the score, which is horrible to think about but it exists.

So I say to them, *learn*; run the great films with great film scores of the past; get cassettes, which we were unable to do, and run them again and see what the great men of picture music have done. And then see if you can do it while expressing yourself to the advantage of the film. In other words, have you got a gift? If so, nurture it and then *use* it.

■

APPENDIX

SOURCES

Author interviews with **Elmer Bernstein** (March and October 1991); **Carter Burwell** (March 1998); **Elia Cmiral** (September 1999); **John Corigliano** (April and May 1998); **Patrick Doyle** (September 1999); **Mychael Danna** (October 1999); **Philip Glass** (November 1999); **Elliot Goldenthal** (February 2000); **Jerry Goldsmith** (March 1986, September 1987); **Mark Isham** (March and April 1998); **Michael Kamen** (April 1998); **Alan Menken** (July 1992, November 1999); **Basil Poledouris** (October 1999); **Jocelyn Pook** (November 1999); **David Raksin** (December 1998); **David Shire** (October 1999); and **Robert Townson** (January 1999).

In addition, the following sources were quoted:

9 Corigliano: "My ear is always open . . ." Mark Lehman, "*FI* Interview: John Corigliano," *FI*, November 1997.

13 Goldsmith: "Basically I am looking for the humanistic values . . ." Elmer Bernstein, "A Conversation with Jerry Goldsmith," *Film Music Notebook*, Vol. 3, No. 2, 1977.

20 Shire: "There are nine major themes . . . the theme for Ozma." David Kraft, "David Shire on *Return to Oz*," *CinemaScore*, Winter 1986/Summer 1987.

21 Shire: "Ozma is really Dorothy's alter ego . . . while living in the real world." Ibid.

22 Shire: "I had the Ozma theme early on . . . to be telegraphed at all." Ibid.

22 Shire: "'Tik Tok's Theme' features . . . each of the little characters' themes threaded through it." Ibid.

30 Kamen: "I didn't ever try to set it in . . ." Interview by Sean Wright Anderson for the Criterion Collection laserdisc/DVD of *Brazil*, May 1996.

30 Kamen: "Terry and I had funny conversations . . . Oh, *that's* funny!" Ibid.

30 Kamen: "I finished the score . . ." Ibid, unpublished excerpt.

39 Isham: "Others have had more intention . . ." Michael Gudbaur, "Scoring Big," *Leblanc Bell*, Fall 1996.

44 Doyle: "Ken said, 'I want it to start off . . .'" Patrick Doyle, interviewed by Jim Svejda for *The Record Shelf*, KUSC-FM, Los Angeles, April 1994.

51 Goldsmith: "On *Patton* . . ." Derek Elley, "The Film Composer: Jerry Goldsmith," *Films and Filming*, May and June 1979.

52 Goldsmith: "It was Franklin's idea . . ." Joseph Curley, "A Few Easy Pieces: Interviews with Composers Bill Conti & Jerry Goldsmith," *Millimeter*, April 1979.

83 Goldsmith: "You can't let people pin you down . . ." John Voland, "Settling the Score," *Variety*, September 8, 1995.

91 Goldsmith: "When we were spotting *Freud* . . ." Joseph Curley, "A Few Easy Pieces: Interviews with Composers Bill Conti & Jerry Goldsmith," *Millimeter*, April 1979.

134 Corigliano: "having sounds and sonorities coming out of instruments . . ." John Corigliano, interviewed by Tim Page for *Meet the Composers*, WNYC-FM, New York, March 6, 1985.

148 Glass: "These films have always had a small, passionate following . . ." Fiona Maddocks, "Smashing Master Has Come of Age," *Observer*, London, September 1, 1991.

148 Glass: "I said to [Godfrey] . . ." Ibid.

178 Goldsmith: "Sometimes you get an overall orchestral concept . . ." Elley, "The Film Composer: Jerry Goldsmith."

188 Isham: "That's literally taking . . ." Robert Hershon, "Interview with Mark Isham," *CinemaScore*, Winter 1986/Summer 1987.

258 Corigliano: "The movie is about the passion . . ." Jesse Hamlin,

"Corigliano to Show Off His 'Violin,'" *San Francisco Chronicle*, November 25, 1997.

294 Goldsmith: "Now is certainly not the greatest time . . ." David Mermelstein, "In Hollywood, Discord on What Makes Music," *New York Times*, November 2, 1997.

PHOTOGRAPHS

2 Elmer Bernstein, photo by Christopher Barr; courtesy of Ronnie Chasen.

8 David Raksin, courtesy of the Robert Light Agency.

15 Michael Kamen, courtesy of the composer.

21 David Shire, courtesy of the composer.

23 David Shire conducting the LSO, courtesy of the composer.

37 Elia Cmiral, photo © 1998 Filmtraxx/Joey Skibel. All rights reserved.

42 Patrick Doyle, photo by Alex Norton; courtesy of the composer.

51 Jerry Goldsmith, photo by Matthew Joseph Peak; courtesy of Baker-Winokur-Ryder.

58 Carter Burwell, photo by Todd Kasow; courtesy of the composer.

64 Carter Burwell, from *Assassin(s)*, photo by Adam Smalley; courtesy of the composer.

106 Alan Menken, photo by Suzannah Gold; courtesy of the composer.

111 Recording *Beauty and the Beast,* photo by John Seakwood © Disney Enterprises, Inc.; courtesy of the composer.

133 John Corigliano, photo by Christian Steiner; courtesy of Fine Arts Mangement, Inc.

143 Philip Glass, photo by Barron Claiborne/Nonesuch Records; courtesy of Annie Ohayon Media.

169 Basil Poledouris, photo by Larsen & Talbert; courtesy of the composer.

187 Mark Isham, photo by Eric Tucker; courtesy of Earle-Tones Music, Inc.

199 Elliot Goldenthal, photo courtesy of Ronnie Chasen.

214 Jocelyn Pook © Reprise Records; courtesy of Ronnie Chasen.

228 Basil Poledouris, from *For Love of the Game*, photo by Mi Kyoung Chaing; courtesy of the composer.

246 Mychael Danna, courtesy of the composer.

282 Jerry Goldsmith and the NPO, photo by Matthew Joseph Peak © 1997; courtesy of Varèse Sarabande.

FILM STILLS

■

INDEX

Index

Index

Index

Index

Index

Index

ABOUT THE AUTHOR

DAVID MORGAN has written on film production and media issues for such publications as the *Los Angeles Times*, *Newsday*, *Sight & Sound*, *The Hollywood Reporter*, *Empire*, *The Independent*, *American Cinematographer*, *Millimeter*, *Cinefex*, *Ciak si Gira*, and *Flix*.

He is author of the oral history *Monty Python Speaks!* (Spike Books, 1999), and editor of *Sundancing* by John Anderson (Spike Books, 2000). He also co-produced and wrote the interactive supplementary sections of the Criterion Collection's special edition laserdisk/DVDs of Terry Gilliam's *Brazil* and *The Adventures of Baron Munchausen*, documenting and analyzing the production of those films and recording audio commentary.

He is the author of the Website Wide Angle/Closeup: Conversations with Filmmakers, and is presently a producer at ABCNews.com.

He lives in New York City.

■